MW00342255

The Original Scots Colonists of Early America:

CARIBBEAN SUPPLEMENT 1611–1707

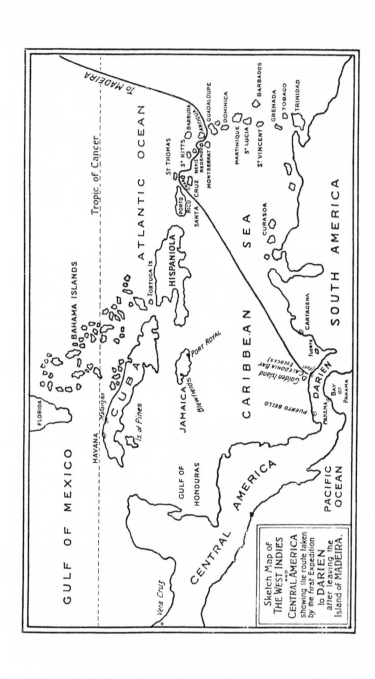

To MADEIRA

ATLANTIC OCEAN

Tropic of Cancer

GULF OF MEXICO

BAHAMA ISLANDS

FLORIDA

HAVANA

Matanzas

CUBA

Is. of Pines

TORTUGA IS.

HISPANIOLA

Port Royal

JAMAICA

Blewfields

GULF OF HONDURAS

CENTRAL AMERICA

Vera Cruz

St THOMAS

St KITTS

BARBUDA

NEVIS

ANTIGUA

REDONDO

MONTSERRAT

GUADALOUPE

DOMINICA

MARTINIQUE

St LUCIA

St VINCENT

BARBADOS

GRENADA

TOBAGO

TRINIDAD

PORTO RICO

SANTA CRUZ

CARIBBEAN SEA

CURASOA

SOUTH AMERICA

CARTAGENA

FUERTE (Isd)

Golden Island

CALEDONIA BAY (Escoces)

DARIEN

PUERTO BELLO

PANAMA

BAY OF PANAMA

PACIFIC OCEAN

Sketch Map of
THE WEST INDIES
AND
CENTRAL AMERICA
showing the route taken
by the first Expedition
to DARIEN
after leaving the
Island of MADEIRA.

The Original Scots Colonists *of* Early America

Caribbean Supplement 1611–1707

By *David Dobson*

Introduction

Y THE LATE seventeenth century there were significant numbers of Scots settled outside Scotland in Europe and America. In Europe the main destinations for emigration were Poland, Scandinavia, the Netherlands and Ireland. Ireland was the most popular destination, in part because of its proximity, but also because it offered refuge and there was encouragement from London that Protestants settle there. For these and other reasons, around 100,000 Scots moved there. The attempt to form an independent Scots colony in Nova Scotia ended in 1632 with King Charles I decreeing that the land be returned to the French as part of a peace settlement.

The Scottish connection with the Caribbean started in 1611 with the voyage to the West Indies of the *Janet of Leith*. It was not, however, until after 1626 that Scots actually settled in the Caribbean. In 1627 King Charles I appointed James Hay, Earl of Carlisle, a Scot, as Governor of the Caribbees, and this led to a steady trickle of Scots to Barbados and other islands. While there was a degree of voluntary emigration, it is likely that the majority of Scots in the West Indies had gone there unwillingly. Five hundred Scots prisoners-of-war were transported to the area by Oliver Cromwell in 1654, and felons or political undesirables such as the Covenanters (militant Protestants) were shipped in chains directly from Scotland. In addition, the English Privy Council regularly received petitions from planters particularly requesting Scottish indentured servants. In consequence a steady stream of Scottish indentured servants sailed from both Scottish and English ports bound for the West Indies. During the 1660s the Glasgow-based organization called the Company Trading to Virginia, the Caribbee Islands, Barbados, New England, St. Kitts, Montserrat, and other Colonies in America established economic links with the West Indies. By the latter part of the seventeenth century Scots merchants, planters, seafarers, and transportees were to be found throughout the English and Dutch colonies of the Caribbean. In total it is believed that as many as 5,000 Scots settled temporarily or permanently in the Caribbean before the Act of Union in 1707.

By the seventeenth century there was a desire in Scotland for the establishment of an independent colony in the Americas, and at one time there was a plan to settle St. Vincent. Impressed by the success of the English and Dutch, Scots were increasingly aware of the substantial economic advantages that would accrue from such a venture.

In 1695 the Scots Parliament passed *An Act in Favour of the Scots Company Trading to Africa and the Indies*. This act gave authority, under the Crown of Scotland, for the establishment of colonies in America, Asia or Africa, to purchase ships, and to open a bank in Edinburgh. Following on this Act, the trading company, commonly known as the Darien Company, was founded. Expectations of profit were high, and the venture caused quite a bit of excitement in the country. Either directly or indirectly, most of Scotland's population became caught up in it, and shareholders were shown to range from landowners, merchants, burgh organizations, crafts guilds, and anyone else with capital to invest. An investor was even found in Virginia, where Benjamin Harrison, a merchant planter, was persuaded to back the scheme.

William Paterson, who had co-founded the Bank of England and made his fortune in the Caribbean, was instrumental in setting up the company, known as the Darien Company, to be established at Darien on the Isthmus of Panama. This was to be a port serving both Atlantic and Pacific trade, and the site of a new Scottish colony. In 1698 and 1699 several ships left Scotland bound for Darien carrying around 3,000 emigrants and soldiers to defend the colony. Darien was opposed by England, who forbad the giving of any assistance or support, and the East India Company also viewed it as a challenge to its monopoly. The Spanish, who had a long-established claim to the area, organized resistance and besieged the settlers. In the meantime, the environment into which the pioneers had innocently ventured was taking its toll. By March 1700 the Scots had been decimated by conditions of excessive humidity where it rained for nine months out of twelve, and by tropical diseases to which they had no resistance. Those who survived after less than two years in the colony, abandoned it. They dispersed; some to Jamaica and other islands of the West Indies; some to Charleston, South Carolina and other ports up to Philadelphia, New York and Boston; and others returned home to Scotland.

Introduction

The failure of the Darien Expedition was a huge blow to Scotland's economy and self-esteem, and contributed to the political union of Scotland and England in 1707. In this way, trade from Scotland, previously blocked by England, was now opened up, and links, both in goods and people, between Scotland and America flourished.

The settlement of Scots in the West Indies was important from the point of view both of the colonist and the home country. Many of the emigrants used these islands as a stopping-off point before continuing to the mainland of America, where they then settled. Alexander Hamilton and Theodore Roosevelt are numbered among those who descend from Scots who initially settled in the Caribbean.

This supplement contains data which expands on some of the information found in my *Original Scots Colonists of Early America, 1612–1783* for the time period 1611–1707; it also contains completely new information gleaned from recent research. The original book, published by GPC in 1989, was based entirely on source material located in the United Kingdom, while this volume contains primary and secondary material from both U.K. and U.S. sources. The focus of the *Caribbean Supplement* is on the period prior to the year 1707, the year marking the political union between Scotland and England. The Act of Union of 1707 eliminated restrictions on trade between Scotland and the American colonies, and in consequence emigration to the West Indies increased rather substantially. This work concentrates, however, on seventeenth-century emigration, a far more difficult period to document than that of the following century.

David Dobson
St. Andrews, Scotland, 1998

References and Abbreviations

Archives

ACA	Aberdeen City Archives	
	APB	Aberdeen Proprinquity Book
BRO	Bristol Record Office	
GAI	General Archives of the Indies, Seville	
NLS	National Library of Scotland, Edinburgh	
NEHGS	New England Historic Genealogical Society	
	Scots Charitable Society papers	
NJSA	New Jersey State Archives, Trenton	
	EJD	East Jersey Deeds
PRO	Public Record Office, London	
	CO	Colonial Office
	PCC	Prerogative Court of Canterbury
SRO	Scottish Record Office, Edinburgh	
	AC	Admiralty Court
	B	Burgh Records
	CC	Commissary Court
	CS	Court of Session
	E	Exchequer Records
	GD	Gifts and Deposits
	NRAS	National Register of Archives of Scotland
	RD	Register of Deeds
WCF	Worshipful Company of Fishmongers, London	

Publications

ACL	Aberdeen Council Letters, L.B. Taylor (London, 1942)
ActsPCCol	Acts of the Privy Council, Colonial, series
APS	Acts of the Parliament of Scotland, series
AUR	Aberdeen University Review, series
BM	The Book of Mackay, A. Mackay (Edinburgh, 1936)
Car	Caribbeana, series
CEC	Exiles of the Covenant, W.H. Carslaw (Helensburgh, 1908)
CFR	Cockburn Family Records, A. Cockburn (Edinburgh, 1913)
DD	Darien Disaster, J. Prebble (London, 1970)
DP	Darien Papers, J.H. Burton (Edinburgh, 1849)
DSP	Darien Shipping Papers, G.P. Insh (Edinburgh, 1924)
EBR	Edinburgh Burgess Records
EMA	List of Emigrant Ministers to America, 1690–1811, G. Fothergill (London, 1904)
ETR	Edinburgh Tolbooth Records
F	Fasti Ecclesiae Scoticanae, H. Scott (Edinburgh, 1915)
GBR	Glasgow Burgess Roll
H	Original Lists ... J. Hotten (Baltimore, 1983)
HMC	Historical Manuscript Commission, series
H2	Omitted Chapters from Hotten's ... J.C. Brandow (Baltimore, 1983)
IBR	Inveraray Burgess Roll
L&J	Letters and Journals 1663–1887, J.G. Dunlop (London, 1953)
MIBWI	Monumental Inscriptions in the British West Indies, J.H. Lawrence-Archer (London, 1875)
OMO	This Old Monmouth of Ours, W.S. Hornor (Freehold, New Jersey, 1932)
OSN	The Old Scots Navy, 1689–1710, J. Grant (London, 1914)
PC	Register of the Privy Council of Scotland, series
RBM	R.B. Miller research papers

Publications

RBS	Extracts from the Records of the Burgh of Stirling, R. Renwick (Glasgow, 1889)
SHR	Scottish Historical Review, series
SPAWI	State Papers, America and the West Indies, series
SPC	State Papers, Colonial, series
SW	Standing Witnesses, T. Campbell (Edinburgh, 1996)
WP	William Paterson and the Darien Company J.S. Barbour (Edinburgh, 1907)
cnf	confirmation of testament
g/s	gravestone inscription
pro	probate

The Original Scots Colonists of Early America: CARIBBEAN SUPPLEMENT 1611–1707

ADAM, JOHN, a Covenanter in Ormidale, Argyll, transported from Leith to Jamaica 7 August 1685. [PC.2.329]

ADAM, WILLIAM, son of James Adam in Bridgeness, Aberdeen, foremastman on the *Caledonia* {600 tons, 50 guns}, from Leith to Darien 14 July 1698, cnf Edinburgh 1707. [SRO.CC8.8.83]

ADAMSON, DAVID, born 1661, emigrated via London as an indentured servant to Jamaica on the *Providence* in March 1684. [CLRO/AIA]

ADARE, JOHN, commander of the *William of Bourbon*, pro.15 July 1696 Barbados. [RB.6.11.373]

ADARE, ROBERT, from Galloway, pro.29 December 1692 Barbados. [RB.6.3.63]

ADDIE, JOHN, a Covenanter in Torpichen, West Lothian, a prisoner in Edinburgh, transported from Leith to Barbados on the *Crown of London*, Captain Thomas Teddico, 27 November 1679, shipwrecked and drowned off Orkney 10 December 1679. [RBM]

AFFLECK, Lieutenant Colonel ANDREW, father of Andrew baptised in St James, Barbados, 27 August 1679; with 20 acres and 7 slaves in St James, Barbados, 20 December 1679. [H#497/500]; commander of a militia company in Barbados 1679. [H2/148]

AGNEW, ANDREW, a minister, to Jamaica 1706, later in Virginia. [EMA#10]

AGNEW, GEORGE, overseer at Darien 1699, cnf Edinburgh 1707. [SRO.CC8.8.84]

AIKEN, ALEXANDER, son of ... Aiken and Susanna Hardy in Bo'ness, West Lothian, a sailor on the *Rising Sun*, from the Clyde to Darien 18 August 1699, cnf Edinburgh 1707. [SRO.CC8.8.83]

1

AIRD, JOHN, passenger on the *James of Ayr*, master James Chalmers, arrived in Ayr 19 September 1681 from the West Indies. [SRO. E72.3.7]

AIRD, JOHN, a planter, died on the voyage to Darien 28 October 1698. [WP#88]

AITCHISON, JAMES, a Covenanter from Nethen, Berwickshire, captured after the Battle of Bothwell Bridge 22 June 1679, transported from Leith to the West Indies on the *Crown of London*, master Thomas Teddico, 27 November 1679, shipwrecked off Muil Head of Deerness, Orkney, 10 December 1679, later transported to Jamaica. [CEC#212/5][SW#203][RBM]

AITKEN, JOHN, a Covenanter from Shotts, Lanarkshire, imprisoned in Edinburgh, transported from Leith to Barbados on the *Crown of London*, master Thomas Teddico, 27 November 1679, shipwrecked and drowned off Orkney 10 December 1679. [RBM]

AITON, ANDREW, a Covenanter from Avondale, Lanarkshire, imprisoned in Edinburgh, transported from Leith on the *Crown of London*, master Thomas Teddico, bound for Barbados 27 November 1679, shipwrecked and drowned off Orkney 10 December 1679. [RBM]

ALDCORN, ADAM, a Covenanter and a minister, transported from Leith to the West Indies on the *St Michael of Scarborough*, master Edward Johnston, 12 December 1678. [PC.6.76]

ALDER, ALEXANDER, a seaman, died on the voyage to Darien September 1698. [DD#143]

ALEXANDER, DUNCAN, a Covenanter in Argyll, transported from Leith to Jamaica 7 August 1685. [PC.11.329]

ALEXANDER, GEORGE, a Covenanter in Newburgh, Fife, transported from Leith to Jamaica on the *St Michael of Scarborough*, master Edward Johnston, 12 December 1678. [PC.6.76]

ALEXANDER, Dr JAMES, militiaman in Captain Richard Vintner's Troop of Horse in Barbados, 1679; with 3 men in Colonel Colleton's Foot Militia March 1680; in St Philip's parish, Barbados, with 2 servants, 44 slaves, and 110 acres, 1680. [H2/3.120. 205]

ALEXANDER, WILLIAM, buried in St Lucy's parish, Barbados, 23 June 1678. [H2/56]

ALICE, a Scots woman, buried in St Philips parish, Barbados, 28 June 1679. [H2/24]

ALISON, ROBERT, a Covenanter from Avondale, Lanarkshire, imprisoned in Edinburgh, transported from Leith on the *Crown of Lon-*

don, master Thomas Teddico, bound for Barbados 27 November 1679, shipwrecked and drowned off Orkney 10 December 1679. [RBM]

ALISON, WILLIAM, a Covenanter from Avondale, Lanarkshire, imprisoned in Edinburgh, transported from Leith on the *Crown of London*, master Thomas Teddico, bound for Barbados 27 November 1679, shipwrecked and drowned off Orkney 10 December 1679. [RBM]

ALLAN, ANDREW, a sailor on the *Endeavour to Darien 1698*. [SRO.GD406, bundle 161.25/10]

ALLAN, DAVID, father of Bessie Allan in Fisherrow, Musselburgh, Midlothian, a sailor on the *Unicorn*, from Leith to Darien 14 July 1698, cnf Edinburgh 1707. [SRO.CC8.8.83]

ALLAN, JOHN, a Covenanter from Torpichen, West Lothian, imprisoned in Edinburgh, transported from Leith on the *Crown of London*, master Thomas Teddico, bound for Barbados 27 November 1679, shipwrecked and drowned off Orkney 10 December 1679. [RBM]

ALLAN, JOHN, a Covenanter in Cumnock, Ayrshire, transported from Leith to Jamaica 7 August 1685. [PC.11.330]

ANDERSON, ADAM, with 5 acres in Christchurch, Barbados, 22 December 1679. [H#473]

ANDERSON, AGNES, transported to Barbados or Virginia, March 1667. [PC.2.263]

ANDERSON, ALEXANDER, a Covenanter and a servant in Kirkliston, West Lothian, transported from Leith to the West Indies on the *St Michael of Scarborough*, master Edward Johnston, 12 December 1678. [PC.6.76]

ANDERSON, ALEXANDER, husband of Jean Edgar, a sailor, from the Clyde to Darien 18 December 1699, cnf Edinburgh 24 September 1707. [SRO.CC8.8.83]

ANDERSON, DAVID, militiaman in Thornhill's Company in Barbados 1679. [H2/151]

ANDERSON, GEORGE, son of Reverend John Anderson in St Andrews, Fife, to Darien 1698, cnf Edinburgh 1707. [SRO.CC8.8.83]

ANDERSON, HARRY, son of Harry Anderson in Glasgow, emigrated to Barbados 1665. [Glasgow Records#67]

ANDERSON, JAMES, and his wife Hanna, had their daughter Martha baptised in Christchurch, Barbados, 24 November 1679. [H#489]

ANDERSON, JAMES, militiaman in Lyne's Regiment of Foot in Barbados 6 January 1679. [H2/99]

ANDERSON, JAMES, a Covenanter from Kilmarnock, Ayrshire, captured after the Battle of Bothwell Bridge 22 June 1679, banished to the Plantations, transported from Leith on the *Crown of London*, master Thomas Teddico, November 1679, shipwrecked and drowned off Orkney December 1679. [Kilmarnock g/s][RBM]

ANDERSON, JAMES, a laborer in Lanarkshire, an indentured servant shipped from London to Jamaica November 1684. [CLRO/AIA]

ANDERSON, JOHN, master of the *Providence of Glasgow* arrived in Glasgow 3 September 1672 from Antigua. [SRO.E72.10.2]

ANDERSON, JOHN, a Covenanter and a servant to a maltman in Glasgow, transported from Leith to the West Indies on the *St Michael of Scarborough*, master Edward Johnston, 12 December 1678. [PC.6.76]

ANDERSON, JOHN, buried in St Peter's, Barbados, ca. 1679. [H2/87]

ANDERSON, JOHN, a mason with 4 servants, 2 slaves and 10 acres in St Peter's All Saints, Barbados, 15 December 1679. [H2/83]

ANDERSON, JOHN, living on Henry Farley's land, with 1 servant, 2 slaves and 15 acres in St Lucy's parish, Barbados, 30 December 1679. [H2/33]

ANDERSON, JOHN, a soldier in Tidcomb's Militia, Barbados, 11 September 1679. [H2/133]

ANDERSON, JOHN, a soldier in Lewgar's Militia January 1679. [H2/145]

ANDERSON, JOHN, a Covenanter, transported from Leith to the West Indies 11 October 1681. [PC.7.219]

ANDERSON, JOHN, a Covenanter in Lanark, transported from Leith to Barbados on the *John and Nicholas*, master Edward Barnes, 17 December 1685. [PC.11.384][ETR#389]

ANDERSON, JOHN, born 1655, captain of the *Endeavour* from Leith to Darien 14 July 1698, captain of the Unicorn *from Darien to New York,* arrived at Sandy Hook 14 August 1699, married Anna Reid in New Jersey, later Governor of East New Jersey 1723, died in Manalapan 6 July 1723, [OMO#112]; witness to the testament of George Calderwood, quartermaster, 16 July 1698.

ANDERSON, JOHN, son of William Anderson and Lillias Strathdee in Boharme, Banffshire, educated at Marischal College, Aberdeen, a physician, emigrated via London to Barbados, settled in St Michael's parish, died there 1718, pro. 2 December 1714 Barbados. [APB.2.139][RB.6.37.406]

ANDERSON, MICHAEL, with 10 acres in St Thomas, Barbados, 3 December 1679. [H2/57]

ANDERSON, ROBERT, a Covenanter from Kilmarnock, Ayrshire, imprisoned in Edinburgh, transported from Leith on the *Crown of London*, master Thomas Teddico, bound for Barbados 27 November 1679, shipwrecked and drowned off Orkney 10 December 1679. [RBM]

ANDERSON, ROGER, with wife, child, and 3 slaves, in St Michael's, Barbados, 1680. [H#442]

ANDERSON, THOMAS, with 2.5 acres in Christchurch, Barbados, 22 December 1679; militiaman in Lieutenant Colonel Andrew Affleck's Company in Barbados, 1679. [H#473][H2/148]

ANDERSON, WILLIAM, buried in St Michael's, Barbados, 4 August 1679. [H#436]

ANDERSON, WILLIAM, with 2 acres in Christchurch, Barbados, 22 December 1679. [H#473]

ANDERSON, WILLIAM, baptised in St Peter's All Saints, Barbados, ca. 1679. [H2/85]

ANDERSON, WILLIAM, from Linktown of Abbotshall, Kirkcaldy, Fife, bosun on the *Endeavour* from Leith to Darien 14 July 1699, cnf Edinburgh 3 October 1707. [SRO.CC8.8.83][SRO.GD406, bundle 161, 25/5]

ANDERSON, WILLIAM, a sailor on the *Endeavour* 1698. [SRO. GD406, bundle 161, 25/9]

ANDERSON, WILLIAM, from Arbroath, Angus, a sailor on the *St Andrew*, from Leith to Darien 14 July 1698, cnf Edinburgh 1707. [SRO.CC8.8.83][SRO.GD406, bundle 160, 4/23]

ANDERSON, WILLIAM, a cordiner in Portsburgh, Edinburgh, from Leith to Darien on the *St Andrew* 14 July 1698, cnf Edinburgh 1707. [SRO.CC8.8.83]

ANDERSON, WILLIAM, a brewer in Leith, from Leith to Darien on the *Endeavour* 14 July 1698, cnf Edinburgh 1707. [SRO.CC8.8. 84]

ANDREW, DAVID, a thief, transported from Ayr to Barbados 1653. [SRO.JC27.10.3]

ANDREW, JAMES, from Edinburgh, a sailor on the *St Andrew*, from Leith to Darien 14 July 1698, cnf Edinburgh 9 October 1707. [SRO.CC8.8.83]

ANGUS, GILBERT, from Burntisland, Fife, a sailor on the *Unicorn* from Leith to Darien 14 July 1698, cnf Edinburgh 9 October 1707. [SRO.CC8.8.83]

ANGUS, JOHN, master's mate on the *Swan of Ayr*, master David Ferguson, which arrived in Ayr from Montserrat and the West Indies 23 September 1678. [SRO.E72.3.4]

ANGUS, JOHN, foremastman on the *Unicorn*, from Leith to Darien 14 July 1698, cnf Edinburgh 1707. [SRO.CC8.8.83]

ANGUS, ROBERT, mariner burgess of Burntisland, Fife, husband of Mausie Doctor, in Barbados, 1651, 1654, 1658. [SRO.GD172. 1814.1/2]

ANGUS, WILLIAM, a Covenanter in Abercorn, West Lothian, transported from Leith to the West Indies on the *St Michael of Scarborough*, master Edward Johnston, 12 December 1678. [PC.6.76]

ARBUTHNOTT, JAMES, a clergyman, emigrated to the Leeward Islands 1705. [EMA#11]

ARCHIBALD, JOHN, from Burntisland, Fife, a sailor on the *Endeavour*, from Leith to Darien 14 July 1698, cnf 8 October 1707. [SRO.CC8.8.83][SRO.GD306, bundle 161, 25/12]

ARMSTRONG, ANN, a time-expired indentured servant emigrated from Barbados to Antigua on the *Francis*, master Peter Jeffreys, 28 April 1679. [H#348]

ARMSTRONG, EDWARD, with 4 slaves and 20 acres in St Lucy's parish, Barbados, 30 December 1678. [H2/33]

ARMSTRONG, ISRAEL, militiaman under Captain Robert Harrison in Barbados 1679. [H2/103]

ARMSTRONG, JOHN, with 3 slaves and 13 acres in St Lucy's parish, Barbados, 30 December 1679. [H2/33]

ARMSTRONG, JOHN, militiaman under Captain Robert Harrison in Barbados 1679. [H2/103]

ARMSTRONG, RACHEL, daughter of John Armstrong, baptised in St Lucy's parish, Barbados, 23 July 1678.

ARMSTRONG, ROBERT, a thief from Jedburgh Tolbooth, Roxburghshire, imprisoned in Edinburgh Tolbooth, transported from Leith to Barbados 17 April 1666. [ETR#106]

ARMSTRONG, SAMUEL, militiaman under Captain Robert Harrison in Barbados 1679. [H2/103]

ARMSTRONG, WILL, militiaman under Colonel Lyne in Barbados 6 January 1679. [H2/99]

ARNETT, DAVID, with 20 acres, 1 servant and 20 slaves in Christchurch, Barbados, 22 December 1679; wife Jane, parents of Samuel baptised in Christchurch, Barbados, 9 September 1679. [H#473/492]

ARNOT, JOHN, a Covenanter in Balgedie, Milnathort, Kinross-shire, transported from Leith to the West Indies 12 December 1678. [PC.6.76]

ARNETT, PATRICK, with 3 acres, 1 servant and 3 slaves in Christchurch, Barbados, 22 December 1679. [H#473]

ASH, JOHN, seaman on the *Swan of Ayr* arrived in Ayr from the Caribee Islands 27 September 1691. [SRO.E72.3.23]

AUCHINCLOSE, WILLIAM, a Covenanter from Paisley, Renfrewshire, imprisoned in Edinburgh, transported from Leith on the *Crown of London*, master Thomas Teddico, bound for Barbados 27 November 1679, shipwrecked and drowned off Orkney 10 December 1679. [RBM]

AULD, ROBERT, a Covenanter from Kilbride, Lanarkshire, imprisoned in Edinburgh, transported from Leith on the *Crown of London*, master Thomas Teddico, bound for Barbados 27 November 1679, shipwrecked and drowned off Orkney 10 December 1679. [RBM]

BAILLIE, ANDREW, a clergyman educated at Edinburgh University 1695, emigrated to Barbados 1709. [EMA#12]

BAILLIE, JOHN, appointed commander of the *Speedy Return* and to sail from the Clyde to Darien October 1699. [SRO.GD406.1]; died in Jamaica September 1700. [DD#325]

BAILLIE, JOHN, surgeon of the *Hope*, died in Jamaica September 1700. [DD#325]

BAILLIE, JOHN, a Lieutenant of Colonel Buchan's Regiment in Flanders before 1697, husband of Margaret Bowden, emigrated to Darien on the *Rising Sun* 1699, died there February 1700. [APS#14, app.127]

BAILLIE, ROBERT, a planter, died on the voyage to Darien 1 September 1698. [WP#87]

BAILLIE, WILLIAM, from Blackbie, a soldier, died at Darien, cnf Edinburgh 1707. [SRO.CC8.8.83]

BAINE, ANGUS, his wife Martha buried in St George's, Barbados, 12 August 1679. [H#468]

BAINE, LAUCHLAN, a physician, emigrated to Barbados before 1697, admitted as an honorary burgess and guildsbrother of Edinburgh 24 August 1697. [Edinburgh Burgh Records#4.217]; with his wife and servant in St Michael's, Barbados, 1680. [H#446]; clerk to Captain Burrow's Company of Militia in Barbados 1679. [H2/182]

7

BAIN, LACHLAN, Lieutenant of the Scottish American Company, subscribed to deeds 1699. [SRO.RD4.85.637] ; died on the voyage from Darien to Jamaica 1700. [DD#325]

BAIN, WILLIAM, son of John Bain in Abbotshall, Fife, a sailor, to Darien on the *Rising Sun* from the Clyde 18 August 1699, cnf Edinburgh 11 October 1707. [SRO.CC8.8.83]

BAIRD, ANDREW, died on the voyage to Darien 28 November 1698. [WP#87]

BAIRD, JAMES, a Covenanter in Calderwood, Lanarkshire, transported from Leith to Jamaica August 1685. [PC.11.330]

BAIRD, ROBERT, a merchant who settled in Surinam before 1689. [SRO.RH1.2.772/3]

BAIRD, WILLIAM, a sailor, died at Darien 24 November 1698. [NLS. RY2b8/19]

BAKER, THOMAS, bosun on the *Dolphin*, then on the *Endeavour*, 1699. [SRO.GD406, bundle 163, C23/3; bundle 161, 25/23]

BALFOUR, JAMES, son in law of Mr Robert Cunningham of Kinghorn, a merchant when on a trading voyage to the West Indies was captured by the Turks and subsequently imprisoned, before 1645. [APS.VI: (i)457]

BALFOUR, JAMES, a time-expired indentured servant, emigrated from Barbados to Antigua on the *True Friendship*, a sloop, master Charles Callaghan, 4 October 1679. [H#355][PRO.CO1.44.47]

BALFOUR, WILLIAM, from Fife, a foremastman on the *Caledonia*, from Leith to Darien 14 July 1698, cnf Edinburgh 8 October 1707. [SRO.CC8.8.83]

BALLENTYNE, GEORGE, son of James Ballentyne of Kellie and Margaret Stewart, a sailor on the *Rising Sun*, from Leith to Darien 14 July 1698, cnf Edinburgh 1708. [SRO.CC8.8.84]

BALLENTYNE, JOHN, from Leith, a sailor on the *St Andrew*, from Leith to Darien 14 July 1698, cnf Edinburgh 1707. [SRO.CC8. 8.83]

BALLENTINE, PATRICK, juryman in New Providence, 1699. [SPAWI.1699/928]

BALLON, ANGELO, a sailor on the *Unicorn*, from Leith to Darien 14 July 1698, cnf Edinburgh 1707. [SRO.CC8.8.83]

BALNAVES, ROBERT, a steward's mate on the *Caledonia*, from Leith to Darien 14 July 1698, cnf Edinburgh 1707. [SRO.CC8.8.83]

BANNATYNE, WILLIAM, son of Captain John Bannatyne and Elizabeth Trotter in the Canongate, Edinburgh, a sailor on the *Cale-*

donia from Leith to Darien 14 July 1698, cnf Edinburgh 1708. [SRO.CC8.8.84]

BAPTIE, JOHN, a steward on the *Unicorn* from Leith to Darien 14 July 1698, cnf Edinburgh 1707. [SRO.CC8.8.83]

BAPTISTA, JOANNES, a sailor on the *Unicorn* from Leith to Darien 14 July 1698, cnf Edinburgh 1707. [SRO.CC8.8.83]

BARCLAY, ADAM, captain's servant on the *St Andrew* 1698. [SRO. GD406, bundle 159, p4/13]

BARCLAY, DAVID, a Covenanter in Courquhally, transported from Leith to the West Indies on the *St Michael of Scarborough*, master Edward Johnston, 12 December 1678. [PC.6.76]

BARCLAY, GEORGE, son of Alexander Barclay in Inverkeithing, Fife, a sailor on the *Olive Branch* to Darien 1699, cnf Edinburgh 28 November 1707. [SRO.CC8.8.83]

BARCLAY, HUGH, steward's mate on the *St Andrew* from Leith to Darien 14 July 1698, cnf Edinburgh 1707. [SRO.CC8.8.83]

BARCLAY, HUGH, sailor, died at Darien 5 November 1698. [NLS. RY2b8/19]

BARCLAY, WILLIAM, from Edinburgh, a sailor on the *Rising Sun* from the Clyde to Darien 18 August 1699, cnf Edinburgh 20 November 1707. [SRO.CC8.8.83]

BARKER, THOMAS, from Burntisland, Fife, emigrated to Darien, later imprisoned in Carthagena and in Spain 1700. [APS.14.app. 114]

BARRON, WILLIAM, a planter, died at Darien 1699. [NLS.RY2b8/19]

BARTON, THOMAS, a Covenanter from Monklands, Lanarkshire, imprisoned in Edinburgh, transported from Leith on the *Crown of London*, master Thomas Teddico, bound for Barbados 27 November 1679, shipwrecked and drowned off Orkney 10 December 1679. [RBM]

BARTRAM, CHRISTIAN, from Burntisland, Fife, a seaman on the *St Andrew* from Leith to Darien 14 July 1698, cnf Edinburgh 23 September 1707. [SRO.CC8.8.83]

BAYNE, AGNES, a prisoner from Edinburgh Correction House, transported by Morris Trent a merchant in Leith from Leith to Barbados on the *Mary*, master David Couston, 4 May 1663. [EBR#186. 13.4]

BAYNE, JOHN, militiaman in Captain Burrow's Company in Barbados 1679. [H2/181]

BEALE, Captain ALEXANDER, with 2 servants, 70 slaves and 111 acres in St John's parish, Barbados, 18 October 1679. [H2/68, 208,126]

BEAL, JOHN, a Covenanter from Newburn, Fife, imprisoned in Edinburgh, transported from Leith on the *Crown of London*, master Thomas Teddico, bound for Barbados 27 November 1679, shipwrecked and drowned off Orkney 10 December 1679. [RBM]

BECK, SAMUEL, a Covenanter from Kirkmabreck, Galloway, imprisoned in Edinburgh, transported from Leith on the *Crown of London*, master Thomas Teddico, bound for Barbados 27 November 1679, shipwrecked and drowned off Orkney 10 December 1679. [RBM]

BELL, JOHN, from Glasgow, pro 9 June 1654 Barbados. [RB.6.13.56]

BELL, JOHN, Lieutenant of the Company of Scotland, husband of Helen Blair, subscribed to a deed 1699. [SRO.RD3.91.567]

BELL, JOHN, a Covenanter from Livingstone, West Lothian, imprisoned in Edinburgh, transported from Leith on the *Crown of London*, master Thomas Teddico, bound for Barbados 27 November 1679, shipwrecked and drowned off Orkney 10 December 1679. [RBM]

BENNET, ADAM, son of Sir William Bennet of Grubbet, a midshipman, died on the voyage to Darien 22 October 1698. [WP#88] [DD#149]

BENNETT, HENRY, a carpenter in Elie, Fife, from Leith to Darien on the *Dolphin* 14 July 1698, died in North America, cnf Edinburgh 1707. [SRO.CC8.8.83]

BENNET, JAMES, from Kirkcaldy, Fife, a sailor on the *Endeavour* from Leith to Darien 14 July 1698. [SRO.GD406, bundle 161, 25/13]

BERRY, FRANCIS, from Leith, a foremastman on the *Caledonia* from Leith to Darien 14 July 1698, cnf Edinburgh 1707. [SRO.CC8.8.83]

BINNEY, ALEXANDER, militiaman in Colonel Lyne's Company in Barbados 6 January 1679; in St Philip's parish, Barbados, with 5 acres, 1680. [H2/4, 113]

BINNEY, JAMES, with 3 slaves in St Andrew's, Barbados, 1680. [H#472]

BIRRELL, JAMES, husband of Bessie Lily in Kinghorn, Fife, a sailor on the *Caledonia* from Leith to Darien 14 July 1698, cnf Edinburgh 1707. [SRO.CC8.8.83]

BISHOP, ALEXANDER, a Covenanter from Torpichen, West Lothian, imprisoned in Edinburgh, transported from Leith on the *Crown of London*, master Thomas Teddico, bound for Barbados 27 November 1679, shipwrecked and drowned off Orkney 10 December 1679. [RBM]

BISHOP, ROBERT, a surgeon's mate, died at Darien 8 December 1698. [NLS.RY2b8/19]

BISSET, ALEXANDER, a Covenanter from West Calder, Midlothian, imprisoned in Edinburgh, transported from Leith on the *Crown of London*, master Thomas Teddico, bound for Barbados 27 November 1679, shipwrecked and drowned off Orkney 10 December 1679. [RBM]

BITCHET, DAVID, a Covenanter from Fenwick, Ayrshire, imprisoned in Edinburgh, transported from Leith on the *Crown of London*, master Thomas Teddico, bound for Barbados 27 November 1679, shipwrecked and drowned off Orkney 10 December 1679. [RBM]

BITCHET, WILLIAM, a Covenanter from Fenwick, Ayrshire, imprisoned in Edinburgh, transported from Leith on the *Crown of London*, master Thomas Teddico, bound for Barbados 27 November 1679, shipwrecked and drowned off Orkney 10 December 1679. [RBM]

BLACK, Mr ANDREW, with 20 acres and 14 slaves in St Andrew's, Barbados, 1680. [H#472]

BLACK, HENRY, a sailor on the *Dolphin*, husband of Janet Renton, from Leith to Darien 14 July 1698, cnf Edinburgh 1707. [SRO. CC8.8.83] [SRO.GD406.bundle 163, C23/11]

BLACK, JAMES, from Edinburgh, a sailor on the *Dolphin*, subscribed to a deed of factory in favor of his sister Jean Black, cnf Edinburgh 1707. [SRO.CC8.8.83][SRO.GD406, bundle 163, C23/10-11]

BLACK, MALCOLM, a Covenanter and a farmer in Achahoish, Argyll, transported from Leith to Jamaica August 1685. [PC.11.136]

BLACK, NEIL, a Covenanter in Melford, Glenbeg, Argyll, transported from Leith to Jamaica August 1685. [PC.11.329]

BLACKIE, DAVID, son of John Blackie and Margaret Japp in Grangepans, West Lothian, a sailor on the *Caledonia* from Leith to Darien 14 July 1698, cnf Edinburgh 20 November 1707. [SRO.CC8.8.83]

BLACKLY, ROBERT, from Ayr to the West Indies on the *James of Ayr* February 1681. [SRO.E72.3.6]

BLACKWOOD, JAMES, a Covenanter in Carmunnock, Lanarkshire, transported from Leith to the West Indies on the *St Michael of Scarborough*, master Edward Johnston, 12 December 1678. [PC. 6.76]

BLAIR, JAMES, a merchant in Vere, Jamaica, pro.25 April 1677 Jamaica

BLAIR, JOHN, a thief, transported from Ayr to Barbados 1653. [SRO. JC27.10.3]

BLAIR, JOHN, a physician from Angus, settled in Port Royal, Jamaica, before 1700. [DP#313]; agent of the Darien Company there 1700. [DD#326]

BLAIR, JOHN, born 1668, to Darien 1699, settled in St Catherine's parish, Jamaica, 1700, husband of (1) Nidime ..., (2) Elizabeth, father of John, Thomas, Christian and Mary, died 27 June 1728. [Spanish Town Cathedral g/s, Jamaica]

BOGIE, ROBERT, a prisoner in Edinburgh Tolbooth, transported from Leith 15 November 1679. [ETR#162]

BOIGS, JOHN, husband of Agnes Dougall in Crawforddykes, Renfrewshire, a sailor on the *Speedy Return* from Greenock, Renfrewshire, to Darien 18 August 1699, cnf Edinburgh 1707. [SRO. CC8.8.83]

BOLTON, JAMES, a sailor to Darien 1699. [SRO.GD406, bundle 162, p39/12]

BONTHRON, JAMES, son of James Bonthron in Brigton of Inverteil, Kinghorn, Fife, bosun on the *Caledonia* from Leith to Darien 14 July 1698, cnf Edinburgh 1707. [SRO.CC8.8.83]

BOOG, ROBERT, a Covenanter from Strathmiglo, Fife, imprisoned in Edinburgh, transported from Leith on the *Crown of London*, master Thomas Teddico, bound for Barbados 27 November 1679, shipwrecked and drowned off Orkney 10 December 1679. [RBM]

BORLAND, FRANCIS, born 1666, son of John Borland in East Kilbride, Lanarkshire, a minister educated at Glasgow University, emigrated before 1685, settled in Surinam 1685–1690, Barbados 1690–1691 and Darien 1699, returned to Scotland 27 July 1701, died in Lesmahagow, Lanarkshire, 1722. [F.7.662][HMC.Laing. I.331] [SRO.NRAS.0118][Glassford Kirk Session Register]

BORLAND JOHN, soldier of Captain Harrison's company of Militia in Barbados 1679. [H2/141]

BORTHWICK, JAMES, a sailor, died at Darien 3 December 1698. [NLS.RY2b8/19]

BORTHWICK, THOMAS, a Covenanter from Linlithgow, West Lothian, imprisoned in Edinburgh, transported from Leith on the *Crown of London*, master Thomas Teddico, bound for Barbados 27 November 1679, shipwrecked and drowned off Orkney 10 December 1679. [RBM]

BOSTOUN, JAMES, a Covenanter from Dreghorn, Ayrshire, imprisoned in Edinburgh, transported from Leith on the *Crown of London*, master Thomas Teddico, bound for Barbados 27 November 1679, shipwrecked and drowned off Orkney 10 December 1679. [RBM]

BOWEN, JAMES, a merchant in Dundee, husband of Elizabeth Blair, father of Thomas, Andrew, Grisell, James, Janet, and John, a steward on the *Hope* to Darien 1699, cnf Edinburgh 1708. [SRO. GD406, bundle 162, C39/21][SRO.CC8.8.84]

BOWIE, JOHN, a Covenanter in Glasgow, transported from Leith to the West Indies on the *St Michael of Scarborough*, master Edward Johnston, 12 December 1678. [PC.6.76]

BOWIE, JOHN, from Newcastle, a sailor on the *St Andrew* from Leith to Darien 14 July 1698, cnf Edinburgh 1707. [SRO.CC8.8.83]

BOWIE, ..., a widow, with 1 servant, in St Michael's, Barbados, 1680. [H#445]

BOWMAN, WILLIAM, settled in Barbados before 1656. [Analecta Hibernia#4/234]

BOYCE, ANDREW, with 3 slaves and 12 acres in St Lucy's parish, Barbados, 1678.[H2/33]

BOYCE, JOHN, on Jacob English's land, with 1 slave in St Lucy's, Barbados, 30 December 1679. [H2/34]

BOYLE, Mr JAMES, with 2 slaves and 9 acres in St Thomas, Barbados, 3 December 1679. [H2/57]

BRAIDIE, ELSPETH, prisoner in Edinburgh Correction House, transported by Morris Trent, a merchant in Leith, from Leith to Barbados on the *Mary*, master David Couston, 8 May 1663. [EBR #186.13.4]

BRAIDWOOD, JAMES, a Covenanter in Carmunock, Lanarkshire, transported from Leith to the West Indies on the *St Michael of Scarborough*, master Edward Johnston, 12 December 1678. [PC.6.76]

BRECKENRIDGE, WILLIAM, a Covenanter from Bothwell, Lanarkshire, imprisoned in Edinburgh, transported from Leith on the *Crown of London*, master Thomas Teddico, bound for Barbados

27 November 1679, shipwrecked and drowned off Orkney 10 December 1679. [RBM]

BRICE, JOHN, a Covenanter from Borgue, Galloway, imprisoned in Edinburgh, transported from Leith on the *Crown of London*, master Thomas Teddico, bound for Barbados 27 November 1679, shipwrecked and drowned off Orkney 10 December 1679. [RBM]

BRISBANE, MATTHEW, in Rosland, guilty of assault, transported from Leith to Barbados on the *St John of Leith* 1 May 1674. [PC.4.144]

BROCK, ANDREW, from Glasgow, gunner's mate on the *St Andrew* from Leith to Darien 14 July 1698, cnf Edinburgh 1707. [SRO.GD406, bundle 160, 4/26][SRO.CC8.8.83]

BRODIE, FRANCIS, son of John Brodie of Windiehills, Morayshire, a sailor on the *Unicorn* from Leith to Darien 14 July 1698, cnf Edinburgh 14 October 1707. [SRO.CC8.8.83]

BRODIE, JAMES, a surgeon in St Michael's, Barbados, reference to in John Anderson's will, pro. 2 December 1714 Barbados, [RB6.37.406]

BROWN, ANDREW, from the Mill of Achiell, Strichen, Aberdeenshire, a sailor on the *St Andrew* from Leith to Darien 14 July 1698, cnf Edinburgh 1707. [SRO.GD406, bundle 159, p4/18][SRO.CC8.8.84]

BROWN, ANDREW, a boy on a French ship, died at Darien 24 December 1698. [NLS.RY28/19]

BROWN, ANDREW, wounded at Darien 6 February 1699. [DP#86]

BROWN, ARCHIBALD, a Covenanter in Argyll, transported from Leith to Jamaica August 1685. [PC.11.330]

BROWN, JAMES, executor of William Powrie's will pro. 4 April 1649 Barbados

BROWN, Colonel JAMES, in Barbados, appointed as a knight baronet of Scotland, 17 February 1664. [RGS.XI.553]

BROWN, Captain JAMES, a Scots privateer in the West Indies, found guilty of piracy and sentenced to death at Jamaica 5 August 1677. [SPAWI.1677#243]

BROWN, JAMES, a Covenanter in Frosk, transported from Leith to the West Indies on the *St Michael of Scarborough*, master Edward Johnston, 12 December 1678. [PC.6.76]

BROWN, JAMES, with 6 slaves and 10 acres in St Lucy's parish, Barbados, 30 December 1678. [H2/33]

BROWN, JAMES, a sailor on the *St Andrew* 1699. [SRO.GD406, bundle 160, 4/20]

BROWN, JAMES, from Edinburgh, pro. 27 November 1703 Barbados. [RB.6.16.53]

BROWN, JOHN, trading between Scotland and Barbados 1663/1666. [NLS.MS#7003, fo.3/7033, fo.29/31, etc]

BROWN, JOHN, a Covenanter in Buchlivie, Stirlingshire, transported from Leith to the West Indies on the *St Michael of Scarborough*, master Edward Johnston,12 December 1678. [PC.6.76]

BROWN, JOHN, a Covenanter from Midcalder, Midlothian, imprisoned in Edinburgh, transported from Leith on the *Crown of London*, master Thomas Teddico, bound for Barbados 27 November 1679, shipwrecked and drowned off Orkney 10 December 1679. [RBM]

BROWNE, JOHN, from Edinburgh, a gentleman in St Michael's parish, Barbados, pro.2 February 1696 Barbados. [RB.6.11.422]

BROWN, ROBERT, a Covenanter from Kirkmabreck, Galloway, imprisoned in Edinburgh, transported from Leith on the *Crown of London*, master Thomas Teddico, bound for Barbados 27 November 1679, shipwrecked and drowned off Orkney 10 December 1679. [RBM]

BROWN, THOMAS, a Covenanter from Gargunnock, Stirlingshire, imprisoned in Edinburgh, transported from Leith on the *Crown of London*, master Thomas Teddico, bound for Barbados 27 November 1679, shipwrecked and drowned off Orkney 10 December 1679. [RBM]

BROWN, WILLIAM, trading between Scotland and Barbados 1663–1666. [NLS.MS#7003 fo.3/7033 fo.29/31, etc]

BROWN, WILLIAM, a Covenanter in Kilmarnock, captured after the Battle of Bothwell Bridge 22 June 1679, banished to the Plantations, transported from Leith on the *Crown of London*, master Thomas Teddico bound for Barbados, 27 November 1679, shipwrecked and drowned off Orkney 10 December 1679. [Kilmarnock g/s][RBM]

BROWN, WILLIAM, a sailor on the *Unicorn* from Leith to Darien 14 July1698, cnf Edinburgh 10 October 1707. [SRO.CC8.8.83]

BROWNLEE, THOMAS, a Covenanter from Avondale, Lanarkshire, imprisoned in Edinburgh, transported from Leith on the *Crown of London*, master Thomas Teddico, bound for Barbados 27 November 1679, shipwrecked and drowned off Orkney 10 December 1679. [RBM]

BRUCE, MICHAEL, transported to Virginia or Barbados July 1668. [PC.2.478]

BRUCE, WILLIAM, from Peterhead, Aberdeenshire, a sailor on the *St Andrew*, from Leith to Darien 14 July 1698, cnf Edinburgh 1707. [SRO.CC8.8.83]

BRUNTON, ROBERT, husband of Mary Brunton in Bo'ness, West Lothian, a sailor on the *Olive Branch* to Darien 1699, cnf Edinburgh 24 September 1707. [SRO.CC8.8.83]

BRYCE, JOHN, a Covenanter from Kirkmichael, Ayrshire, imprisoned in Edinburgh, transported from Leith on the *Crown of London*, master Thomas Teddico, bound for Barbados 27 November 1679, shipwrecked and drowned off Orkney 10 December 1679. [RBM]

BRYCE, ROBERT, a Covenanter from Borgue, Galloway, imprisoned in Edinburgh, transported from Leith on the *Crown of London*, master Thomas Teddico, bound for Barbados 27 November 1679, shipwrecked and drowned off Orkney 10 December 1679. [RBM]

BUCHAN, WILLIAM, a Covenanter from Paisley, Renfrewshire, imprisoned in Edinburgh, transported from Leith on the *Crown of London*, master Thomas Teddico, bound for Barbados 27 November 1679, shipwrecked and drowned off Orkney 10 December 1679. [RBM]

BUCHANAN, ALEXANDER, a Covenanter in Buchlivie, Stirlingshire, transported from Leith to the West Indies on the *St Michael of Scarborough*, master Edward Johnston, 12 December 1678. [PC.6.76]

BUCHANAN, GEORGE, executor—James Foulis, a merchant in London, reference to brother Robert Buchanan, sister Janet Buchanan, brother William Buchanan, and his brother's son George, also to James Brodie, subscribed 6 January 1678, pro.27 May 1679 Nevis.

BUCHANAN, GILBERT, a Covenanter and a baker in Glasgow, son of Walter Buchanan, transported to the West Indies June 1678. [PC.65.474]

BUCHANAN, JAMES, a Covenanter from Gargunnock, Stirlingshire, imprisoned in Edinburgh, transported from Leith on the *Crown of London*, master Thomas Teddico, bound for Barbados 27 November 1679, shipwrecked and drowned off Orkney 10 December 1679. [RBM]

BUCHANAN, ROBERT, son of Robert Buchanan in Craigward of Alloway, a sailor on the *Unicorn*, from Leith to Darien 14 July 1698, cnf Edinburgh 23 October 1707. [SRO.CC8.8.83]

BUCHANAN, WALTER, from Kilmarnock, Ayrshire, a sailor on the *St Andrew*, from Leith to Darien 14 July 1698, died in Jamaica, cnf Edinburgh 8 October 1707. [SRO.GD406, bundle 159, p4/12] [SRO.CC8.8.83]

BUCKLE, ANDREW, a Covenanter from Fenwick, Ayrshire, imprisoned in Edinburgh, transported from Leith on the *Crown of London*, master Thomas Teddico, bound for Barbados 27 November 1679, shipwrecked and drowned off Orkney 10 December 1679. [RBM]

BUIST, JOHN, from Auchterderran, Fife, a sailor on the *Caledonia* from Leith to Darien 14 July 1698, cnf Edinburgh 1707. [SRO.CC8.8.83]; witness to the testament of James Watson, sailor.

BURBAUX, THOMAS, coxswain of the *Unicorn* from Leith to Darien 14 July 1698, cnf Edinburgh 10 October 1707. [SRO.CC8.8.83]

BURDEN, ALEXANDER, a Covenanter from Barr, Ayrshire, imprisoned in Edinburgh, transported from Leith on the *Crown of London*, master Thomas Teddico, bound for Barbados 27 November 1679, shipwrecked and drowned off Orkney 10 December 1679. [RBM]

BURLEY, WILLIAM, a planter on Nevis, pro.1658 PCC.

BURNETT, ALEXANDER, sent from Darien to Jamaica for supplies 1699. [DSP#109]

BURNETT, ALEXANDER, a court clerk in Barbados 1705. [SPAWI. 1705.409]

BURNS, GEORGE, husband of Margaret Watson in Dysart, Fife, a sailor on the *St Andrew*, from Leith to Darien 14 July 1698, cnf Edinburgh 1707. [SRO.GD406, bundle 160, 2/3][SRO.CC8.8.83]

BURNS, JOHN, a sailor on the *Hope* to Darien 1698. [SRO.GD406, bundle 162, p39/21-25]

BURNSIDE, ANDREW, a victualler in Port Royal, Jamaica, pro.21 April 1676 Jamaica

BURROL, JOHN, a sailor, died at Darien December 1698. [NLS. RY2b8/19]

BURT, EDWARD, master of the *Margaret of Leith* 180 tons, 20 guns, with 70 man crew, was impressed by the Governor of Barbados for service against the French in the Leeward Islands where the ship was wrecked by a hurricane, petitioned the Privy Council in 1665. [PC#2.353/642]

BURT, THOMAS, a clerk on the *Unicorn* from Leith to Darien 14 July 1698, cnf Edinburgh 1707. [SRO.CC8.8.83]

BURT, THOMAS, husband of Margaret Gray in Burntisland, Fife, a cook on the *Unicorn* from Leith to Darien 14 July 1698, cnf Edinburgh 1707. [SRO.CC8.8.83]

BYRES, JAMES, a merchant from Edinburgh, instructed to sail from Greenock to Caledonia, Darien, 20 September 1699. [SRO. GD406]; from Darien via Jamaica to Charleston, South Carolina, on the *Rising Sun* August 1700.

CADDELL, CHRISTIAN, a prisoner from Edinburgh Correction House, transported by Morris Trent a merchant in Leith from Leith to Barbados on the *Mary of Leith*, master David Couston, 4 May 1663. [EBR#186.13.4]

CAIRNDUFF, JOHN, a Covenanter from Avondale, Lanarkshire, imprisoned in Edinburgh, transported from Leith on the *Crown of London*, master Thomas Teddico, bound for Barbados 27 November 1679, shipwrecked and drowned off Orkney 10 December 1679. [RBM]

CAIRNS, THOMAS, a Covenanter from Sprostoun, Roxburghshire, imprisoned in Edinburgh, transported from Leith on the *Crown of London*, master Thomas Teddico, bound for Barbados 27 November 1679, shipwrecked and drowned off Orkney 10 December 1679. [RBM]

CALDERWOOD, GEORGE, quartermaster of the *St Andrew* from Leith to Darien 14 July 1698, cnf Edinburgh 22 September 1707. [SRO.CC8.8.83]

CALDOW, ROBERT, a Covenanter from Balmaghie, Galloway captured after the Battle of Bothwell bridge 22 June 1679, transported from Leith to the West Indies on the *Crown of London*, master Thomas Teddico, November 1679, shipwrecked off Muil Head of Deerness, Orkney, 10 December 1679, later transported to Jamaica. [CEC#212/5][SW#202][RBM]

CALDWELL, JOHN, husband of Marion Orrock in Burntisland, Fife, a sailor on the *Caledonia* from Leith to Darien 14 July 1698, cnf Edinburgh 1707. [SRO.CC8.8.83]

CALDWELL, JOHN, a sailor on the *Caledonia* from Leith to Darien 14 July 1698, cnf Edinburgh 1707. [SRO.CC8.8.83]

CALDWELL, MARTHA, buried in Christchurch, Barbados, 28 July 1679. [H#496]

CALDWELL, ROBERT, from Glasgow, a sailor on the *Rising Sun* from the Clyde to Darien 18 August 1698, cnf Edinburgh 1707. [SRO. CC8.8.83]

CALDWELL, WILLIAM, a Covenanter from Girvan, Ayrshire, imprisoned in Edinburgh, transported from Leith on the *Crown of London*, master Thomas Teddico, bound for Barbados 27 November 1679, shipwrecked and drowned off Orkney 10 December 1679. [RBM]

CALDWELL, WILLIAM, a merchant, pro.3 May 1694 Barbados. [RB. 6.2.119]

CALHOUN, WILLIAM, assemblyman in St Kitts 10 September 1677. [SPAWI.1678/741]

CALLENDAR, GEORGE, pro.17 May 1694 Jamaica

CALLENDAR, JOHN, with 11 acres in St Lucy's, Barbados, 30 December 1679. [H2/35]

CALLENDAR, RICHARD, with 4 servants, 6 slaves and 11 acres in St Lucy's, Barbados, 30 December 1679. [H2/35]

CAMBY, JACOB, a sailor on the *Unicorn* from Leith to Darien 14 July 1698, cnf Edinburgh 1707. [SRO.CC8.8.83]

CAMERON, HENRY, a surgeon, emigrated to Darien, later imprisoned in Carthagena and in Spain 1700. [APS.14, app.114]

CAMERON, HUGH, a Covenanter in Dalmellington, Ayrshire, captured after the Battle of Bothwell Bridge 22 June 1679, transported from Leith to the West Indies on the *Crown of London*, master Thomas Teddico, November 1679, shipwrecked off Orkney December 1679, later transported to Jamaica. [CEC#212/5] [SW#199][RBM]

CAMERON, JOHN, with 45 acres in St James, Barbados, 20 December 1679. [H#501]

CAMERON, JOHN, with 2 servants, 6 slaves and 40 acres in St Peter's parish, Barbados, 1679. [H2/78]

CAMERON, JOHN with 2 militiamen in Colonel Bayley's Regiment in Barbados 6 January 1679. [H2/138]

CAMPBELL, ALEXANDER, died at Fort St Andrew, Darien, 20 December 1699. [DP#209]

CAMPBELL, ALEXANDER, a sailor on the *Rising Sun* from the Clyde to Darien 18 August 1699, cnf Edinburgh 27 October 1707. [SRO.CC8.8.83] [SRO.GD406, bundle 162, p39/14]

CAMPBELL, Captain ALEXANDER, of Fonabb, appointed as a Councillor of Caledonia, Darien, 20 October 1699. [SRO.GD406]; Lieutenant Colonel Alexander Campbell, late of the Duke of Argyll's Regiment and of the Earl of Portmore's Regiment, then in Darien, [APS#14.174]; cnf Edinburgh 4 October 1739.

CAMPBELL, ANN, wife of Patrick Campbell, buried in St Michael's, Barbados, 4 August 1679. [H#436]

CAMPBELL, COLIN, son of Reverend Patrick Campbell in Kenmore, Perthshire, a soldier, to Darien, died in Jamaica 1699, cnf Edinburgh 1707. [SRO.CC8.8.83]

CAMPBELL, COLIN, wrote from Caledonia Bay, Darien, describing the voyage of the *Unicorn* from Scotland to Darien 1698. [NLS. MS846]

CAMPBELL, COLIN, mate of the *St Andrew* from Leith to Darien 14 July 1698, cnf Edinburgh 1707. [SRO.CC8.8.83]

CAMPBELL, COLIN, son of Colin Campbell of Monzie, a sailor on the *Hope* bound for Darien, signed a deed of factory 31 May 1698; later imprisoned in Carthagena and in Spain. [SRO.GD406, bundle 162, p40/13][APS.14.app114]

CAMPBELL, COLIN, a Captain of the Darien Company, from the Clyde to Darien 1699, from Darien bound for Scotland on the *Little Hope*, shipwrecked off Cuba and imprisoned by the Spanish in Havanna and in Cuba, petitioned Parliament in Edinburgh 10 March 1707. [APS.XI.441, app.113]

CAMPBELL, DONALD, a Covenanter, transported from Leith to Jamaica August 1685. [PC.11.330]

CAMPBELL, DOUGALL, and his wife Mary, parents of Mary baptised in Christchurch, Barbados, 8 September 1678; a militiaman in Colonel Lyne's Regiment in Barbados 6 January 1679. [H#489] [H2/103]

CAMPBELL, DUNCAN, a gentleman in St Thomas, Jamaica, pro. July 1693 Jamaica

CAMPBELL, DUNCAN, formerly an Ensign of the Earl of Argyll's Regiment, died at Darien 1699, cnf Edinburgh 22 September 1707. [SRO.CC8.8.83]

CAMPBELL, GEORGE, a Covenanter in Irvine, transported 1679. [Irvine g/s]

CAMPBELL, GEORGE, a Covenanter from Galston, Ayrshire, imprisoned in Edinburgh, transported from Leith on the *Crown of London*, master Thomas Teddico, bound for Barbados 27 November 1679, shipwrecked and drowned off Orkney 10 December 1679. [RBM]

CAMPBELL, GILBERT, a militiaman in Colonel Lyne's Regiment in Barbados 6 January 1679. [H2/103]

CAMPBELL, HEW, a merchant trading from Port Glasgow to the West Indies on the *Walter of Glasgow* February 1683. [SRO.E72.19.8]

CAMPBELL, HUGH, with 1 slave and 3 acres in St Lucy's parish, Barbados, 1678; a militiaman in Colonel Bayley's Regiment in Barbados 8 January 1680. [H2/35,137]

CAMPBELL, JAMES, a militiaman in Colonel Thornhill's Regiment in Barbados 6 January 1680. [H2/148]

CAMPBELL, JAMES, a sailor on the *Rising Sun* to Darien, cnf Edinburgh 1707. [SRO.CC8.8.83]

CAMPBELL, JAMES, son of Colin Campbell of Monzie, a surgeon on the *Hope* bound for Darien, signed a deed of factory 31 May 1698. [SRO.GD406, bundle 162, p40/13]

CAMPBELL, JAMES, a sailor on the *Hope* from Leith to Darien 1698, cnf Edinburgh 27 October 1707. [SRO.GD406, bundle 162, p39/14] [SRO.CC8.8.83]

CAMPBELL, JANET, daughter of James Campbell, baptised in St Joseph's parish, Barbados, 9 July 1679.[H2/30]

CAMPBELL, JOHN, a militiaman in Colonel Lyne's Regiment in Barbados 6 January 1679. [H2/106]

CAMPBELL, JOHN, a militiaman in Colonel Bate's Regiment in Barbados 6 January 1679. [H2/179]

CAMPBELL, JOHN, a Covenanter from Muirkirk, Ayrshire, imprisoned in Edinburgh, transported from Leith on the *Crown of London*, master Thomas Teddico, bound for Barbados 27 November 1679, shipwrecked and drowned off Orkney 10 December 1679. [RBM]

CAMPBELL, JOHN, a Covenanter in Dunalter, Kintyre, son of Walter Campbell, transported from Leith to Jamaica August 1685. [PC.11.329]

CAMPBELL, JOHN, a Covenanter in Auchenchrydie, Cowal, son of Donald Campbell, transported from Leith to Jamaica August 1685. [PC.11.329]

CAMPBELL, JOHN, a Covenanter in Lochwoar, Lorne, son of Robert Campbell, transported from Leith to Jamaica August 1685. [PC.11.136]

CAMPBELL, JOHN, a Covenanter in Carrisk, Lochfynesyde, Argyll, transported from Leith July 1685. [PC.11.329]

CAMPBELL, JOHN, in Port Royal, Jamaica, pro.12 September 1692 Jamaica

CAMPBELL, JOHN, son of Reverend Patrick Campbell and Jean Campbell, born in Inveraray, Argyll, 1674, from Leith to Darien 1699, settled at Black River, Jamaica, as a planter, husband of (1)

Katherine Clayborn, (2) Elizabeth Gaines, father of Colin, admitted as a burgess of Glasgow 1716 and of Inveraray 1716, died in St Elizabeth, Jamaica, 29 January 1740, buried at Black River Church, Jamaica. [MIBWI#340][F.4.9][SRO.RS4.396][GBR] [IBR][Black River g/s, St Elizabeth parish, Jamaica]

CAMPBELL, ROBERT, a militiaman in Colonel Thornhill's Regiment in Barbados 6 January 1679. [H2/156]

CAMPBELL, WILLIAM, mariner, from Dunbarton to Barbados November 1667. [DBR#9]

CAMPBELL, WILLIAM, to Darien 1699, cnf Edinburgh 1707. [SRO. CC8.8.83]

CAMPBELL, WILLIAM, son of John Campbell and Elizabeth McNeil in Kildallogs, Argyll, undershipman on the *Rising Sun* from the Clyde to Darien 18 August 1699, cnf Edinburgh 1708. [SRO. CC8.8.84]

CAMPBELL, WILLIAM, a soldier who died at Darien 1699, cnf Edinburgh 1707. [SRO.CC8.8.83]

CANNIE, JOHN, a sailor, died at Darien 16 November 1698. [NLS. 2b8/19]

CARMICHAEL, Captain ARCHIBALD, with 11 slaves and 16 acres in St John's parish, Barbados, 1679. [H2/68]

CARMICHAEL, ARCHIBALD, surgeon general and councillor of Barbados 20 March 1680. [SPAWI.1679/1251]

CARMICHAEL, ARCHIBALD, Provost Marshal of Barbados May 1683. [SPAWI.1683/1094]; Clerk of the Naval Office in Barbados, granted leave of one year to go to England 27 November 1690. [ActsPCCol#391]

CARMICHAEL, WILLIAM, son of Archibald Carmichael, a merchant in Barbados by 1695. [SRO.RD2.80.10; RD4.78.1253]

CARMICHAEL, WILLIAM, husband of Jean Herd, a cook's mate on the *Unicorn* from Leith to Darien 14 July 1698, cnf Edinburgh 1707. [SRO.CC8.8.83]

CARNEGIE, JOHN, son of William Carnegie in Edinburgh, bosun's yeoman, died at Darien 22 October 1699, cnf Edinburgh 22 October 1707. [SRO.CC8.8.83]

CARNEGY, JOHN, husband of Margaret Wilson in Edinbugh, a cook on the *Caledonia* from Leith to Darien 14 July 1698, cnf Edinburgh 7 October 1707. [SRO.CC8.8.83]

CARNOCHAN, EDMOND, transported from Leith to Barbados on the *John and Nicholas*, master Edward Barnes, 17 December 1685. [PC.11.389][ETR#389]

CARR, MALCOLM, a militiaman in Colonel Lyne's Regiment in Barbados 6 January 1679. [H2/101]

CARRUTHERS, JOHN, settled in Antigua, died 1700, pro.5/740:11/449 PCC.

CARSE, EDWARD, a merchant trading from Ayr to Barbados, Montserrat and the Caribee Islands on the *Rebecca of Dublin*, 35 tons, master James Gollier, 18 November 1642. [SRO.RD1.544.6]

CASKIE, WILLIAM, quartermaster on the *Unicorn* from Leith to Darien 14 July 1698, cnf Edinburgh 1707. [SRO.CC8.8.83]

CASSELLS, JOHN, sr., from Bo'ness, West Lothian, a sailor on the *St Andrew* from Leith to Darien 14 July 1698, cnf Edinburgh 1707. [SRO.GD406, bundle 160, 4/25][SRO.CC8.8.83]

CATHCART, ALLAN, a soldier who died at Darien 1699, cnf Edinburgh 1707. [SRO.CC8.8.83]

CATHCART, ANDREW, a passenger on the *James of Ayr*, master James Chalmers, which arrived in Ayr from the West Indies 19 September 1673, [SRO.E72.3.4]; a merchant, from Ayr to the West Indies on the *James of Ayr*, February 1681, also March 1683. [SRO.E72.3.6/12]

CATHRO, SAMUEL, a shipmaster in Port Royal, Jamaica, pro. 4 September 1690 Jamaica

CAVERS, JOHN, a Covenanter, transported from Leith to the West Indies on the *St Michael of Scarborough*, master Edward Johnston, 12 December 1678. [PC.6.76]

CHALMERS, JAMES, master of the *James of Ayr*, arrived in Ayr 19 September 1673 and on 19 September 1681 from Montserrat and the West Indies. [SRO.E72.4/7]

CHALMERS, JOHN, son of John Chalmers in Kirkcaldy, Fife, a sailor on the *Endeavour* to Darien, testament 1707. [SRO.GD406, bundle 161, 25/21]

CHALMERS, ROBERT, a Covenanter from Shotts, Lanarkshire, imprisoned in Edinburgh, transported from Leith on the *Crown of London*, master Thomas Teddico, bound for Barbados 27 November 1679, shipwrecked and drowned off Orkney 10 December 1679. [RBM]

CHAMBERLAIN, WILLIAM, a passenger on the *James of Ayr*, master John Hodgson, which arrived in Ayr from the West Indies 19 September 1673. [SRO.E72.3.4]

CHAPMAN, DAVID, born 1687, a thief imprisoned in Crieff and Perth Tolbooths, banished to the American Plantations, transported by

William Ritchie a skipper in Bo'ness, West Lothian, 12 September 1699. [SRO.B59.26.11.6/8]

CHARTERS, HENRY, a volunteer, died on the voyage to Darien 16 October 1698. [WP#88]

CHIESLY, JOHN, a volunteer, died on the voyage to Darien 27 October 1698. [WP#88]

CHRISTIE, ROBERT, a merchant from Culross, Fife, husband of Margaret Sands, in Florida possibly heading for Mexico 1667. [PC.4.297]

CHRISTIE, PETER, wounded at Darien 6 February 1699. [DP#86]

CHRISTY, WILLIAM, son of John Christy, buried in St Philips parish, Barbados, 8 October 1678. [H2/23]

CHRISTY, WILLIAM, in St Philips parish, Barbados, with 5 acres and 1 slave, 1680. [H2/5]

CHRISTISON, JOHN, a Covenanter from Kilmadock, Perthshire, imprisoned in Edinburgh, transported from Leith on the *Crown of London*, master Thomas Teddico, bound for Barbados 27 November 1679, shipwrecked and drowned off Orkney 10 December 1679. [RBM]

CLANDANNING, ADAM, buried in St Philips parish, Barbados, 11 August 1678. [H2/22]

CLARK, JAMES, a Covenanter from Kilbride, Lanarkshire, imprisoned in Edinburgh, transported from Leith on the *Crown of London*, master Thomas Teddico, bound for Barbados 27 November 1679, shipwrecked and drowned off Orkney 10 December 1679. [RBM]

CLARK, JAMES, a planter, died at Darien 7 November 1698. [NLS. 2b8/19]

CLARK, JOHN, a writer in Edinburgh, transported from Leith to the West Indies on the *St Michael of Scarborough*, master Edward Johnston,12 December 1678. [PC.6.76]

CLARK, JOHN, a Covenanter from Kilbride, Lanarkshire, imprisoned in Edinburgh, transported from Leith on the *Crown of London*, master Thomas Teddico, bound for Barbados 27 November 1679, shipwrecked and drowned off Orkney 10 December 1679. [RBM]

CLARK, JOHN, jr., from Bo'ness, West Lothian, a sailor on the *Rising Sun* from the Clyde to Darien 18 August 1699, cnf Edinburgh 11 October 1707. [SRO.CC8.8.83]

CLARK, JOHN, the purser on the *St Andrew* 1698. [SRO.GD406, bundle 160, 2/16]

CLELAND, JAMES, a merchant in Edinburgh, from the Clyde to Darien on the *Rising Sun* 18 August 1699, cnf Edinburgh 28 November 1707. [SRO.CC8.8.83]

CLELLAND, JOHN, in Barbados, son of David Clelland a surgeon in Edinburgh, 1706. [SRO.RD4.99.32/34]

CLELAND, Colonel WILLIAM, Assemblyman of Barbados 24 January 1699. [SPAWI.1699/53]; reference to in Lawrence Trent's will, pro.23 March 1693 Barbados; subscribed to his will 24 August 1718, reference to his wife Sarah, his sister Margaret Cleland, widow of Arthur Bruce possibly in Edinburgh, etc., pro. 15 July 1719 Barbados. [RB6.4.519]

CLELONE, ROBERT, a sailor on the *Caledonia* from Leith to Darien 14 July 1698, cnf Edinburgh 10 October 1707. [SRO.CC8.8.83]

CLERK, ANDREW, a Covenanter from Lochruttan, Galloway, captured after the Battle of Bothwell Bridge 22 June 1679, transported from Leith to the West Indies on the *Crown of London*, master Thomas Teddico, November 1679, shipwrecked off Muil Head of Deerness, Orkney, 10 December 1679, later transported to Jamaica. [CEC#212/5][SW#203][RBM]

CLERK, DOUGAL, a Covenanter and a farmer in Otter Gallachie, Argyll, transported from Leith to Jamaica 12 August 1685. [ETR #373][PC.2.330]

CLERK, MARY, a Covenanter in Kirkcudbright 1684, transported from Leith to Jamaica August 1685, landed at Port Royal, Jamaica, November 1685. [PC.9.573;11.329][LJ#30]

CLINTRIE, ARCHIBALD, a sailor on the *Unicorn* from Leith to Darien 14 July 1698, cnf Edinburgh 1707. [SRO.CC8.8.83]

CLYDESDALE, RICHARD, a Covenanter and a chapman, transported from Leith to the West Indies on the *St Michael of Scarborough*, master Edward Johnston,12 December 1678. [PC.6.76]

CLYDESDALE, ROBERT, a passenger on the *James of Ayr*, master James Chalmers, arrived in Ayr from the West Indies 19 September 1673. [SRO.E72.3.4]

CLYDESDALE, ROBERT, son of the late William Clydesdale, surgeon burgess of Glasgow, to the West Indies 1680. [SRO.B10.15.1743]

CLYDESDALE, ROBERT, a merchant trading from Port Glasgow to the West Indies on the *Walter of Glasgow* February 1683. [SRO. E72.19.8]

COCHRANE, Lieutenant ARCHIBALD, representative in Antigua June 1678. [SPAWI.1678/741]; Councillor of Antigua 30 September 1684. [SPAWI.1684/1879]

COCHRANE, ELIAZER, freeman and militiaman in Colonel Standfast's regiment in Barbados 6 January 1679; with 11 acres in St Thomas parish, Barbados, 3 December 1679. [H2/58/161]

COCHRANE, JAMES, a cook on the *Unicorn* from Leith to Darien 14 July 1698, cnf Edinburgh 1707. [SRO.CC8.8.83]

COCHRAN, JOHN, a Covenanter from Avondale, Lanarkshire, imprisoned in Edinburgh, transported from Leith on the *Crown of London*, master Thomas Teddico, bound for Barbados 27 November 1679, shipwrecked and drowned off Orkney 10 December 1679. [RBM]

COCHRANE, JOHN, and Robert Cochrane, sons of William Cochrane, V. Garret Powell and his wife Elizabeth, former wife of Colonel Archibald Cochrane, in Antigua 29 June 1699. [ActsPCCpl.#751]

COCHRAN, JOHN, died in Montserrat, pro.1699 PCC [PAB158/130][130, Pett]

COCHRANE, MUNGO, husband of Christine Rattoun, a Covenanter and a merchant burgess of Glasgow, transported from Leith to the West Indies on the *St Michael of Glasgow*, master Edward Johnston, 12 December 1678. [PC.6.76]

COCKBURN, Dr JAMES, son of Sir Archibald Cockburn of Langton, apprenticed to John Jossie an Edinburgh apothecary in 1690, married Sarah ..., father of Archibald (born 1708), William, Thomas, Frances, and Sarah, settled in Jamaica before 1711, died 1717. [CFR#256]

COCKBURN, JAMES, from Lasswade, Midlothian, a sailor on the *St Andrew* from Leith to Darien 14 July 1698, cnf Edinburgh 23 October 1707. [SRO.GD406, bundle 160, 2/1][SRO.CC8.8.83]

COCKBURN, WILLIAM, son of William Cockburn and Isobel Landreth in Langton Mill, settled in Grenada, died there 1687. [CFR#257]

COGLE, DAVID, from Gallowhill, Wick, Caithness, a sailor on the *Unicorn* from Leith to Darien 14 July 1698, cnf Edinburgh 1708. [SRO.CC8.8.84]

COLT, ANDREW, from Quarrell, Stirlingshire, a mariner on the *Unicorn* from Leith to Darien 14 July 1698, died at Darien, cnf Edinburgh 24 September 1707. [SRO.CC8.8.84]

COLQUHOUN, OWEN, buried in St James, Barbados, 29 July 1679. [H#499]

COLQUHOUN, WILLIAM, a resident of Glasgow, who had for 20 years been a planter in the Caribee Islands, 1681. [PC.7.664]

COLVILLE, ARCHIBALD, a planter who died in Barbados 1647, testimonial re his daughter Mary, wife of Lieutenant Colonel William Carmichael, and his grandsons William and Archibald Carmichael, 1659. [EBR.9.2.1659]

COLVILL, JAMES, a Covenanter from Glencairn, Nithsdale, imprisoned in Edinburgh, transported from Leith on the *Crown of London*, master Thomas Teddico, bound for Barbados 27 November 1679, shipwrecked and drowned off Orkney 10 December 1679. [RBM]

COLVILL, JOHN, son of John Colvill, a midshipman on the *Rising Sun* from Leith to Darien 14 July 1698, cnf Edinburgh 1707. [SRO. CC8.8.83]

COMIN, JAMES, a schoolmaster, emigrated to the Leeward Islands 1695. [EMA#21]

CONGILTON, JAMES, a prisoner in Edinburgh Tolbooth, transported by Morris Trent a merchant in Leith from Leith to Barbados on the *Mary*, master David Couston, 4 May 1663. [EBR#186.13.4]

CONRODSMEYER, DANIEL, a trumpeter on the *St Andrew* from Leith to Darien 14 July 1698, cnf Edinburgh 1707. [SRO.CC8. 8.83]

COOK, ALEXANDER, a sailor on the *Unicorn* from Leith to Darien 14 July 1698, died at Darien, cnf Edinburgh 3 October 1707. [SRO.CC8.8.83]

COOK, ANDREW, a Covenanter from Melrose, Roxburghshire, imprisoned in Edinburgh, transported from Leith on the *Crown of London*, master Thomas Teddico, bound for Barbados 27 November 1679, shipwrecked and drowned off Orkney 10 December 1679. [RBM]

COOK, JOHN, a sailor on the *Endeavour* to Darien 1698. [SRO. GD406, bundle 161, 25/8]

COOK, JOHN, sr., father of James Cook in Kirkcaldy, Fife, a sailor on the *Caledonia* from Leith to Darien 14 July 1698, died in the West Indies, cnf Edinburgh 6 October 1707. [SRO.CC8.8.83]

COPLAND, PATRICK, born in Aberdeen 1572, educated at Aberdeen Grammar School and at Marischal College, Aberdeen; in London 1615, enrolled as a chaplain to the East India Company, chaplain on the *Royal James* in the East Indies 1618; appointed as Rector of Henrico College, Virginia, and as a member of the Virginia Council, granted land in Virginia; settled in Bermuda as a schoolmaster 1626; in Paget's Tribe, Somer Islands 1632; moved to the Bahamas 1648, died there during 1650s. [AUR][SRO. NRAS#0486][ACL#1.133/185/225/342]

CORBET, HUGH, witnessed a document in St Kitts 21 January 1700. [SRO.GD84.Sec.1/22/9B]

CORCORAN, WILLIAM, militiaman in Colonel Colleton's Regiment in Barbados 6 March 1680. [H2/127]

CORSAN, JAMES, a Covenanter from Kirkcudbrightshire, imprisoned in Edinburgh Tolbooth, transported from Leith on the *Crown of London*, master Thomas Teddico, bound for Barbados 27 November 1679, shipwrecked and drowned off Orkney 10 December 1679. [RBM][ETR#79]

COULTER, ADAM, a passenger on the *Swan of Ayr*, master David Ferguson, arrived in Ayr from the West Indies 23 September 1678. [SRO.E72.3.4]

COUPAR, JAMES, a Covenanter from Carnwath, Lanarkshire, imprisoned in Edinburgh, transported from Leith on the *Crown of London*, master Thomas Teddico, bound for Barbados 27 November 1679, shipwrecked and drowned off Orkney 10 December 1679. [RBM]

COUPAR, JAMES, from Park of Erskine, a carpenter's mate on the *Rising Sun* from the Clyde to Darien 18 August 1699, cnf Edinburgh 13 November 1707. [SRO.CC8.8.83]

COUSTOUN, DAVID, master of the *Mary* from Leith to Barbados 4 May 1663. [EBR#186.13.4]

COUSTON, JAMES, a Covenanter from Southdean, Roxburghshire, imprisoned in Edinburgh, transported from Leith on the *Crown of London*, master Thomas Teddico, bound for Barbados 27 November 1679, shipwrecked and drowned off Orkney 10 December 1679. [RBM]

COUSTOUN, ROBERT, from St Ninian's parish, Stirlingshire, a sailor on the *Caledonia* from Leith to Darien 14 July 1698, cnf Edinburgh 5 December 1707. [SRO.CC8.8.83]

CRACHTER, JOHN, son of James Crachter in Newcastle, a sailor on the *St Andrew* from Leith to Darien 14 July 1698, cnf Edinburgh 1707. [SRO.CC8.8.83]

CRAFFORD, ALEXANDER, in Antigua, died on the Queen's frigate at sea 1707. [pro.5/4913; 11/497 PCC]

CRAG, JOHN, and his wife Susanna, parents of John baptised in St Michael's, Barbados, 30 March 1679. [H#424]

CRAGE, JOHN buried in St George's, Barbados, 12 February 1679. [H#467]

CRAG, WILLIAM, with 1 slave, in St Michael's, Barbados, 1680. [H#443]; a militiaman on Colonel Bate's Regiment in Barbados 1679. [H2/181]

CRAICH, JOHN, a weaver in Peebles, father of Thomas Craich, from Leith to Darien on the *Dolphin* 14 July 1698, cnf Edinburgh 1707. [SRO.CC8.8.83]

CRAIG, JAMES, a Covenanter from Glassford, Lanarkshire, imprisoned in Edinburgh, transported from Leith on the *Crown of London*, master Thomas Teddico, bound for Barbados 27 November 1679, shipwrecked and drowned off Orkney 10 December 1679. [RBM]

CRAIG, PATRICK, from Kirkwall, Orkney, a sailor on the *St Andrew* from Leith to Darien 14 July 1698, cnf Edinburgh 1708. [SRO.CC8.8.84] [SRO.GD406, bundle 159, p4/12]

CRAWFORD, HUGH, born 1680, a merchant in Kingston, Jamaica, died 17 December 1719. [Kingston g/s]

CRAWFORD, JAMES, a seaman in Leith, from Leith to Darien on the *St Andrew*, subscribed to a deed of factory in favor of his wife Margaret Gardner 2 January 1699. [SRO.GD406, bundle 159, p4/6]

CRAWFORD, JAMES, son of ... Crawford and Jean Gordon in Grangepans, West Lothian, a sailor on the *Rising Sun* from the Clyde to Darien 18 August 1699, died at Darien, cnf Edinburgh 23 September 1707. [SRO.CC8.8.83]

CRAWFORD, JOHN, a merchant trading from Port Glasgow to the West Indies on the *Mayflower of Glasgow* October 1684. [SRO.E72.19.9]

CRAWFORD, JOHN, a Covenanter in Otter, Argyll, transported from Leith to Jamaica 12 December 1685. [PC.11.136][ETR#373]

CRAWFORD, JOHN, merchant on the *Swan of Ayr*, master John Miliken, arrived in Ayr 27 September 1691 from the Caribee Islands. [SRO.E72.3.23]

CRAWFORD, JOHN, son of Thomas Crawford in Kirkcaldy, Fife, a sailor on the *Rising Sun* from the Clyde to Darien 18 August 1699, cnf Edinburgh 24 September 1707. [SRO.CC8.8.83]

CRAWFORD, THOMAS, a freeman and militiaman in Colonel Stanfast's Regiment in Barbados 6 January 1679. [H2/157]

CRAWFORD, THOMAS, buried in Christchurch, Barbados, 21 October 1679. [H#494]

CRAWFORD, THOMAS, master of the *Swan of Dunbarton*, from Port Glasgow to the Caribee Islands with coal, butter, thread, playing cards, stockings, hats, beef, cloth, grinding stones, and gloves, 18 March 1685. [SRO.E72.19.9]

CRAWFORD, Mr WILLIAM, had his children Esther born 1665, Caesar born 1666, Mary born 1667, baptised in St Philips parish, Barbados, 1 June 1678; Lieutenant of Captain Vintner's Troop of Horse Militia 6 January 1679; resident in St Philips parish, Barbados, with 30 acres, 1 servant and 22 slaves, 1680. [H2/5.18.205]

CRAWFORD, WILLIAM, a Militia Lieutenant in Barbados 5 January 1679. [H2/205]

CRAWFORD, WILLIAM, transported from Leith to Jamaica 12. December 1685. [PC.11.148][ETR#373]

CRIGHTON, THOMAS, from Carnwath, Lanarkshire, a Covenanter imprisoned in Edinburgh Tolbooth, transported from Leith bound for Barbados on the *Crown of London*, master Thomas Teddico, 15 November 1679, shipwrecked and drowned off Orkney 10 December 1679. [ETR#162][RBM]

CROAKER, ROBERT, a seaman on the *St Andrew* from Leith to Darien 14 July 1698, cnf Edinburgh 1707. [SRO.CC8.8.83]

CROOKS, JAMES, from Garturk, a soldier who died at Darien 1699, cnf Edinburgh 1707. [SRO.CC8.8.83]

CROOKSHANKS, ALEXANDER, had his daughter Hester baptised in St George's, Barbados, 3 November 1678. [H#465]

CRUICKSHANK, ALEXANDER, a merchant from Aberdeen, died in Antigua 1713. [APB#2.111]

CROSBIE, DAVID, a Covenanter in Carmunnock, Lanarkshire, transported from Leith to the West Indies on the *St Michael of Scarborough*, master Edward Johnston,12 December 1678. [PC.6.76]

CROW, Reverend FRANCIS, born 1627, son of Patrick Crow of Heughhead and Elizabeth Clapperton, minister of Chirnside, Berwickshire, 1653–1658, emigrated to Jamaica 1686, died in Essex, England, 1692. [F.2.33]

CUMIN, JOHN, a Covenanter and a weaver in the Bridgend of Glasgow, transported from Leith to the West Indies on the *St Michael of Scarborough*, master Edward Johnston, 12 December 1678. [PC.6.76]

CUMMINS, ROBERT, a householder and militiaman in Barbados 1679. [H2/165]

CUMMING, DANIEL, from Edinburgh, a sailor on the *Unicorn* from Leith to Darien 14 July 1698, cnf Edinburgh 1707. [SRO.CC8. 8.83]

CUMMING, THOMAS, with 1 slave and 6 acres in St Lucy's parish, Barbados, 1678; father of Jane baptised in St Lucy's, Barbados, 6 October 1678, [H2/51]; a militiaman in Colonel Bayley's Regiment in Barbados 1679. [H2/143].

CUMMING, THOMAS, son of John Cumming in Valleyfield, Culross, Fife, a sailor on the *Endeavour* from Leith to Darien 14. July 1698, cnf Edinburgh 8 October 1707. [SRO.CC8.8.83]

CUMMING, THOMAS, from Irvine, Ayrshire, skipper of the *Speedy Return* from the Clyde to Darien 12 October 1699, cnf Edinburgh 1708. [SRO.CC8.8.84]

CUNNINGHAM, ADAM, brother of Sir William Cunningham of Caprington, a midshipman, died on the voyage to Darien 22 October 1698. [WP#88][DD#149]

CUNNINGHAM, ALEXANDER, Captain of Militia in Barbados 6 January 1679. [H2/106]

CUNNINGHAM, ALEXANDER, from Dysart, Fife, sailor on the *Unicorn* from Leith to Darien 14 July 1698, cnf. Edinburgh 1707. [SRO.CC8.8.83]

CUNNINGHAM, ARCHIBALD, a thief imprisoned in Edinburgh Tolbooth, transported from Leith on William Johnston's ship, 23 December 1680. [ETR#178]

CUNNINGHAM, CHARLES, a minister, emigrated to Jamaica 1707. [EMA#22]

CUNNINGHAM, DANIEL, a Covenanter from Drummond, Stirlingshire, imprisoned in Edinburgh, transported from Leith on the *Crown of London*, master Thomas Teddico, bound for Barbados 27 November 1679, shipwrecked and drowned off Orkney 10 December 1679. [RBM]

CUNNINGHAM, DANIEL, from Edinburgh, a sailor on the *Unicorn* from Leith to Darien 14 July 1698, cnf Edinburgh 10 October 1707. [SRO.CC8.8.83]

CUNNINGHAM, DAVID, transported from Leith November 1679. [ETR#162]

CUNNINGHAM, EDWARD, in Barbados, before 1676. [PC#4.671]

CUNNINGHAM, GEORGE, with 5 acres in St Joseph's parish, Barbados, 1680. [H2/28]

CUNNINGHAM, J., wrote to the Directors of the Company of Scotland trading to Africa and the Indies from Caledonia, New Edinburgh, Darien, 28 December 1698. [SRO.GD406.1.6489]

CUNNINGHAM, JAMES, a Covenanter from Eastwood, Renfrewshire, imprisoned in Edinburgh, transported from Leith on the *Crown of London*, master Thomas Teddico, bound for Barbados 27 November 1679, shipwrecked and drowned off Orkney 10 December 1679. [RBM]

CUNNINGHAM, JAMES, transported from Leith to Jamaica 17 August 1685, landed at Port Royal, Jamaica, died in Jamaica. [ETR #390][LJ#35]

CUNNINGHAM, JAMES, a prisoner in Edinburgh Tolbooth, transported from Leith to Barbados on the *John and Nicholas*, master Edward Barnes, 12 December 1685. [ETR#390]

CUNNINGHAM, Major JAMES, of Aiket, arrived in Edinburgh from America with news of the Scots Colony at Darien and was admitted as a burgess of Edinburgh on 17 May 1699. [Edinburgh Burgess Roll]

CUNNINGHAM, JOHN, militiaman in Colonel Lyne's Regiment 6 January 1679. [H2/101]

CUNNINGHAM, Mr JOHN, buried in St Michael's, Barbados, 11 July 1679. [H#435]

CUNNINGHAM, JOHN, transported from Leith to Jamaica 11 August 1685. [PC#11.329][ETR#369]

CUNNINGHAM, ROBERT, son of Robert Cunningham in Glengarnock, Ayrshire, emigrated ca.1700, a soldier and a planter, settled in St Kitts, married Judith Bonnefaut, father of Richard, Elizabeth, Daniel and Robert, died after 1727. [SRO.CS230.15.7][Caribeanna#1.101]

CUNNINGHAM, WILLIAM, baptised in St Peter's parish, Barbados, 1679. [H2/85]

CUNNINGHAM, WILLIAM, a militiaman in Colonel Bayley's Regiment in Barbados 11 September 1679. [H2/132]

CUNNINGHAM, WILLIAM, soldier of Major William Foster's Company of Militia 6 January 1679. [H2/134]

CUNNINGHAM, WILLIAM, a sailor on the *Hope* from the Clyde to Darien 18 August 1699, cnf Edinburgh 11 October 1707. [SRO. CC8.8.83] [SRO.GD406, bundle 162, p40/1]

CUNNINGHAM, ... Captain, with 4 men in Lieutenant Thomas Maxwell's troop of horse militia in Barbados 6 January 1679. [H2/211]

CURREY, PATRICK, son of Patrick Currey, baptised in St Joseph's parish, Barbados, 9 July 1679. [H2/30]

CURRIE, DAVID, a Covenanter from Fenwick, Ayrshire, imprisoned in Edinburgh, transported from Leith on the *Crown of London*, master Thomas Teddico, bound for Barbados 27 November 1679, shipwrecked and drowned off Orkney 10 December 1679. [RBM]

CURRIE, JOAN, prisoner in Edinburgh Correction House, transported by Morris Trent, a merchant in Leith, from Leith to Barbados on the *Mary*, master David Couston, 8 May 1663. [EBR#186.13.4]

CURRY, ROBERT, militiaman in Colonel Thornhill's Regiment in Barbados 6 January 1679. [H2/156]

CUSSINS, JOHN, a sailor on the *St Andrew* from Leith to Darien 14 July 1698, cnf Edinburgh 1707. [SRO.CC8.8.83]

CUTHBERT, ALEXANDER, his daughter Elizabeth baptised in St James, Barbados, 8 September 1678. [H#497]

CUTHBERTSON, JOHN, a Covenanter from Kilmarnock, Ayrshire, imprisoned in Edinburgh, transported from Leith on the *Crown of London*, master Thomas Teddico, bound for Barbados 27 November 1679, shipwrecked and drowned off Orkney 10 December 1679. [RBM]

DALGLEISH, ALEXANDER, a minister educated at Edinburgh University, emigrated from Leith to Darien 14 July 1698, died on Montserrat November 1698. [F.7.663]

DALLING, RICHARD, master of the *Hope of Bo'ness*, surrendered to the Spanish at Carthagena April 1700. [DD#348]

DALRYMPLE, THOMAS, a planter, died on the voyage to Darien 5 October 1698. [WP#87]

DALZIELL, CHARLES, son of the Earl of Carnwath, died at Darien 1699, cnf Edinburgh 1707. [SRO.CC8.8.83]

DANIEL, JOHN, a planter, died on the voyage to Darien 24 October 1698. [WP#88]

DAVIDSON, JAMES, a planter, died on the voyage to Darien 24 October 1698. [WP#88]

DAVIDSON, JOHN, from Aberdeen, a former exile in Barbados, who was admitted as a burgess of Aberdeen 14 November 1666. [ABR]

DAVIDSON, JOSEPH, son of Patrick Davidson and Katherine Cathcart in Ayr, gunner on the *Dolphin* from Leith to Darien 14 July 1698, cnf Edinburgh 1707. [SRO.CC8.8.84][SRO.GD406, bundle 163, C23/4/8]

DAVIDSON, ROBERT, from Edinburgh, a sailor on the *Dolphin* from Leith to Darien 14 July 1698. cnf Edinburgh 7 October 1707. [SRO.CC8.8.83]

DAVIDSON, WILLIAM, emigrated from Ayr to the West Indies on the *James of Ayr* February 1681. [SRO.E72.3.6]

DAVIDSON, WILLIAM, bosun of the *St Andrew* from Leith to Darien 14 July 1698, cnf Edinburgh 1707. [SRO.CC8.8.83]; witness to the testament of George Calderwood, quartermaster, 16 July 1698.

DEANS, JOHN, a Covenanter from Nenthorn, Berwickshire, imprisoned in Edinburgh, transported from Leith on the *Crown of London*, master Thomas Teddico, bound for Barbados 27 November 1679, shipwrecked and drowned off Orkney 10 December 1679. [RBM]

DEMPSTER, EDWARD, a shipmaster, pro.2 June 1669 Jamaica

DEWAR, STEPHEN, a soldier of Colonel Carter's Militia Troop in Barbados 5 January 1679; a time-expired indentured servant, emigrated from Barbados to Antigua on the bark *Resolution*, master Thomas Gilbert, 15 November 1679. [H#365][H2/51

DICK, EDWARD, from Airth, Stirlingshire, a sailor on the *Caledonia* from Leith to Darien 14 July 1698, cnf Edinburgh 1707. [SRO. CC8.8.83]

DICK, JOHN, son of George Dick in Airth, Stirlingshire, cook on the *Caledonia* from Leith to Darien 14 July 1698, cnf Edinburgh 1707. [SRO.CC8.8.83]

DICK, ROBERT, from Edinburgh, transported from Leith to the West Indies on the *St Michael of Scarborough*, master Edward Johnston, 12 December 1678. [PC.6.76]

DOD, RALPH, a soldier, to Jamaica on the *Grantham* 1659. [SPC. 1659.126]

DONALD, DAVID, from Kincardine on Forth, a sailor on the *Rising Sun* from Greenock, Renfrewshire, to Darien 18 August 1699, cnf Edinburgh 1707. [SRO.CC8.8.83]

DONALD, DAVID, husband of Isabel Turnbull in Lochbank, son of David Donald or McDonald of Shangzie, to Darien 1699, "who stayed at Darien till it was deserted and thereafter deceased abroad", cnf Edinburgh 6 July 1709. [SRO.CC8.8.84]

DONALD, MATHEW, transported from Glasgow to Jamaica 13 February 1669. [GBR]

DONALDSON, ANDREW, a Covenanter from Girthorn, Kirkcudbrightshire, imprisoned in Edinburgh, transported from Leith on the *Crown of London*, master Thomas Teddico, bound for Barbados 27 November 1679, shipwrecked and drowned off Orkney 10 December 1679. [RBM]

DONALDSON, JAMES, a Covenanter from Kelton, Kirkcudbrightshire, imprisoned in Edinburgh, transported from Leith on the *Crown of London*, master Thomas Teddico, bound for Barbados 27 November 1679, shipwrecked and drowned off Orkney 10 December 1679. [RBM]

DONALDSON, JOHN, a Covenanter from Kincardine, Perthshire, imprisoned in Edinburgh, transported from Leith on the *Crown of London*, master Thomas Teddico, bound for Barbados 27 November 1679, shipwrecked and drowned off Orkney 10 December 1679. [RBM]

DONALDSON, ROBERT, a planter, died on the voyage to Darien 22 August 1698. [WP#87]

DOUGALL, ARTHUR, a Covenanter and a wright in Glasgow, husband of Katherine Hall, transported from Leith to the West Indies on the *St Michael of Scarborough*, master Edward Johnston, 13 June 1678. [PC.6.76]

DOUGALL, DANIEL, with 1 slave in St Andrew's, Barbados, 1680. [H#472]

DOUGALL, JOHN, from Crawforddykes, Renfrewshire, a sailor on the *Speedy Return* to Darien 1699, cnf 7 December 1707. [SRO.CC8. 8.83]

DOUGALL, ROBERT, from Crawforddykes, Renfrewshire, carpenter's mate on the *Rising Sun* from the Clyde to Darien 18 August 1699, cnf Edinburgh 7 December 1707. [SRO.CC8.8.83]

DOUGLAS, EDWARD, soldier in Captain Elliot's Company of Militia in Barbados 1679. [H2/188]

DOUGLAS, GEORGE, an Ensign, died at Darien, cnf Edinburgh 6 October 1707. [SRO.CC8.8.83]

DOUGLAS, JAMES, husband of Katherine Waterstone, father of James and Christian in Edinburgh, a carpenter on the *St Andrew* from Leith to Darien 14 July 1698, cnf Edinburgh 1707. [SRO.CC8. 8.83]

DOUGLAS, JOHN, a Covenanter from Kirkmichael, Ayrshire, imprisoned in Edinburgh, transported from Leith on the *Crown of London*, master Thomas Teddico, bound for Barbados 27 November 1679, shipwrecked and drowned off Orkney 10 December 1679. [RBM]

DOUGLAS, NATHAN, soldier of Captain Burton's Company of Militia in Barbados 1679. [H2/184]

DOUGLAS, SAMUEL, a Covenanter from Cavers, Roxburghshire, imprisoned in Edinburgh, transported from Leith on the *Crown of London*, master Thomas Teddico, bound for Barbados 27 November 1679, shipwrecked and drowned off Orkney 10 December 1679. [RBM]

DOUGLAS, WILLIAM, indentured in Bristol for 4 years service in Nevis, 19 November 1670. [BRO]

DOUGLAS, WILLIAM, soldier in Captain Hackett's Company of Militia in Barbados 6 March 1680. [H2/128]

DOW, JAMES, coxswain on the *Caledonia* from Leith to Darien 14 July 1698, "died in English service in the West Indies", cnf Edinburgh 10 October 1707. [SRO.CC8.8.83]

DOWNIE, JAMES, from Peterhead, Aberdeenshire, a sailor on the *Unicorn* from Leith to Darien 14 July 1698, cnf Edinburgh 21 October 1707. [SRO.CC8.8.83]

DOWNIE, JOHN, a Covenanter, transported from Leith to Jamaica August 1685. [PC.11.130]

DRAFIN, GEORGE, a Covenanter from Lesmahagow, Lanarkshire, captured after the Battle of Bothwell Bridge 22 June 1679, transported from Leith to the West Indies on the *Crown of London*, master Thomas Teddico, November 1679, shipwrecked off Muil Head of Deerness, Orkney 10 December 1679, later transported to Jamaica. [CEC#212/5][SW#199][RBM]

DREDDAN, Captain GEORGE, master of the merchant ship *Glasgow* bound for Barbados and the Caribee Islands, together with John Anderson and Archibald Scott, merchants in Glasgow, petitioned the Privy Council for vagabonds etc for shipment there, 8 December 1670. [PC#3.259]

DRENNAN, WILLIAM, a Covenanter transported from Leith to Jamaica 11 August 1685.(probably on the *John and Nicholas*, master Edward Barnes) [PC.11.329][ETR#369]

DRIPS, WILLIAM,, a Covenanter from Mauchline, Ayrshire, imprisoned in Edinburgh, transported from Leith on the *Crown of London*, master Thomas Teddico, bound for Barbados 27 November 1679, shipwrecked and drowned off Orkney 10 December 1679. [RBM]

DRUMMOND, ARCHIBALD, a sailor on the *Caledonia* bound for Darien, witness to the teatament of Henry Gilchrist 16 August 1698.

DRUMMOND, GEORGE, signed a deposition describing the conditions at the Darien Settlement in May 1699. [Audienca de Panama, General Archives of the Indies, Seville, #160{2535}969-6-5]

DRUMMOND, GEORGE, from Kirkwall, Orkney, now of Barbados, surgeon on the ship *Blessing*, will subscribed 16 May 1701, pro.23 May 1701 Barbados. [RB6.43.269]

DRUMMOND, Captain LAURENCE, from Darien to New York, from Sandy Hook 12 October 1699 on the *Endeavour*, arrived at Islay 20 November 1699, from there to Edinburgh with news of Darien. [DSP#108]

DRUMMOND, ROBERT, a sergeant, wounded at Darien 6 February 1699. [DP#86]

DRUMMOND, ROBERT, a cornet in Lord Jedburgh's Regiment, later Captain of the *Caledonia*, Admiralty Court decree 29 May 1702. [SRO.NRAS.0364/63]; from Darien via New York to Islay on the *Caledonia*1699. [DSP#109/113]

DRUMMOND, Captain THOMAS, councillor in Caledonia [Darien], subscribed to an agreement in St Thomas 27 October 1699. [SPAWI.1699/902]; wrote from Darien of supplies received from Barbados, New England, and Scotland. [SRO.NRAS#859.21.5]

DRUMMOND, THOMAS, from Edinburgh, a soldier, to Darien, cnf Edinburgh 1707. [SRO.CC8.8.83]

DRYSDALE, DAVID, husband of Jean Archibald in Culross, Fife, a sailor on the *Rising Sun* from Greenock to Darien 18 August 1699, cnf Edinburgh 7 October 1707. [SRO.CC8.8.83]

DRYSDALE, JOHN, a Covenanter, transported to the West Indies October 1681. [PC.7.219]

DUFFUS, JOHN, a sailor who died on the voyage to Darien 1 October 1699. [WP#87]

DUNBAR, ALEXANDER, in St Elizabeth, Jamaica, pro.30 January 1679 Jamaica

DUNBAR, GEORGE, a Covenanter from Craigie, Ayrshire, captured after the Battle of Bothwell Bridge 22 June 1679, imprisoned in Edinburgh, transported from Leith to the West Indies on the *Crown of London*, master Thomas Teddico, November 1679, shipwrecked off Muil Head of Deerness, Orkney, 10 December 1679, later shipped to Jamaica. [SW#200][RBM]

DUNBAR, JAMES, a merchant bound for Barbados, petitioned the Privy Council for felons in Edinburgh, Leith and Canongate Tolbooths for shipment to there, 11 January 1666. [PC.2.128]

DUNBAR, JOHN, a passenger on the *Unity of Ayr*, master John Hodgson, which arrived in Ayr from Montserrat 2 September 1673; passenger on the *Swan of Ayr,* master David Ferguson, arrived in Ayr from Montserrat and the West Indies 23 September 1678. [SRO.E72.3.3/4]

DUNBAR, ROBERT, master of the *Tidewell* galley, died in Nevis, pro.1700 PCC; [DP#335]

DUNCAN, ANDREW, soldier of Captain Dent's Company of Militia in Barbados 6 January 1679; in St Philips parish Barbados, with 10 acres and 4 slaves, 1680. [H2/6.104]

DUNCAN, GEORGE, in Barbados 1700. [SPAWI.1700.88/133]

DUNCAN, HECTOR, in St Thomas, Jamaica, pro.30 August 1684 Jamaica

DUNCAN, JAMES, a Covenanter in Grange, transported August 1670. [PC.3.206]

DUNCAN, JAMES, born 1671, a mariner in Barbados, appointed master of the *Amity* there in 1697. [PRO.HCA.Exams.#82, 24.6.1700]

DUNCAN, THOMAS, soldier of Captain Burrow's Company of Militia in Barbados 1679. [H2/181]

DUNCAN, WALTER, husband of Helen Hill in Bo'ness, West Lothian, skipper of the *Duke of Hamilton* at Darien, from Darien via Jamaica to Carolina 1700, shipwrecked at Charleston, South Carolina, August 1700, cnf Edinburgh 5 December 1707. [SRO.CC8. 8.83]

DUNCAN, WILLIAM, soldier of Pinket's Company of Militia in Barbados 6 January 1679. [H2/109]

DUNDAS, WALTER, son of Robert Dundas in Harbiston, a soldier, died at Darien, cnf 1707 Edinburgh. [SRO.CC8.8.83]

DUNDAS, WILLIAM, a time-expired indentured servant, emigrated from Barbados to Virginia on the *Young William*, master Thomas Cornish, 1 August 1679. [H#364]

DUNLOP, ALEXANDER, of Dunlop, from Kelburn, Ayrshire, to Antigua on the *Richard and John of London* 4 March 1686, landed there 15 May 1686, left there 27 July 1686 possibly via Port Royal, South Carolina, [WLClements Lib., Misc. Bound Collections, University of Michigan]

DUNLOP, JAMES, a merchant in Garnkirk, died in Curacao, pro.1684 PCC.

DUNLOP, ..., an Ensign, wounded at Darien 6 February 1699. [DP#86]

DUNN, QUENTIN, a Covenanter, transported from Leith to Jamaica 11 August 1685. [PC.11.329][ETR#369]

DUNNIE, JAMES, a planter, died on the voyage to Darien 16 September 1698. [WP#87]

DURHAM, ARCHIBALD, soldier of Captain Thornhill's Company of Miitia in Barbados 6 January 1679. [H2/151]

DURY, MARGARET, a Covenanter in Edinburgh, wife of James Kello, transported July 1668. [PC.2.500]

EAGLETON, ARCHIBALD, from Fisherrow, Edinburgh, a sailor on the *Unicorn* from Leith to Darien 14 July 1698, cnf Edinburgh 1707. [SRO.CC8.8.83]

EASTON, ANDREW, a Covenanter from Torpichen, West Lothian, imprisoned in Edinburgh, transported from Leith on the *Crown of London*, master Thomas Teddico, bound for Barbados 27 November 1679, shipwrecked and drowned off Orkney 10 December 1679. [RBM]

EASTON, JAMES, a Covenanter from Torpichen, West Lothian, imprisoned in Edinburgh, transported from Leith on the *Crown of London*, master Thomas Teddico, bound for Barbados 27 November 1679, shipwrecked and drowned off Orkney 10 December 1679. [RBM]

EASTON, JOHN, a Covenanter from Torpichen, West Lothian, captured after the Battle of Bothwell Bridge 22 June 1679, transported from Leith to the West Indies on the *Crown of London*, master Thomas Teddico November 1679, shipwrecked off Muil Head of Deerness, Orkney, 10 December 1679, later shipped to Jamaica. [SW#201][RBM]

ECCLES, MUNGO, a Covenanter from Maybole, Ayrshire, imprisoned in Edinburgh, transported from Leith on the *Crown of London*, master Thomas Teddico, bound for Barbados 27 November 1679, shipwrecked and drowned off Orkney 10 December 1679. [RBM]

EDGAR, JOHN, a Covenanter from Balmaclennan, Galloway, captured after the Battle of Bothwell Bridge 22 June 1679, transported from Leith to the West Indies on the *Crown of London*, master Thomas Teddico, November 1679, shipwrecked off the Muil Head of Deerness, Orkney, 10 December 1679, later shipped to Jamaica. [SW#203][RBM]

EDMONSTONE, PATRICK, son of the laird of Ednam, late of the Darien Company's Service, 1707. [APS.14, app.114]

ELDER, ALEXANDER, died on the voyage to Darien 25 September 1698. [WP#87]

ELLIOT, HENRY, a time-expired indentured servant, emigrated from Barbados to Antigua on the sloop *True Friendship*, master Charles Callaghan, 2 October 1679. [H#367]

ELLIOT, JOHN, in Port Royal, Jamaica, pro.16 May 1671 Jamaica

ELLIOT, JOHN, a Covenanter from Southdean, Roxburghshire, imprisoned in Edinburgh, transported from Leith on the *Crown of London*, master Thomas Teddico, bound for Barbados 27 November 1679, shipwrecked and drowned off Orkney 10 December 1679. [RBM]

ELLIOT, JOHN, a Covenanter in Teviotdale, transported from Leith to Jamaica August 1685, landed at Port Royal, Jamaica. [PC.11.329] [LJ#44]

ELLIOT, Captain JOHN, with 5 servant, 131 slaves, and 200 acres in St Thomas parish, Barbados, 1679. [H2/58]

ELLIOT, MARY, wife of Thomas Elliot, buried in St Philips parish, Barbados, 20 September 1679. [H2/25]

ELLIOT, PETER, with 4 slaves and 10 acres in St Lucy's parish, Barbados, 1678. [H2/37]

ELLIOT, RICHARD, son of Richard and Jane Elliot, buried in St Michael's, Barbados, 25 September 1679. [H#438]; with 1 servant and 20 slaves in Christchurch, Barbados, 22 December 1679. [H#477]

ELLIOT, ROBERT, with 2 slaves and 5 acres in St Philip's parish, Barbados, 1680. [H2/6]

ELLIOT, THOMAS, and his wife Anne had their son Thomas baptised in St Philips, Barbados, 29 September 1678 and buried there 26 July 1679. [H2/19]

ELLIOT, WALTER, a midshipman on the *St Andrew,* died on the voyage to Darien 20 October 1698, [WP#88]; witness to the testament of George Calderwood, quartermaster, 16 July 1698.

ERSKINE, HENRY, brother-in-law to Haldane of Gleneagles, to Darien on the *Unicorn* 1698, captured by the Spanish, remained at Darien in 1700. [DD#322]

ERSKINE, WILLIAM, a planter who died at Darien 7 December 1698. [WP#89]

ESPLIN, JOHN, a soldier. Emigrated from Leith to Darien on the *Unicorn* 14 July 1698, died at Darien 1 July 1700. [DP#352]

EWAN, JOHN IRVINE or, a sailor on the *Endeavour* to Darien 1698. [SRO.GD406, bundle 161, 25/30]

EWART, JAMES, soldier in Captain Burrow's Company of Militia in Barbados 1679. [H2/181]

FAIRBAIRN, JOHN, a Covenanter in Kirkliston, West Lothian, transported from Leith to the West Indies on the *St Michael of Scarborough*, master Edward Johnston, 12 December 1678. [PC.6.76]

FAIRWEATHER, WILLIAM, a skipper in Dundee, master of the *Margaret of Dundee* to Darien 1700. [SRO.GD406]

FARQUHAR, MARY, baptised in St Peter's parish, Barbados, 1679. [H2/85]

FARQUHAR, THOMAS, in St David's, Jamaica, pro.3 January 1694 Jamaica

FENNER, THOMAS, clerk to Mr Paterson, died on the voyage to Darien 2 November 1698. [WP#88]

FERGUSON, AGNES, transported from Leith to Jamaica August 1685, landed at Port Royal, Jamaica, November 1685. [PC.11.136] [LJ#18]

FERGUSON, ALEXANDER, a soldier from Maybole, Ayrshire, died at Darien 1699, cnf Edinburgh 1707. [SRO.CC8.8.83]

FERGUSON, ANGUS, transported from Leith to Jamaica August 1685. [PC.11.149]

FERGUSON, ARTHUR, son of William Ferguson, buried in St Philips parish, Barbados, 1 April 1679. [H2/24]

FERGUSON, DAVID, a Covenanter at the Bridgend of Glasgow, transported from Leith to the West Indies on the *St Michael of Scarborough*, master Edward Johnston, 12 December 1678. [PC.6.76]

FERGUSON, DAVID, master and merchant of the *Swan of Ayr*, arrived in Ayr from Montserrat 23 September 1678, [SRO.E72.3.4]; a merchant, from Ayr to the Caribee Islands on the *James of Ayr* March 1683. [SRO.E72.3.12]

FERGUSON, DAVID, Dean of Guild in Ayr, authorised to recruit servants in Edinburgh for Barbados 1693. [EBR.29.11.1693]

FERGUSON, DONALD, a Covenanter in Ruchoard, transported from Leith to Jamaica August 1685. [PC.11.136]

FERGUSON, DUNCAN, a Covenanter, transported from Leith to Jamaica 5 August 1684. [PC.9.95]

FERGUSON, DUNCAN, a farmer in Polmaise, St Ninian's, Stirlingshire, transported from Leith to Jamaica August 1685. [PC.11.136][ETR#373]

FERGUSON, JAMES, husband of Anna Abercromby in Fife, a mariner on the *Caledonia* from Leith to Darien 14 July 1698, cnf Edinburgh 1707. [SRO.CC8.8.83]

FERGUSON, JOHN, a Covenanter from Glencairn, Dumfriesshire, imprisoned in Edinburgh, transported from Leith on the *Crown of London*, master Thomas Teddico, bound for Barbados 27 November 1679, shipwrecked and drowned off Orkney 10 December 1679. [RBM]

FERGUSON, THOMAS, and his wife Elizabeth, parents of Thomas baptised in St Michael's, Barbados, 8 January 1679; with 5 children, 2 servants and 17 slaves, in St Michael's, Barbados, 1680. [H#423/444]

FERGUSON, WILLIAM, a Covenanter from Glencairn, Nithsdale captured after the Battle of Bothwell Bridge 22 June 1679, imprisoned in Edinburgh, transported from Leith to the West Indies on the *Crown of London*, master Thomas Teddico, 27 November 1679, shipwrecked off Muil Head of Deerness, Orkney, 10 December 1679, later transported to Jamaica. [CEC#212/5] [SW#202][RBM]

FERGUSON, WILLIAM, freeman and soldier of Colonel Standfast's Company of Militia in Barbados 6 January 1679. [H2/158]

FIFE, ALEXANDER, soldier of Colonel Colleton's Company of Militia in Barbados 9 March 1680. [H2/119]

FIFE, WILLIAM, soldier of Captain Davies' Company of Militia in Barbados 6 January 1679. [H2/166]

FINDLAY, ALEXANDER, a Covenanter in Buchlivie, Stirlingshire, transported from Leith to the West Indies on the *St Michael of Scarborough*, master Edward Johnston, 12 December 1678. [PC.6.76]

FINDLAY, ALEXANDER, son of ... Findlay and Elspeth Reid in Queensferry, West Lothian, a seaman, from the Clyde to Darien August 1699, cnf Edinburgh 1707. [SRO.CC8.8.83]

FINLAY, ARCHIBALD, from Leith, a seaman on the *Royal William* discharged to join the Darien Company 12 November 1696. [OSN#226]

FINLAY, COLIN, a sailor on the *Hope* to Darien 1699. [SRO.GD406, bundle 162, C39/8]

FINDLAY, THOMAS, a Covenanter in Kilmarnock, Ayrshire, captured after the Battle of Bothwell Bridge 22 June 1679, imprisoned in Edinburgh, banished to the Plantations, transported from Leith on the *Crown of London*, master Thomas Teddico, 27 November

1679, shipwrecked and drowned off Orkney 10 December 1679. [Kilmarnock g/s] [RBM]

FINLAYSON, JAMES, a Covenanter in New Kilpatrick, Dunbartonshire, captured after the Battle of Bothwell Bridge 22 June 1679, imprisoned in Edinburgh, banished to the Plantations, transported from Leith on the *Crown of London*, master Thomas Teddico, 27 November 1679, shipwrecked and drowned off Orkney 10 December 1679. [RBM]

FINLAYSON, WILLIAM, from Stirling, died in America, cnf Edinburgh 1707, [SRO.CC8.8.83]

FINNEY, Mr SAMUEL, in St Philips parish, Barbados, with 100 acres, 2 servants and 40 slaves, 1680; Assemblyman for St Philip's, Barbados, 25 April 1682. [SPAWI.1682/488][H2/7]

FINNEY, WILLIAM, a mariner on the *Dorothy*, died in Barbados 1693. [Pro.5/889; 11/417 PCC]

FINNISON, JOHN, a Covenanter, transported from Leith to Jamaica August 1685. [PC.11.329]

FLEMING, ALEXANDER, from Dysart, Fife, a sailor on the *St Andrew* from Leith to Darien 14 July 1698, cnf Edinburgh 7 October 1707. [SRO.CC8.8.83][SRO.GD406, bundle 159, p4/19]

FLEMING, GEORGE, son of George Fleming in Edinburgh, formastman on the *Caledonia*, died at Darien 1699, cnf Edinburgh 1707. [SRO.CC8.8.83]

FLEMING, THOMAS, and other merchants bound for Barbados were granted vagabonds and idle persons in Edinburgh for shipment there, 1659. [EBR, 9.2.1659]

FLETCHER, DANIEL, a Captain in Barbados, trading with Edwin Taylor, the King's printer in Scotland, 1644. [SRO.RD1.553.406]

FLETCHER, DUNCAN, a Covenanter, transported from Leith to Jamaica August 1685. [PC.11.136]

FLETCHER, JOHN, a Covenanter in Rumcadle, Kintyre, Argyll, transported from Leith to Jamaica August 1685. [PC.11.329]

FLETCHER, JOHN, a planter who died at Darien 11 November 1698. [NLS.RY2b8/19]

FOGO, DAVID, from the Almshouse, buried in St Michael's, Barbados, 9 July 1679. [H#435]

FOORD, WILLIAM, husband of Euphane Robertson in Burntisland, Fife, a sailor on the *Caledonia* from Leith to Darien 14 July 1698, cnf Edinburgh 9 October 1707. [SRO.CC8.8.83]

FORBES, CHARLES, former Captain of Hill's Regiment, Councillor at Darien, died at Matanzas Bay, Cuba, on the voyage back to Scotland 1700. [DD#225]

FORBES, JAMES, a time-expired indentured servant, emigrated from Barbados to Jamaica on the *Two Brothers*, master Rice Jeffreys, 13 February 1678. [H#367][PRO.CO1.44.47]

FORBES, JAMES, a drummer who was wounded at Darien 6 February 1699. [DP#86]

FORBES, JOHN, Marshal of the Assembly of Barbados, March 1681. [SPAWI.1681/58]

FORBES, Mrs JUDITH, in Nevis 14 August 1699. [SPAWI.1699/714]

FORBES, THOMAS, Captain of Collingwood's Regiment, died in the West Indies 1703. pro.5/1158 PCC.

FORBES, WILLIAM, a witness to John Innes's will, pro.14 April 1716 Barbados. [RB6.35.551]

FORBES, Captain ..., wrote an account of the abandonment of Caledonia, Darien, 1700. [SRO.GD406.1.4883]

FORBES, Captain ..., a soldier emigrated from Leith to Darien on the *Unicorn* 14 July 1698, died at the Bay of Matanzas, Cuba, 25 July 1699. [DP#196]

FORD, JAMES, a Covenanter in Crichton, Midlothian, captured after the Battle of Bothwell Bridge 22 June 1679, imprisoned in Edinburgh, banished to the Plantations, transported from Leith on the *Crown of London*, master Thomas Teddico, 27 November 1679, shipwrecked and drowned off Orkney 10 December 1679. [RBM]

FORREST, JAMES, son of James and Marion Forrest, a Covenanter in Cambusnethan, Lanarkshire, transported from Leith to Jamaica August 1685, landed at Port Royal, Jamaica, November 1685. [PC.11.329][LJ#17]

FORRESTER, JOHN, a planter who died on the voyage to Darien 11 September 1698. [WP#87]

FORSYTH, JAMES, wounded at Darien 6 February 1699. [DP#86]

FORTUNE, JOSEPH, son of Thomas Fortune, baptised in St Lucy's parish, Barbados, 16 September 1679. [H2/53]

FORTUNE, THOMAS, in St Lucy's parish, Barbados, 1678; soldier in Captain Thorburne's Company of Militia in Barbados 6 January 1679. [H2/38.140]

FOULLAR, THOMAS, husband of Janet Bannatyne in Greenock, Renfrewshire, a sailor on the *Speedy Return* to Darien 12 October 1698, cnf Edinburgh 1708. [SRO.CC8.8.84]

FRAME, WILLIAM, a Covenanter from Calder, Clydesdale, captured after the Battle of Bothwell Bridge 22 June 1679, transported from Leith to the West Indies on the *Crown of London*, master Thomas Teddico, November 1679, shipwrecked off Orkney December 1679, later transported to Jamaica. [CEC#212/5][SW#198][RBM]

FRAME, WILLIAM, with 10 acres in Christchurch, Barbados, 22 December 1679. [H#478]

FRASER, ALEXANDER, a soldier who was killed at Darien 1699, cnf Edinburgh 1707. [SRO.CC8.8.84]

FRASER, ALEXANDER, husband of Margaret Simpson in Newhaven, Midlothian, a sailor on the *Unicorn* from Leith to Darien 14 July 1698, cnf Edinburgh 1708. [SRO.CC8.8.84]

FRASER, DONALD, prisoner in Edinburgh Correction House, transported from Leith by Morris Trent, a merchant in Leith, to Barbados on the *Mary*, master David Couston, 4 May 1663. [EBR #186.13.4]

FRASER, EDMOND, in Barbados, Admin.1649 PCC.

FRASER, GEORGE, son of Captain William Fraser, an overseer at Darien 1698. [SRO.RD4.101.632]

FRASER, HUGH, a sailor on the *Caledonia* from Leith to Darien 14 July 1698, cnf Edinburgh 20 November 1707. [SRO.CC8.8.83]

FRASER, JOHN. Supplication by Elizabeth Fraser, wife of John Fraser, carpenter on the *Conclusion* which had sailed to Barbados in 1679 but had been captured by Turkish pirates on the return voyage and imprisoned, awaiting a ransom. [PC.7.152]

FRASER, JOHN, born in Aberdeen 1678, deserted from the colony at Darien to the Spanish, a prisoner at Rancho Vieja Bay 28 March 1700. [Audiencia de Panama, Archives of the Indies, L#164, Sevill]

FRASER, WILLIAM, in Barbados 6 November 1683. [SPAWI.1683/1365]

FRASER, WILLIAM, mariner, bosun of the *Amity of London*, died in Barbados, pro.1698 PCC.

FRASER, WILLIAM, father of George in Inverness-shire, an overseer at Darien 1698, died in the West Indies 1699, cnf Edinburgh 1707. [SRO.CC8.8.83]

FRASER, Captain ..., at Darien 16 December 1698. [DSP#93]

FREELAND, PETER, a sailor on the *Caledonia* from Leith to Darien 14 July 1698. [see William Foord's testament]

FRENCH, ANDREW, a Covenanter, transported from Leith to Barbados on the *John and Nicholas*, master Edward Barnes, December 1685. [PC.11.232][ETR#389]

FRISSELL, DANIEL, and his wife Elizabeth, parents of Francis baptised in St Michael's, Barbados, 15 December 1678; son Thomas buried 15 April 1679. [H#423/433]; with 3 acres in St Lucy's parish, Barbados, 1678. [H2/38]; father of Ann baptised in St Lucy's, Barbados, 14 October 1678. [H2/51]; soldier of Colonel Lewis' Company of Militia in Barbados 6 January 1679. [H2/101]

FRIZELL, ISAAC, son of Owen Frizell, baptised in St Thomas's, Barbados, 8 March 1679. [H2/64]

FRIZELL, JACOB, son of Owen Frizell, baptised in St Thomas's, Barbados, 8 March 1679. [H2/64]

FRIZELL, JOHN, soldier of Pinket's Company of Militia in Barbados 6 January 1679. [H2/109]; in St Philip's parish, Barbados, with 12 acres and 6 slaves, 1680. [H2/7]

FRISSELL, JOHN, witness to John Innes's will, pro.14 April 1716 Barbados. [RB6.35.551]

FRISSELL, WILLIAM, pro.25 June 1677 Jamaica

FULLARTON, ROBERT, a passenger on the *James of Ayr*, master James Chalmers, arrived in Ayr from the West Indies 19 September 1673; a merchant, from Ayr to the West Indies on the *James of Ayr* 20 February 1681; merchant, arrived in Ayr from the West Indies on the *James of Ayr*, master James Chalmers, 19 September 1681. [SRO.E72.3.4/6/7]

FULLARTON, THOMAS, brother of John Fullerton in Montrose, Angus, emigrated to New York, later around 1691 settled in Barbados. [NJSA.EJD/D]

FULLARTON, THOMAS, husband of Isabel Hodgson, Captain of the *Dolphin* from Leith to Darien 14 July 1698, died at Darien 25 December 1698. [SRO.GD406, bundle 163, C23/1] [SRO.CC8. 8.83][NLS.RY2b8/19]

FYFFE, PATRICK, authorised to recruit emigrants for Virginia and Barbados in Edinburgh 1667. [EBR.15.11.1667]; Patrick Fyffe and James Hamilton, merchants in Edinburgh, owners of the *Charles of Leith* petitioned the Privy Council for beggars, gypsies and other undesirables for shipment to Virginia or Barbados 3 June 1669. [PC#3.21]

GALBRAITH, JAMES, a Covenanter in Kippen, Stirlingshire, captured after the Battle of Bothwell Bridge 22 June 1679, imprisoned in Edinburgh, banished to the Plantations, transported from Leith on the *Crown of London*, master Thomas Teddico, 27 November 1679, shipwrecked and drowned off Orkney 10 December 1679. [RBM]

GALLOWAY, BRIAN, soldier in Colonel Thorburn's Company of Militia in Barbados 6 January 1679; with 2 acres and 3 slaves in St Thomas's parish, Barbados, 3 December 1679. [H2/58.152]

GALLOWAY, EDWARD, with 6 acres in St Lucy's parish, Barbados, 1678. [H2/38]

GALLOWAY, JOHN, son of John Galloway in Culross, Fife, bosun's mate on the *Rising Sun* from the Clyde to Darien 18 August 1699, cnf Edinburgh 11 October 1707. [SRO.CC8.8.83]

GARDINER, CHRISTINE, guilty of infanticide, imprisoned in Edinburgh Tolbooth, transported from Leith to Jamaica August 1685. [PC.11.330][ETR#369]

GARDNER, JOHN, a Covenanter from Monklands, Lanarkshire, captured after the Battle of Bothwell Bridge 22 June 1679, transported from Leith to the West Indies on the *Crown of London*, master Thomas Teddico, November 1679, shipwrecked off Orkney December 1679, later transported to Jamaica. [CEC#212/5][RBM]

GARDNER, WILLIAM, husband of Agnes Davidson in Abbotshall, Fife, a sailor on the *Unicorn* from Leith to Darien 14 July 1698, cnf Edinburgh 1707. [SRO.CC8.8.83]

GARGE, WILLIAM, from Kirkwall, Orkney, father of Alexander, settled in New Scotland, Barbados, died before 1683. [SRO.S/H 19 November 1683] {cf William George a soldier of Captain Archibald Johnstone's Company of Militia in Barbados 6 January 1679. [H2/164]}

GARNER, RICHARD, master of the *Isobel of Belfast*, arrived in Port Glasgow from Barbados with sugar and tobacco October 1682. [SRO.E72.19.5]

GARVY, WILLIAM, a sailor on the *Hope* to Darien 1699. [SRO. GD406, bundle 162, p39/15]

GASCOIGN, FRANCIS, son of Robert Gascoign and Isabel Smith in Newcastle upon Tyne, a sailor on the *St Andrew* from Leith to Darien 14 July 1698, cnf Edinburgh 1707. [SRO.CC8.8.83]

GAUDIE, ROBERT, a planter who died on the voyage to Darien 28 October 1698. [WP#88]

GAVINE, JAMES, a Covenanter in Douglas, Lanarkshire, husband of Helen Dickson, transported from Leith to Jamaica August 1685, died after 1695 in Douglas. [PC.11.330][ETR#369][Douglas g/s]

GAY, EDWARD, a Covenanter in the Bridgend of Glasgow, transported from Leith to the West Indies on the *St Michael of Scarborough*, master Edward Johnston, 12 December 1678. [PC.6.76]

GAY, JOHN, bosun of the *Hope* bound for Darien, subscribed to a deed at Greenock 1699. [SRO.GD406, bundle 162, c39/4]

GEDDES, WILLIAM, from Edinburgh, emigrated via London to Barbados 1684; postmaster in Barbados, 1699. [WCF#MS6679] [SPAWI.1699/880.iv]

GEMMILL, JOHN, a Covenanter, transported from Leith to Barbados on the *John and Nicholas*, master Edward Barnes, September 1685. [PC.11.255][ETR#389]

GEMMILL, JOHN, a Covenanter in Cumnock, Ayrshire, captured after the Battle of Bothwell Bridge 22 June 1679, imprisoned in Edinburgh, banished to the Plantations, transported from Leith on the *Crown of London*, master Thomas Teddico, 27 November 1679, shipwrecked and drowned off Orkney 10 December 1679. [RBM]

GERMONT, THOMAS, a Covenanter in Kirkoswald, Ayrshire, captured after the Battle of Bothwell Bridge 22 June 1679, imprisoned in Edinburgh, banished to the Plantations, transported from Leith on the *Crown of London*, master Thomas Teddico, 27 November 1679, shipwrecked and drowned off Orkney 10 December 1679. [RBM]

GIBB, JAMES, a Covenanter in Abercorn, West Lothian, captured after the Battle of Bothwell Bridge 22 June 1679, imprisoned in Edinburgh, banished to the Plantations, transported from Leith on the *Crown of London*, master Thomas Teddico, 27 November 1679, shipwrecked and drowned off Orkney 10 December 1679. [RBM]

GIBB, JAMES, from Abercorn, West Lothian, a sailor on the *Rising Sun* from the Clyde to Darien 18 August 1699, cnf Edinburgh 15 October 1707. [SRO.CC8.8.83]

GIBB, JOHN a Covenanter in Cavers, Roxburghshire, captured after the Battle of Bothwell Bridge 22 June 1679, imprisoned in Edinburgh, banished to the Plantations, transported from Leith on the *Crown of London*, master Thomas Teddico, 27 November 1679, shipwrecked and drowned off Orkney 10 December 1679. [RBM]

GIBB, JOHN, a Covenanter, transported from Leith to Jamaica August 1685. [PC.11.329]

GIBB, JOHN, from Bo'ness, West Lothian, a foremastman on the *Caledonia* from Leith to Darien 14 July 1698, cnf Edinburgh 15 October 1707. [SRO.CC8.8.8]

GIBSON, ANDREW, Captain of the brigantine *Dispatch* from Leith to Darien January 1699, wrecked off Islay, Argyll, February 1699. [DD#235]

GIBSON, GEORGE, son of Thomas Gibson in Edinburgh, a surgeon's mate on the *Rising Sun* from Leith to Darien 14 July 1698, cnf Edinburgh 1707. [SRO.CC8.8.83]

GIBSON, Captain JAMES, commander of the *Rising Sun* instructed to sail from Greenock to Caledonia, Darien, 20 September 1699. [DSP#55] [SRO.GD406]; witness to the testaments of David Drysdale and of John Clark jr. sailors 17 August 1699; drowned in the wreck of the *Rising Sun* at Charleston, South Carolina, 3 August 1700. [DD#329]

GIBSON, JAMES, from Prestonpans, East Lothian, a foremastman on the *Caledonia* from Leith to Darien 14 July 1698, cnf Edinburgh 22 July 1707. [SRO.CC8.8.83]

GIBSON, MALCOLM, son of Sir Alexander Gibson of Pentland, surgeon's mate on the *Rising Sun* from the Clyde to Darien 18 August 1699, cnf Edinburgh 1707. [SRO.CC8.8.83]

GIBSON, ..., a planter in Nevis 1683. [ActsPCCol#118]

GIBSON, NINIAN, master of the *Jean of Largs*, from Port Glasgow to the West Indies with cloth, hats, gloves, candles, shoes, linen, buttons, damask, blankets and nails, April 1684. [SRO.E72.19.9]

GIBSON, WALTER, merchant on the *James of Ayr*, master James Chalmers, which arrived in Ayr from Montserrat and the West Indies 19 September 1673. [SRO.E72.3.4]

GIFFARD, JOHN, a schoolmaster, educated at Edinburgh University 1702, emigrated to the Leeward Islands 1703. [EMA#29]

GILCHRIST, HENRY, from Burntisland, Fife, a seaman on the *Caledonia* from Leith to Darien 14 July 1698, cnf Edinburgh 23 September 1707. [SRO.CC8.8.83]

GILCHRIST, PATRICK, a Covenanter in Gargunnock, Stirlingshire, captured after the Battle of Bothwell Bridge 22 June 1679, imprisoned in Edinburgh, banished to the Plantations, transported from Leith on the *Crown of London*, master Thomas Teddico, 27 November 1679, shipwrecked and drowned off Orkney 10 December 1679. [RBM]

GILCHRIST, ROBERT, son of John Gilchrist in Duns, Berwickshire, a merchant, emigrated from Ayr to Barbados, died in Barbados, 1649, cnf Edinburgh 1653. [SRO.CC8.8.67]

GILCHRIST, THOMAS, a Covenanter in Calder, Midlothian, captured after the Battle of Bothwell Bridge 22 June 1679, imprisoned in Edinburgh, banished to the Plantations, transported from Leith on the *Crown of London*, master Thomas Teddico, 27 November 1679, shipwrecked and drowned off Orkney 10 December 1679. [RBM]

GILCHRIST, WILLIAM, in St Andrew's, Jamaica, pro.10 December 1677 Jamaica

GILHAGIE, NINIAN, a passenger on the *James of Ayr* which arrived in Ayr from the West Indies 19 September 1673, [SRO.E72.3.4]; from Ayr to the West Indies on the *James of Ayr* February 1681. [SRO.E72.3.6]

GILMOUR, JOHN, a foremastman on the *Caledonia* from Leith to Darien 14 July 1698, died after July 1699, cnf Edinburgh 1707. [SRO.CC8.8.83]

GIVEIN, ROBERT, from Leith, a sailor on the *Unicorn* from Leith to Darien 14 July 1698, cnf Edinburgh 9 October 1707. [SRO.CC8. 8.83]

GIRVAN, THOMAS, a passenger on the *James of Ayr*, master James Chalmers, which arrived in Ayr 19 September 1681 from the West Indies. [SRO.E72.3.7]

GLASGOW, JOHN, a Covenanter from Cavers, Roxburghshire, captured after the Battle of Bothwell Bridge 22 June 1679, transported from Leith to the West Indies on the *Crown of London*, master Thomas Teddico, 27 November 1679, shipwrecked off Muil Head of Deerness, Orkney, 10 December 1679, later transported to Jamaica. [CEC#212/5][SW#203][RBM]

GLASGOW, JOHN, a minister, emigrated to Antigua 1707. [EMA#30]

GLASGOW, WILLIAM, a Covenanter from Cavers, Roxburghshire, captured after the Battle of Bothwell Bridge 22 June 1679, transported from Leith to the West Indies on the *Crown of London*, master Thomas Teddico, 27 November 1679, shipwrecked off Muil Head of Deerness, Orkney, 10 December 1679, later transported to Jamaica. [CEC#212/5][SW#203][RBM]

GLEN, DUNCAN, from Edinburgh, a steward on the *Unicorn* from Leith to Darien 14 July 1698, cnf Edinburgh 1707. [SRO.CC8. 8.83]

GLEN, HENRY, from Edinburgh, a foremastman on the *Unicorn* from Leith to Darien 14 July 1698, cnf Edinburgh 1707. [SRO.CC8. 8.83]

GLENDENNING, AGNES, prisoner in Edinburgh Correction House, transported from Leith, by Morris Trent a merchant in Leith, to Barbados on the *Mary*, master David Couston, 4 May 1663. [EBR#186.13.4]

GLENFIELD, ROBERT, master of the *Benjamin of Glasgow*, arrived in Port Glasgow from the West Indies with sugar, tobacco and indigo June 1681; from Glasgow to the West Indies with 60 grindstones, hats, thread, buttons, coal, cloth, pipes, candles and gloves, August 1681. [SRO.E72.19.1/2]

GLOVER, JOHN, master of the *Salmond of Chester*, arrived in Port Glasgow from Nevis with sugar, indigo, tobacco, and 4 "elephant teeth" November 1681, [SRO.E72.19.5]

GOOD, JOHN, a minister sent to Darien April 1699. [Letters and Journals pp88/89]

GORDON, AGNES, a prisoner in Edinburgh Tolbooth, transported by Morris Trent a merchant in Leith from Leith to Barbados on the *Mary*, master David Couston, 4 May 1663. [EBR#186.13.4]

GORDON, GEORGE, with 3 slaves and 20 acres in St Peter's parish, Barbados, 15 December 1679. [H2/77]

GORDON, GEORGE, a time-expired indentured servant, emigrated from Barbados to Carolina on the *Plantation*, master Aser Sharpe, 9 August 1679. [H#372]

GORDON, GILBERT, a gentleman, from London to Barbados on the *Hopewell* February 1683. [CLRO/AIA/MR.E593]

GORDON, ISABEL, with 3 slaves in St Peter's parish, Barbados, 1679. [H2/79]

GORDON, JAMES, buried in St Thomas's parish, Barbados, 23 December 1678. [H2/66]

GORDON, JAMES, quartermaster of the *St Andrew* from Leith to Darien 14 July 1698, cnf Edinburgh 1707. [SRO.CC8.8.83]

GORDON, JAMES, sailor on the *Unicorn* from Leith to Darien 14 July 1698, cnf Edinburgh 20 November 1707. [SRO.CC8.8.83]

GORDON, PETER, soldier of Captain Brown's Company of Militia in Barbados 6 January 1679. [H2/106]; with 8 acres in Christchurch, Barbados, 22 December 1679. [H#478]

GORDON, THOMAS, a merchant in St Michael's, Barbados, reference to in John Anderson's will, pro.2 December 1714 Barbados. [RB6.37.406]

GORDON, WILLIAM, a minister, emigrated to Barbados 1699. [EMA#30]

GOURDON, GEORGE, in St John's, Jamaica, pro.16 July 1685 Jamaica

GOURDON, JOHN, a schoolmaster, emigrated to Barbados 1700. [EMA#30]

GOVAN, JOHN, a Covenanter in Neilston, Renfrewshire, captured after the Battle of Bothwell Bridge 22 June 1679, imprisoned in Edinburgh Tolbooth, banished to the Plantations, transported from Leith on the *Crown of London*, master Thomas Teddico, 27 November 1679, shipwrecked and drowned off Orkney 10 December 1679. [RBM][ETR#162]

GOVAN, JOHN, a Covenanter in Kirkliston, West Lothian, captured after the Battle of Bothwell Bridge 22 June 1679, imprisoned in Edinburgh, banished to the Plantations, transported from Leith on the *Crown of London*, master Thomas Teddico, 27 November 1679, shipwrecked and drowned off Orkney 10 December 1679. [RBM]

GOWRY, RICHARD, freeman in Colonel Christopher Lyne's Company of Militia in Barbados 6 January 1679. [H2/100]

GRAHAM, CHARLES, a mariner on the *St Andrew*, subscribed to a deed of factory 1698. [SRO.GD406, bundle 159, p2/8]

GRAHAME, GEORGE, juryman in New Providence 1699. [SPAWI. 1699/928]

GRAHAM, IVOR, a Covenanter in Innerneil, Argyll, transported from Leith to Jamaica August 1685. [PC.11.329]

GRAHAM, JAMES, a volunteer who died on the voyage to Darien 25 October 1698. [WP#88]

GRAHAM, JAMES, first mate of the *Dolphin* witnessed James Black's deed on 16 July 1698. [SRO.GD406, bundle 163, c23/11]; later imprisoned in Carthagena and in Seville accused of piracy, sentenced to death May 1700 but released 20 September 1700. [SRO.GD406.1.4541][APS.14.app114][DD#332]

GRAHAM, JAMES, son of Patrick Graham in Edinburgh, a midshipman on the *St Andrew* from Leith to Darien 14 July 1698, cnf Edinburgh 1707. [SRO.CC8.8.83]

GRAHAM, JOHN jr., in Ledlevan, transported from Leith to the West Indies on the *St Michael of Scarborough*, master Edward Johnston, 12 December 1678. [PC.6.76]

GRAHAM, JOHN, soldier of Captain Brown's Company of Militia in Barbados 6 January 1679. [H2/107]

GRAHAM, JOHN, son of ... Graham and Euphan Watson in Burntisland, Fife, a sailor on the *Endeavour*, from Leith to Darien 14 July 1698, cnf Edinburgh 1707. [SRO.CC8.8.83] [SRO.GD406, bundle 161, 25/11]

GRAHAM, WILLIAM, transported from Leith to Barbados on the *John and Nicholas*, master Edward Barnes, December 1685. [ETR#390]

GRAME, CHARLES, from Valleyfield, Fife, a sailor on the *St Andrew*, deed of factory 1698. [SRO.GD406, bundle 159, p2/9]

GRANT, ALEXANDER, with 1 slave in St Peter's parish, Barbados, 1679. [H2/80]

GRANT, ARTHUR, indented for 5 years service in Nevis or Virginia, in Bristol 25 July 1679, sailed on the *Bristol Merchant*. [BRO]

GRANT, DAVID, freeman in Lieutenant Colonel Alexander Riddoch's Company of Militia in Barbados 1679. [H2/159]

GRANT, GEORGE, from Prestonpans, East Lothian, a sailor on the *Union* from Leith to Darien 14 July 1698, died at Darien 1699, cnf Edinburgh 1707. [SRO.CC8.8.83]

GRANT, HUGH, soldier in Captain Stephen Brown's Company of Militia in Barbados 6 January 1679. [H2/108]

GRANT, JAMES, master of the ...., arrived at Port Findhorn from the Plantations with a cargo of tobacco 4 May 1690. [SRO.E72.11.16]

GRANT, JOHN, with 8 acres in St Lucy's parish, Barbados, 1678. [H2/38]

GRANT, JOHN, freeman in Colonel Lyne's Company of Militia in Barbados 6 July 1679. [H2/99, 107]

GRANT, JOHN, sr., householder and soldier of Lieutenant Colonel Alexander Riddoch's Company of Militia in Barbados 6 January 1679. [H2/159]

GRANT, RICHARD, from Edinburgh, emigrated via Bristol to St Kitts ca.1660. [BRO#04220]

GRANT, THOMAS, buried in St Michael's, Barbados, 26 November 1678. [H#431]

GRANT, THOMAS, a butcher from Edinburgh, emigrated to Darien from the Clyde on the *Rising Sun* 18 August 1699, cnf Edinburgh 16 October 1707. [SRO.CC8.8.83]

GRANT, THOMAS, a ships carpenter from Jamaica, died 1700 in Deptford, Kent, pro.5/1148 PCC.

GRANT, Mr WILLIAM, with 5 servants, 3 freemen, 40 slaves, and 30 acres in St Joseph's parish, Barbados, 1680; with 1 man soldier in Lieutenant Colonel Carter's Troop of Militia February 1679. [H2/ 28, 201]

GRAPES, HENRY, a trumpeter who died at Darien 5 November 1698. [NLS.RY.2b8/19]

GRAY, JAMES, prisoner in Edinburgh Tolbooth, transported by George Hutcheson a merchant in Edinburgh from Leith 7 December 1665. [ETR#104]

GRAY, JAMES, a Covenanter in Fenwick, Ayrshire, captured after the Battle of Bothwell Bridge 22 June 1679, imprisoned in Edinburgh, banished to the Plantations, transported from Leith on the *Crown of London*, master Thomas Teddico, 27 November 1679, shipwrecked and drowned off Orkney 10 December 1679. [RBM]

GRAZE, JAMES, a Covenanter in Calder, Midlothian, captured after the Battle of Bothwell Bridge 22 June 1679, imprisoned in Edinburgh, banished to the Plantations, transported from Leith on the *Crown of London*, master Thomas Teddico, 27 November 1679, shipwrecked and drowned off Orkney 10 December 1679. [RBM]

GREENSHIELDS, JOHN, a Covenanter in Cavers, Roxburghshire, captured after the Battle of Bothwell Bridge 22 June 1679, imprisoned in Edinburgh, banished to the Plantations, transported from Leith on the *Crown of London*, master Thomas Teddico, 27 November 1679, shipwrecked and drowned off Orkney 10 December 1679. [RBM]

GREG, THOMAS, son of William Greg, a minister educated at the University of St Andrews, emigrated to Darien 1699, died in the West Indies, cnf Edinburgh 1707. [SRO.CC8.8.83]

GRIER, JAMES, a Covenanter in Dalry, transported from Leith to Jamaica September 1685, landed at Port Royal, Jamaica, November 1685. [PC.11.153][LJ#17]

GRIEVE, JACOB, a passenger on the *James of Ayr*, master James Chalmers, which arrived in Ayr from the West Indies 19 September 1673. [SRO.E72.3.4]

GRIEVE, WILLIAM, from Leith, Midlothian, a sailor on the *Rising Sun* died at Darien, cnf Edinburgh 13 October 1707. [SRO.CC8. 8.83]

GRIG, PETER, son of William Grig, buried in St Joseph's parish, Barbados, 20 May 1679. [H2/31]

GRIGG, ROBERT, and Alice Grigg, time expired indentured servants, emigrated from Barbados to Carolina on the *Mary*, master Nicholas Lockwood, 10 March 1678. [H#370]

GRINDLAY, WILLIAM, a Covenanter in Cavers, Roxburghshire, captured after the Battle of Bothwell Bridge 22 June 1679, imprisoned in Edinburgh Tolbooth, banished to the Plantations, transported from Leith on the *Crown of London*, master Thomas Teddico, 27 November 1679, shipwrecked and drowned off Orkney 10 December 1679. [RBM][ETR#162]

GRINTOUN, ALEXANDER, jr., from Bo'ness, West Lothian, a sailor on the *Rising Sun*, from the Clyde to Darien 18 August 1699, cnf Edinburgh 23 October 1707. [SRO.CC8.8.81]

GROAT, DANIEL, son of William Groat in Burntisland, Fife, a seaman on the *Unicorn* from the Clyde to Darien 14 July 1698, cnf Edinburgh 23 October 1707. [SRO.CC8.8.83]

GUNN, DANIEL, and his wife Sarah, parents of Henry baptised in St George's, Barbados, 14 September 1678, and of Thomas baptised in St Michael's, Barbados, 25 July 1679; soldier in Captain Francis Burton's Company of Militia in Barbados 1679. [H#424/465][H2/184]

GUNN, JOHN, with 1 slave and 15 acres in St Peter's parish, Barbados, 1679; householder with 10 acres, in Lieutenant Colonel Alexander Riddoch's Company of Militia in Barbados 1679. [H2/76, 159]

GUTHRIE, JAMES, from Largo, Fife, a mariner on the *Rising Sun* from the Clyde to Darien 18 August 1699, died at Darien, cnf Edinburgh 4 October 1707. [SRO.CC8.8.83]

GUTHRIE, JOHN, master of the *Ewe and Lamb* petitioned the Privy Council for felons from Edinburgh, Leith and Canongate Tolbooths for shipment to Virginia or Barbados, 7 November 1667. [PC.2.358]

HACKSTONE, WILLIAM, a Covenanter and a tailor in Edinburgh, transported from Leith to the West Indies on the *St Michael of Scarborough*, master Edward Johnston, 12 December 1678. [PC.6.76]

HADDEN, ..., transported to Barbados or Virginia 28 February 1667. [PC.2.263]

HADDOWAY, ARCHIBALD, a Covenanter in Glasgow, transported from Leith to the West Indies on the *St Michael of Scarborough*, master Edward Johnston, 12 December 1678. [PC.6.76]

HAIG, WILLIAM, born 20 June 1670, son of Anthony Haig of Bemersyde, Berwickshire, a merchant in Antigua. ["Haigs of Bemersyde", p443, {Edinburgh, 1881}]

HALKETT, JOHN, a sailor on the *Olive Branch* to Darien 1699, cnf Edinburgh 17 October 1707. [SRO.CC8.8.83]

HALL, JAMES, a Covenanter in Kintyre, Argyll, transported from Leith to Jamaica August 1685. [PC.11.136]

HALLYBURTON, WILLIAM, an Ensign, husband of Janet Allan, died at Darien 6 December 1698, cnf Edinburgh 1707. [SRO.CC8.8.83][WP#89]

HAMILTON, ADAM, a time-expired indentured servant, emigrated from Barbados to New England on the ketch *William and Susan*, master Ralph Parker, 21 March 1678. [H#374]

HAMILTON, {"HAMBLETON"}, ALEXANDER, with 2 slaves and 10 acres in St Lucy's parish, Barbados, 1678. [H2/39]

HAMILTON, ALEXANDER, settled in Nevis before 1700. [DP#308]

HAMILTON, Mr ALEXANDER, from Bo'ness, West Lothian, appointed as a Councillor of Caledonia, Darien, 20 October 1699, died there 1699. [SRO.GD406][SRO.CC8.8.83]

HAMILTON, ALEXANDER, dispatched from Darien bound for Scotland via France on the *Pink* 25 December 1698, [DSP#94]; arrived in Edinburgh from America with news of the Scots Colony at Darien 25 March 1699, [DSP#107] and was admitted as a burgess 17 May 1699. [EBR]

HAMILTON, ALEXANDER, a merchant in Bo'ness, West Lothian, mate of the *Dolphin* 1699. [SRO.GD406, bundle 163, c23/2] [SRO.CC8.8.83]

HAMILTON, ALEXANDER, son of George Hamilton in Inveresk, Midlothian, a midshipman on the *Caledonia* from Leith to Darien 14 July 1698, cnf Edinburgh 1707. [SRO.CC8.8.83]

HAMILTON, ANDREW, emigrated from Ayr to the West Indies on the *James of Ayr* 20 February 1681. [SRO.E72.3.6]

HAMILTON, ANDREW, a midshipman who died at Darien 22 November 1698. [NLS.RY2b8/19]

HAMILTON, ARCHIBALD, from Carriden, West Lothian, a sailor on the *Dolphin* from Leith to Darien 14 July 1698, cnf Edinburgh 27 October 1707. [SRO.CC8.8.83]

HAMILTON, CHARLES, son of Frederick Hamilton in Edinburgh, a midshipman on the *Union*, died on the voyage to Darien 10 October 1698, cnf Edinburgh 1707. [SRO.CC8.8.83][WP#87]

HAMILTON, ISABEL, a prisoner in Edinburgh Tolbooth, transported by George Hutcheson a merchant in Edinburgh from Leith to Barbados December 1665. [ETR#104]

HAMILTON, JAMES, son of Frederick Hamilton in Edinburgh, a sailor on the *Rising Sun* from the Clyde to Darien 10 October 1698, cnf Edinburgh 1707. [SRO.CC8.8.83][WP#87]

HAMILTON, JOHN, of Boighall, trading in the West Indies before 1644. [APS.V: (i)227]

HAMILTON, JOHN, representative in Antigua June 1678, [SPAWI.1678/741]; in Antigua 1699. [SPAWI/1699/658]; appointed a Councillor of Antigua 22 August 1699. [ActsPCCol]

HAMILTON, MARGARET, late of West Bow in Edinburgh, a servant in Barbados 1676. [PC.4.674]

HAMILTON, MATTHEW, a Covenanter and a husbandman in Kintyre, Argyll, a prisoner in Edinburgh Tolbooth, transported from Leith to Jamaica August 1685. [PC.11.329][ETR#369]

HAMILTON, PATRICK, a Covenanter in Livingstone, West Lothian, captured after the Battle of Bothwell Bridge 22 June 1679, imprisoned in Edinburgh, banished to the Plantations, transported from Leith on the *Crown of London*, master Thomas Teddico, 27 November 1679, shipwrecked and drowned off Orkney 10 December 1679. [RBM]

HAMILTON, THOMAS, son of Frederick Hamilton in Edinburgh, an overseer at Darien 1698, cnf Edinburgh 1707. [SRO.CC8.8.83]

HAMILTON, THOMAS, from Bathgate, West Lothian, formerly a Captain of Sir John Hill's Regiment, then an assistant overseer at Darien, cnf Edinburgh 14 November 1707. [SRO.CC8.8.83]

HAMILTON, Colonel WALTER, in Nevis 14 August 1699. [SPAWI.1699/714]; appointed a Councillor of Nevis 22 August 1699. [ActsPCCol]

HAMILTON, WILLIAM, soldier of Captain William Allamby's Company of Militia in Barbados 6 January 1679. [H2/155]

HAMILTON, WILLIAM, a merchant in St Kitts, pro.1698 PCC.

HAMILTON, WILLIAM, from Crombie, Fife, a sailor on the *Unicorn* from Leith to Darien 14 July 1698, cnf Edinburgh 7 October 1707. [SRO.CC8.8.83]

HAMILTON, WILLIAM, an Ensign, died at Darien 1698. [NLS. RY2b8/19]

HAMILTON, ..., a schoolmaster, emigrated to the Leeward Islands 1700. [EMA#32]

HANDYSIDE, JAMES, from Edinburgh, a foremastman on the *St Andrew* from Leith to Darien 14 July 1698, cnf Edinburgh 1707. [SRO.CC8.8.83]

HANDYSIDE, JOHN, a sailor on the *St Andrew* to Darien 1698. [SRO.GD406, bundle 160, 4/22]

HANNAH, ANDREW, a servant of William Strickland, emigrated from Barbados to Antigua on the sloop *Katherine*, master Andrew Gall, 27 November 1679. [H#379]

HANNAY, GEORGE, with wife, 2 children, 6 servants, and 10 slaves, in St Michael's, Barbados, 1680. [H#446]; Provost Marshal of Barbados, December 1681; 2 December 1682. [SPAWI.1681/343; 1682/826]; Provost Marshal of Barbados 21 January 1696. [Rawl.MS.A241pp122]

HANNAY, JAMES, Clerk of Chancery in Barbados 1699. [SPAWI. 1699/880.iv]

HANNAY, SAMUEL, a Covenanter in Kirkmabreck, Kirkcudbrightshire, captured after the Battle of Bothwell Bridge 22 June 1679, imprisoned in Edinburgh, banished to the Plantations, transported from Leith on the *Crown of London*, master Thomas Teddico, 27 November 1679, shipwrecked and drowned off Orkney 10 December 1679. [RBM]

HARDIE, WILLIAM, a Covenanter in Kelso, Roxburghshire, captured after the Battle of Bothwell Bridge 22 June 1679, imprisoned in Edinburgh, banished to the Plantations, transported from Leith on the *Crown of London*, master Thomas Teddico, 27 November 1679, shipwrecked and drowned off Orkney 10 December 1679. [RBM]

HARDING, JOHN, yeoman of the powder on the *St Andrew* to Darien 1698. [SRO.GD406, bundle 15, p4/6]

HARDY, JAMES, son of Patrick and Agnes Hardy in Kinneil, West Lothian, a sailor on the *Rising Sun* from the Clyde to Darien 18 August 1699, cnf Edinburgh 1707. [SRO.CC8.8.83]

HARDY, JOHN, witness to William Milne's disposition 9 July 1699. [SRO.GD406, bundle 159, p2/12]

HARDY, ROBERT, a volunteer who died on the voyage to Darien 19 September 1698. [WP#87]

HARPER, DAVID, son of ... Harper and Bessie Salmond in Kirkcaldy, Fife, a foremastman on the *Caledonia* from Leith to Darien 14 July 1698, cnf Edinburgh 1707. [SRO.CC8.8.83]

HARRIS, WILLIAM, master of the *Walter of Glasgow*, arrived in Port Glasgow from the Caribees with tobacco January 1683. [SRO. E72.19.8]

HARRIS, ..., a deserter from Darien 1 April 1699. [SRO.GD406. 1.6484]

HARRISON, BENJAMIN, in James County, Virginia, a shareholder in the Darien Company, 1706. [SRO.AC.Decreets, #13.1076/1102]

HARRISON, JOHN, master's mate on the *James of Ayr, 120 tons,* arrived in Ayr 19 September 1681 from the West Indies; master of the *James of Ayr*, from Ayr to the Caribees March 1683; arrived in Ayr from Montserrat September 1683. [SRO.E72.3.7/11/12]

HARROWAY, JOHN, transported from Leith to the West Indies on the *St Michael of Scarborough*, master Edward Johnston, 12 December 1678. [PC.6.76]

HASTIE, WILLIAM, a Covenanter in Carluke, Lanarkshire, transported from Leith to Jamaica July 1685. [PC.11.136]

HAY, ANDREW, son of Andrew Hay in Dysart, Fife, a sailor on the *St Andrew* from Leith to Darien 14 July 1698, cnf Edinburgh 1707. [SRO.CC8.8.83]

HAY, ARCHIBALD, in St Lucia 1639. [SRO.GD34.479.2]

HAY, ARCHIBALD, a planter in Barbados, pro.13 January 1652 PCC.

HAY, DAVID, a volunteer who died on the voyage to Darien 1 November 1698. [WP#88]

HAY, GEORGE, an engineer and Provost Marshal in Barbados 1705. [SPAWI.1705.409]

HAY, DAVID, a soldier who died at Darien, cnf Edinburgh 1707. [SRO. CC8.8.83]

HAY, Sir JAMES, in St Lucia 1639. [SRO.GD34.479.2]

HAY, JOHN, appointed as Provost Marshal of Barbados for 7 years, 1 April 1638. [SRO.GD34.927]

HAY, JOHN, soldier of Captain Thomas Liston's Company of Militia in Barbados 1679. [H2/143]

HAY, JOHN, buried in St John's parish, Barbados, 19 July 1679. [H2/75]

HAY, Lieutenant JOHN, died on the voyage to Darien 28 October 1698, cnf Edinburgh 1707. [SRO.CC8.8.83][WP#88]

HAY, Mrs ..., wife of Lieutenant John Hay, died on the voyage to Darien 19 October 1698. [WP#88]

HAY, PATRICK, from Edinburgh, formerly a Lieutenant of Lord Lindsay's Regiment of Foot, an overseer at Darien, cnf Edinburgh 17 November 1707. [SRO.CC8.8.83]

HAY, PETER, appointed as Receiver of Rents of Plantations and Ports of Barbados 13 June 1636. [SRO.GD34.920.921/922/923]

HAY, ROBERT, master of the *Janet of Leith*, from Leith to the West Indies 1611. [SRO.E71.29.6, fo.22]

HAY, Sir ROBERT, late of the Darien Company's Service, 1707. [APS. 14.app.114]

HAY, WILLIAM, settled in Barbados before 1645. [SRO.GD34.945]

HAY, WILLIAM, transported from Leith to the West Indies on the *St Michael of Scarborough*, master Edward Johnston, 12 December 1678. [PC.6.76]

HAY, WILLIAM, soldier of Captain Francis Cleaver's Company of Militia in Barbados 1679. [H2/127]

HAY, WILLIAM, from Edinburgh, a sailor on the *Rising Sun* from the Clyde to Darien 18 August 1699, cnf Edinburgh 16 October 1707. [SRO.CC8.8.83]

HAY, WILLIAM, wrote a letter from Fort St Andrew, Darien, 26 February 1700. Also wrote from Jamaica to his brother John Hay of Alderston 26 July 1707. [SRO.NRAS.0181, deed 3.1]

HAY, WILLIAM, born 1681, settled in Westmoreland, Jamaica, died 16 April 1717. [Kingston g/s, Jamaica]

HEATHERSGILL, ROBERT, from Jedburgh, Roxburghshire, a prisoner in Edinburgh Tolbooth, transported from Leith to Barbados 17 April 1666. [ETR#106]

HEDDERWICK, JOHN, born 20 September 1679, son of John Hedderwick and Elspet Hay in Aberdeen, a sailor on the *Caledonia* from Leith to Darien 14 July 1698, cnf Edinburgh 1707. [SRO.CC8.8.83]

HEDDERWICK, WILLIAM, son of Andrew Hedderwick in Edinburgh, a surgeon's mate on the *Duke of Hamilton* from the Clyde to Darien 18 August 1699, cnf Edinburgh 16 October 1707. [SRO. CC8.8.83]

HEIDSHOIP, ANTHONY, from Jedburgh, Roxburghshire, a prisoner in Edinburgh Tolbooth, transported from Leith to Barbados 17 April 1666. [ETR#106]

HENDERSON, ALEXANDER, in Nevis 14 June 1682. [SPAWI.1682/602]

HENDERSON, DAVID, from Burntisland, Fife, a sailor on the *Caledonia* died on the voyage to Darien 25 October 1698, cnf Edinburgh 23 September 1707. [WP#88][SRO.CC8.8.83]

HENDERSON, FRANCIS, with 5 acres in Christchurch, Barbados, 22 December 1679. [H#479]

HENDERSON, JOHN, soldier of Lieutenant Colonel Samuel Tidcom's Company of Militia in Barbados 11 September 1679. [H2/133]

HENDERSON, MATTHEW, soldier of Captain Ely's Company of Militia in Barbados 1679. [H2/179]

HENDERSON, RICHARD, soldier of Colonel Timothy Thornhill's Company of Militia in Barbados 6 January 1679. [H2/146]

HENDERSON, ROBERT, died in Barbados, Admin.1653 PCC.

HENDERSON, THOMAS, with 5 acres in St Lucy's parish, Barbados, 1678. [H2/39]

HENDERSON, WILLIAM, a Covenanter in Livingstone, West Lothian, captured after the Battle of Bothwell Bridge 22 June 1679, imprisoned in Edinburgh, banished to the Plantations, transported from Leith on the *Crown of London*, master Thomas Teddico, 27 November 1679, shipwrecked and drowned off Orkney 10 December 1679. [RBM]

HENDERSON, WILLIAM, with 1 slave in St Andrew's, Barbados, 1680. [H#472]

HENDERSON, WILLIAM, from Edinburgh, formerly a Captain of Colonel George McGill's Regiment, then an overseer at Darien, died there 1699, cnf Edinburgh 7 October 1707. [SRO.CC8.8.83]

HENDRY, ALEXANDER, from Linlithgow, West Lothian, a sailor on the *Rising Sun* from the Clyde to Darien 18 August 1698, cnf Edinburgh 1707. [SRO.CC8.8.83]

HENDRY, GEORGE, soldier of Captain John Lewgar's Company of Militia in Barbados January 1679. [H2/145]

HENDRIE, ROBERT, a Covenanter in Airth, Stirlingshire, captured after the Battle of Bothwell Bridge 22 June 1679, imprisoned in Edinburgh, banished to the Plantations, transported from Leith on the *Crown of London*, master Thomas Teddico, 27 November 1679, shipwrecked and drowned off Orkney 10 December 1679. [RBM]

HENRY, ALEXANDER, a prisoner in Edinburgh Tolbooth, transported from Leith to Barbados on the *John and Nicholas*, master Edward Barnes, December 1685. [ETR#390]

HENSHAW, WILLIAM, born 12 September 1643 in Glasgow son of James Henshaw and Janet Neill, a Covenanter and a merchant, transported to the West Indies June 1678. [PC.5.474]

HEPBURN, PATRICK, soldier of Major William Foster's Company of Militia in Barbados 6 January 1679. [H2/134]

HERD, WALTER, a foremastman on the *Unicorn* from Leith to Darien 14 July 1698, cnf Edinburgh 1707. [SRO.CC8.8.83]

HERD, WILLIAM, a Covenanter in Ashkirk, Roxburghshire, captured after the Battle of Bothwell Bridge 22 June 1679, imprisoned in Edinburgh, banished to the Plantations, transported from Leith on the *Crown of London*, master Thomas Teddico, 27 November 1679, shipwrecked and drowned off Orkney 10 December 1679. [RBM]

HERMAN, MATTHEW, a seaman on the *St Andrew* from Leith to Darien 14 July 1698, cnf Edinburgh 1707. [SRO.CC8.8.83]

HERRIES, ROBERT, a Covenanter and a surgeon in Dunbarton, transported to the West Indies November 1678. [PC.6.53]

HERRIES, WALTER, a surgeon from Dunbarton, late of the Royal Navy, to Darien 1698, from Darien on the *Dolphin* December 1699, later in London. [DD]

HILL, ADAM, a planter who died on the voyage to Darien 20 October 1698. [WP#88]

HISLOP, RICHARD, bosun of the *Royal William* discharged 12 November 1696 to join the Darien Company. [OSN#226]

HODGESON, JOHN, master of the *Unity of Ayr*, arrived in Ayr from Montserrat 2 September 1673. [SRO.E72.3.3]

HOGG, JOHN, a Covenanter imprisoned in Edinburgh Tolbooth, transported from Leith to Barbados on the *John and Nicholas*, master Edward Barnes, December 1685. [PC.11.255][ETR#389]

HOGG, MARK, son of James Hogg in Bonhardpans, West Lothian, a sailor on the *Rising Sun* from the Clyde to Darien 18 August 1699, cnf Edinburgh 1707. [SRO.CC8.8.83]

HOGG, PATRICK, a sailor on the *St Andrew* from Leith to Darien 14 July 1698, cnf Edinburgh 1707. [SRO.CC8.8.83]

HOLLAND, WILLIAM, son of Ralph Holland in Ayr, a sailor on the *Rising Sun* from the Clyde to Darien 18 August 1699, cnf Edinburgh 1708. [SRO.CC8.8.84]

HOLMES, JOHN, a seaman on the *Hope* to Darien 1699. [SRO. GD406, bundle 162, p39/19]

HOLMES, MARGARET, a prisoner in Edinburgh Tolbooth, transported from Leith to Jamaica August 1685. [ETR#369][PC. 11.330]

HOPE, THOMAS, son of Alexander Hope of Kerse, a soldier shipped from Leith to Darien on the *Unicorn* 14 July 1698, died in Jamaica, cnf Edinburgh 1707. [SRO.CC8.8.83]

HOPKIRK, JAMES, a Covenanter in Cavers, Roxburghshire, captured after the Battle of Bothwell Bridge 22 June 1679, imprisoned in Edinburgh, banished to the Plantations, transported from Leith on the *Crown of London*, master Thomas Teddico, 27 November 1679, shipwrecked and drowned off Orkney 10 December 1679. [RBM]

HORN, THOMAS, a Covenanter in Maybole, Ayrshire, captured after the Battle of Bothwell Bridge 22 June 1679, imprisoned in Edinburgh, banished to the Plantations, transported from Leith on the *Crown of London*, master Thomas Teddico, 27 November 1679, shipwrecked and drowned off Orkney 10 December 1679. [RBM]

HORNE, WILLIAM, a prisoner in Edinburgh Tolbooth, transported from Leith to the West Indies on the *John and Nicholas*, master Edward Barnes, December 1685. [ETR#390]

HORRORRISON,{?}, JOHN, master of the *James of Wairwater*, from Port Glasgow to the Caribees with textiles, stockings, gloves, buttons, coats, hats, shoes, bed-feathers, thread, spoons, pins, hose, beef, brass candlesticks, drugs, pipes, and buttons, February 1682. [SRO.E72.19.6]

HOUSTON, JAMES, a Covenanter in Balmaghie, Kirkcudbrightshire, captured after the Battle of Bothwell Bridge 22 June 1679, imprisoned in Edinburgh, banished to the Plantations, transported from Leith on the *Crown of London*, master Thomas Teddico, 27 November 1679, shipwrecked and drowned off Orkney 10 December 1679. [RBM]

HOUSTON, J., petitioned the King on behalf of the General Council of the Company of Scotland trading to Africa and the Indies {the Darien Company} re losses sustained at Darien. [SRO.GD26. 13.119]

HOUSTON, ROBERT, with 2 servants, 2 slaves and 10 acres in St Peter's parish, Barbados, 1679. [H2/79]

HOUSTON, SAMUEL, with 4 servants and 1 slave in St Peter's parish, Barbados, 1679. [H2/89]

HOWIE, JOHN, a prisoner in Edinburgh Tolbooth, transported from Leith to Barbados 22 December 1665, on Edward Burd's ship the *Margaret of Leith* {?}. [ETR#104]

HOWIE, JOHN, a Covenanter imprisoned in Edinburgh Tolbooth, transported from Leith to Jamaica August 1685. [ETR#369]

HOWIE, SAMUEL, a Covenanter imprisoned in Edinburgh Tolbooth, transported from Leith to Jamaica August 1685. [ETR#369] [PC.11.329]

HOWNAME, WALTER, a Covenanter in Teviotdale, transported from Leith to Jamaica August 1685, landed at Port Royal, Jamaica, 1685. [PC.11.330][LJ#15/17]

HUMPER, WALTER, a Covenanter in Dalmellington, Ayrshire, captured after the Battle of Bothwell Bridge 22 June 1679, imprisoned in Edinburgh, banished to the Plantations, transported from Leith on the *Crown of London*, master Thomas Teddico, 27 November 1679, shipwrecked and drowned off Orkney 10 December 1679. [RBM]

HUMPER, WALTER, jr., in Dalmellington, Ayrshire, a Covenanter, captured after the Battle of Bothwell Bridge 22 June 1679, transported from Leith to the West Indies on the *Crown of London*, master Thomas Teddico, 27 November 1679, shipwrecked off Orkney 10 December 1679, later transported to Jamaica. [CEC#212/5][SW#199]

HUNTER, JOHN, a passenger on the *Unity of Ayr*, master John Hodgson, which arrived in Ayr from Montserrat 2 September 1673; merchant on the *James of Ayr*, master James Chalmers, which arrived in Ayr 19 September 1681 from the West Indies. [SRO.E72.3.3/7]

HUNTER, JOHN, soldier of Captain William Walley's Company of Militia in Barbados 8 January 1679. [H2/80]

HUNTER, JOHN, with 1 slave and 6 acres in St Philip's parish, Barbados, 1680. [H2/8]

HUNTER, JOHN, a Covenanter imprisoned in Edinburgh Tolbooth, transported from Leith to Barbados on the *John and Nicholas*, master Edward Barnes, December 1685. [ETR#389][PC.11.166]

HUNTER, JOHN, a merchant, trading from Ayr to the West Indies on the *James of Ayr* February 1681, and from Ayr to the Caribee Islands also on the *James of Ayr* March 1683. [SRO.E72.3.6; E72.3.12]

HUNTER, JOHN, died at Darien 1700. [DD#325]

HUNTER, ROBERT, a baker from Perth, husband of Maria Henderson, died at Darien 1703 (sic!), cnf Edinburgh 1708. [SRO.CC8.8.84]

HUNTER, WILLIAM, soldier of Captain John Adam's Company of Militia in Barbados 6 January 1679. [H2/115]

HUNTLEY, WILLIAM, with 2 slaves and 5 acres in St Philip's parish, Barbados, 1680. [H2/9]

HUNTLEY, WILLIAM, buried in St Philip's parish, Barbados, 1 August 1679. [H2/25]

HUSSIE, MICHAEL, a sailor on the *Unicorn* from Leith to Darien 14 July 1698, cnf Edinburgh 1707. [SRO.CC8.8.83]

HUTCHISON, ALEXANDER, a sailor on the *Rising Sun* from the Clyde to Darien 18 August 1699, cnf Edinburgh 1707. [SRO. CC8.8.83]

HUTCHISON, GEORGE, a merchant in Edinburgh, petitioned the Privy Council for prisoners in Edinburgh for shipment to Jamaica and Barbados 2 November 1665; allocated prisoners in Edinburgh Tolbooth 7 December 1665. [PC#2.101, 111]

HUTCHESON, GEORGE, a Covenanter in Straiton, Ayrshire, captured after the Battle of Bothwell Bridge 22 June 1679, imprisoned in Edinburgh, banished to the Plantations, transported from Leith on the *Crown of London*, master Thomas Teddico, 27 November 1679, shipwrecked and drowned off Orkney 10 December 1679. [RBM]

HUTCHESON, ROBERT, transported from Leith to Jamaica August 1685. [PC.11.136]

HUTCHISON, WILLIAM, in Jamaica 1694; settled in Port Royal, Jamaica, before 1700. [SPAWI/1699/443][DP#352]

HUTTON, JAMES, son of John Hutton in Cleish, Kinross-shire, a sailor on the *St Andrew* from Leith to Darien 14 July 1698, cnf Edinburgh 1707. [SRO.CC8.8.83]

HUTTON, JOHN, son of John Hutton or Seaton in Chapel Lauder, Berwickshire, a minister, from Leith to Darien on the *Caledonia* cnf Edinburgh 25 September 1707. [SRO.CC8.8.83]

INGLIS, CHARLES, son of James Inglis in St Andrews, Fife, a sailor on the *Rising Sun* from the Clyde to Darien 18 August 1699, cnf Edinburgh 1707. [SRO.CC8.8.83]

INGLIS, HENRY, from Kinghorn, Fife, a sailor on the *St Andrew* from Leith to Darien 14 July 1698, cnf Edinburgh 26 November 1707. [SRO.CC8.8.83][SRO.GD406, bundle 159, p2/9]

INGLIS, JAMES, a Lieutenant who died on the voyage to Darien 3 November 1698. [WP#88][DD#157]

INGLIS, JAMES, from Calder, Midlothian, an overseer who was killed at Darien 1699, cnf Edinburgh 1707. [SRO.CC8.8.83]

INGLIS, ROBERT, son of James Inglis in St Andrews, Fife, a sailor on the *Rising Sun* from the Clyde to Darien 18 August 1699, cnf Edinburgh 1707. [SRO.CC8.8.83]

INGLIS, THOMAS, merchant burgess of Edinburgh, trading from Leith to the West Indies 1611. [SRO.E71.29.6]

INGLIS, THOMAS, a Covenanter in Livingston, West Lothian, captured after the Battle of Bothwell Bridge 22 June 1679, imprisoned in Edinburgh, banished to the Plantations, transported from Leith on the *Crown of London*, master Thomas Teddico, 27 November 1679, shipwrecked and drowned off Orkney 10 December 1679. [RBM]

INGLIS, WILLIAM, from Farr?, Sutherland, emigrated via Liverpool to Barbados 5 May 1698. [LRO.HQ325.2.FRE]

INNES, ALEXANDER, from West Lothian, a gunner's boy on the *St Andrew* from Leith to Darien 14 July 1698, cnf Edinburgh 11 November 1707. [SRO.CC8.8.83]

INNES, JAMES, buried in St James, Barbados, 14 July 1679. [H#499]

INNES, JOHN, a merchant in Port Royal, Jamaica, pro.16 September 1692 Jamaica

INNES, JOHN, soldier of Thornhill's Company of Militia in Barbados 6 January 1679. [H2/151]

INNES, JOHN, overseer of Colonel John Hallet's Cliff Plantation, St John's parish, Barbados, will subscribed 20 February 1713, pro.14 April 1716 Barbados [RB6/35/551]

INNES, PHILIP, with 4 acres and 3 slaves in Christchurch, Barbados, 22 December 1679. [H#477]

INNES, TIMOTHY, and his wife Margaret, parents of Timothy baptised in St Michael's, Barbados, 10 August 1679. [H#424]

INNES, WILLIAM, soldier of Colonel Affleck's Company of Militia in Barbados 6 January 1679. [H2/148]

IRELAND, JOHN, a Covenanter imprisoned in Edinburgh Tolbooth, transported from Leith to Jamaica 11 August 1685. [PC.11.114] [ETR#369]

IRVINE, ANDREW, born 1668 son of Andrew Irvine in the Shetland Islands, emigrated via London to Barbados August 1684. [CLRO/AIA]

IRVINE, CHARLES, of Cults, in Barbados, 1703. [JGD]

IRVINE, JOHN, son of Charles Irvine of Cults, in Barbados 1703. [JGD]

ISAAC, ALEXANDER, from Tulliallan, Clackmannanshire, a sailor on the *Unicorn* from Leith to Darien 14 July 1698, cnf Edinburgh 1707. [SRO.CC8.8.83]

IVAR, JOHN, transported from Leith to Jamaica August 1685. [PC.11.136]

IVAR, MALCOLM, a Covenanter, transported July 1685. [PC.11.126]

JACKSON, JAMES, son of Charles Jackson a merchant in Edinburgh, a sailor on the *Olive Branch* from the Clyde to Darien May 1699, cnf Edinburgh 8 October 1707. [SRO.CC8.8.83]

JACKSON, JOHN, a Covenanter in Braestob, Glasgow, transported from Leith to Jamaica August 1685, landed at Port Royal, Jamaica, November 1685, settled in Spanish Town, Jamaica. [PC.11.329][LJ#81]

JAFFRAY, ANDREW, killed at Darien 6 February 1699. [DP#86] [DD#189]

JAFFREY, JOHN, firemaster at Darien, wife and daughter Mary at Darien 1699. [DD#245]

JAMES, THOMAS, a minister who died on the voyage to Darien 23 October 1698. [WP#88]

JAMIESON, ALEXANDER, a Covenanter and a servant in Mauchline, Ayrshire, imprisoned in Edinburgh Tolbooth, transported from Leith to Jamaica August 1685. [PC.11.136][ETR#369]

JAMIESON, ALEXANDER, born 1678, son of Reverend Alexander Jamieson and Grizel Maxwell in Govan, died in the West Indies before 1706. [F.3.412]

JAMIESON, JAMES, son of James Jamieson in Burntisland, Fife, a sailor on the *Unicorn* from Leith to Drien 14 July 1698, cnf Edinburgh 9 October 1707. [SRO.CC8.8.83]

JAMIESON, JOHN, a merchant trading from Port Glasgow to the West Indies on the *Walter of Glasgow* February 1683. [SRO.E72.19.8]

JAMIESON, WILLIAM, Captain of the *Olive Branch* from the Clyde to Darien 12 May 1699, arrived there August 1699. [OSN#202]; witness to the testaments of James Troup, George Barclay, and of Patrick Young, 5 May 1699; ship burnt in Caledonia Bay, Darien, November 1699. [DD#256]

JANSEN, JAN, arrived in Leith from the West Indies with a consignment of tobacco July 1643. [EBR.26.7.1643]

JANSON, ADRIAN, master of the *Nicolas Jan of Flushing* from Findhorn to Surinam with a cargo of 39 horses 4 August 1684. [SRO.E72.11.9]

JANSON, PETER, a seaman on the *St Andrew* from Leith to Darien 14 July 1698, cnf Edinburgh 1707. [SRO.CC8.8.83]

JARDINE, JOHN, born in "Monte", a laborer, emigrated to Darien on the *Caledonia*, deserted but captured by the Spanish, signed a deposition in Panama 15 February 1700. [Audienca de Panama, Archives of the Indies, L#164, Seville, Spain][DD#274]

JARDEN, WILLIAM, a passenger on the *James of Ayr*, master James Chalmers, arrived in Ayr from Montserrat 19 September 1673.[SRO.E72.3.4]

JARDEN, WILLIAM, in Antigua, died 1705, pro.5/618 PCC.

JERVY, JOHN, a wright in Falkirk, transported from Leith to the West Indies on the *St Michael of Scarborough*, master Edward Johnston, 12 December 1678. [PC.6.76]

JOHNSON, ROBERT, a schoolteacher, his wife and son, died at Darien 1700. [DD#325]

JOHNSTONE, ALEXANDER, a soldier who died at Darien 1699, cnf Edinburgh 1707. [SRO.CC8.8.83]

JOHNSTON, ANDREW, a schoolmaster, emigrated to Jamaica 1706. [EMA#37]

JOHNSTON, Mrs ANN, with 110 acres in Barbados 1679. [H2/162, 204]

JOHNSTON, ARCHIBALD, Captain of a Company of Militia in Barbados 1679, [H2/164]; with 2 sons, 60 acres, 3 menservants and 36 slaves in St Andrew's, Barbados, 1680. [H#469]; a merchant in Barbados and father of Archibald by 1694. [SRO.PC2.25.98]

JOHNSTON, ARCHIBALD, from Musselburgh, Midlothian, to Barbados 12 July 1682. [PRO.C66.3228.15]

JOHNSTON, DONALD, a Covenanter, transported from Leith to Jamaica August 1685. [PC.11.136]

JOHNSTON, JAMES, a merchant from Glasgow, on Montserrat 1691. [SRO.RD2.104.958]

JOHNSTONE, JAMES, from Queensferry, West Lothian, a foremastman on the *Caledonia* from Leith to Darien 14 July 1698, cnf Edinburgh 1707. [SRO.CC8.8.83]

JOHNSTONE, JAMES, from Leith, Midlothian, a sailor on the *Unicorn* from Leith to Darien 14 July 1698, cnf Edinburgh 28 July 1709. [SRO.CC8.8.84]

JOHNSTON, JOHN, a weaver, from the Clyde to Darien on the *Speedy Return* 12 October 1698, cnf Edinburgh 1708. [SRO.CC8.8.84]

JOHNSTON, JUDITH, buried in St Lucy's, Barbados, 12 May 1679. [H2/155]

JOHNSTON, THOMAS, a passenger on the *James of Ayr*, master James Chalmers, which arrived in Ayr from the West Indies 19 September 1673; passenger on the *Swan of Ayr* which arrived in Ayr from the West Indies 23 September 1678. [SRO.E72.3.4]

JOHNSTON, THOMAS, with 8 slaves in St Andrew's, Barbados, 1680. [H#472]

JOHNSTON, THOMAS, a merchant trading between Port Glasgow and the Caribee Islands on the *Walter of Glasgow* February 1683 and on the *Mayflower of Glasgow* March 1685. [SRO.E72.19.8/9]

JOHNSTONE, WALTER, son of James Johnstone of Corhead in Edinburgh, surgeon's mate, died at Darien 29 November 1699, cnf Edinburgh 26 November 1707. [SRO.CC8.8.83][WP#87]

JOHNSTON, WILLIAM, with 2 slaves in St Peter's parish, Barbados, 1679. [H2/79]

JOHNSTONE, WILLIAM, Ensign of Colonel Stanfast's Regiment of Militia in Barbados 6 January 1679. [H2/157]

JOHNSTONE, WILLIAM, Captain's servant on the *St Andrew* to Darien 1698. [SRO.GD406, bundle 159, p4/16]

JOLLY, ALEXANDER, from Prestonpans, Midlothian, a seaman on the *Royal William* who was discharged to join the Darien Company 12 November 1696. [OSN#228]

JOLLY, JOHN, from Prestonpans, Midlothian, a seaman on the *Royal William* who was discharged to join the Darien Company 12 November 1696. [OSN#228]

JOLLY, ROBERT, wrote to the directors of the Darien Company from Caledonia, New Edinburgh, Darien, 28 December 1698. [SRO. GD406.1.6489]; arrived at Gravesend, Kent, England, from Caledonia, Darien, 12 August 1699. [SRO.GD406.1.4427]

JONES, MOSES, master of the *Merchants Adventurers of Belfast*, arrived in Port Glasgow from Barbados with sugar August 1682. [SRO.E72.19.5]

KEIL, ROBERT, a goldsmith, died at Darien 1700. [DD#325]

KEIN, PATRICK, a prisoner in Edinburgh Tolbooth, transported from Leith 27 November 1679. [ETR#162]

KEIR, JAMES, a merchant from Stirling, emigrated to Darien 1699. [RBS#91]

KEIR, PATRICK, a Covenanter in Kincardine on Forth(?), captured after the Battle of Bothwell Bridge 22 June 1679, imprisoned in Edinburgh, banished to the Plantations, transported from Leith on the *Crown of London*, master Thomas Teddico, 27 November 1679, shipwrecked and drowned off Orkney 10 December 1679. [RBM]

KEITH, ELIZABETH, daughter of Dr James Keith, baptised in St John's, Barbados, 9 December 1678, buried there 11 December 1678. [H2/74]

KEITH, HENRY, a time-expired indentured servant, emigrated from Barbados to Virginia on the *Young William*, master Thomas Cornish, 2 August 1679. [H#383]

KEITH, Dr JAMES, father of Elizabeth baptised in St John's, Barbados, 9 December 1678. [H#508]; with 3 servants, 20 slaves and 20 acres in St John's parish, Barbados, 1679. [H2/70]

KEITH, ROBERT, a mariner on the *Olive Branch* from the Clyde to Darien 5.1699, cnf Edinburgh 11 October 1707. [SRO.CC8.8.83]

KEITH, THOMAS, soldier of Captain Robert Bowcher's Company of Militia in Barbados 6 January 1679; in St Philips parish, Barbados, with 15 acres, 1680. [H2/9, 112]

KELL, NEIL, transported from Leith to Jamaica 7 August 1685. [PC. 11.130]

KELSO, ARCHIBALD, from Edinburgh, a sailor on the *Dolphin* from Leith to Darien 14 July 1698, cnf Edinburgh 17 October 1707. [SRO.CC8.8.83]

KENNEDY, ADAM, settled in Antigua, died before 1698, pro.1698 PCC.

KENNEDY, CHARLES, died in Barbados, Admin.1652 PCC.

KENNEDY, DANIEL, soldier of Captain John Thorburn's Company of Militia in Barbados 1679. [H2/140]

KENNEDY, HUMPHREY, soldier of Captain John Thorburn's Company of Militia in Barbados 1679, with 5 acres of land in St Lucy's parish, Barbados, 30 December 1679. [H2/41, 141]

KENNEDY, JAMES, soldier in Captain Lewgar's company of Militia in Barbados 6 January 1679. [H2/138]

KENNEDY, JOHN, a militiaman in Colonel Lyne's Regiment in Barbados 6 January 1679. [H2/103]

KENNEDY, JOHN, a defaulter from Captain Woodward's company of Militia in Barbados 6 January 1679. [H2/156]

KENNEDY, JOHN, and his wife Ellinor, time-expired indentured servants, emigrated from Barbados to Bristol on the *Society*, master Edmond Ditty, 2 May 1679. [H#383]

KENNEDY, JOHN, trooper of Captain John Leslie's Troop of Militia in Barbados 1679. [H2/208]

KENNEDY, JOHN, a Covenanter in Closeburn, Dumfriesshire, captured after the Battle of Bothwell Bridge 22 June 1679, imprisoned in Edinburgh, banished to the Plantations, transported from Leith on the *Crown of London*, master Thomas Teddico, 27 November 1679, shipwrecked and drowned off Orkney 10 December 1679. [RBM]

KENNEDY, JOHN, a Covenanter, transported from Leith to Jamaica August 1685. [PC.11.329]

KENNEDY, RICHARD, soldier of Lieutenant Colonel Andrew Affleck's Company of Militia in Barbados 1679. [H2/148]

KENNEDY, THOMAS, and wife Ann, parents of Mary baptised in St Michael's, Barbados, 3 November 1678. [H#422]; Thomas Kennedy a soldier in Captain Ely's company of Militia in Barbados 1679. [H2/177]

KENNEDY, WILLIAM, soldier of Captain Merrell's company of Militia in Barbados 1679. [H2/153]

KENNEDY, WILLIAM. soldier of Captain John Adams company of Militia in Barbados 6 January 1679. [H2/115]

KENNEDY, WILLIAM, baptised in St Peter's parish, Barbados, 1679. [H2/85]

KERR, THOMAS, an engineer late from Flanders, emigrated to Darien 1699, died in the West Indies, cnf Edinburgh 1707. [SRO.CC8. 8.83][DD#245]

KEY, JAMES, a sailor on the *Endeavour* to Darien 1698. [SRO.GD406, bundle 161, 25/17]

KIDD, DAVID, a weaver in Logie, transported from Leith to the West Indies on the *St Michael of Scarborough*, master Edward Johnston, 12 December 1678. [PC.6.76]

KIDD, JAMES, soldier of Captain Hall's Company of Militia in Barbados 31 December 1679. [H2/136]

KIDD, WILLIAM, soldier of Captain Woodward's Company of Militia in Barbados 6 January 1680. [H2/156]

KILGOUR, ALEXANDER, from Lochgelly, Fife, a sailor on the *Caledonia* from Leith to Darien 14 July 1698, cnf Edinburgh 22 July 1709. [SRO.CC8.8.84]

KILLEN, JOHN, a Covenanter in Shotts, Lanarkshire, captured after the Battle of Bothwell Bridge 22 June 1679, imprisoned in Edinburgh, banished to the Plantations, transported from Leith on the *Crown of London*, master Thomas Teddico, 27 November 1679, shipwrecked and drowned off Orkney 10 December 1679. [RBM]

KILPATRICK, ROGER, with 3 slaves and 10 acres in St Lucy's parish, Barbados, 30 December 1679. [H2/41]

KINNAIRD of Culbin, Sir ALEXANDER, overseer, witnessed a document in St Kitts 21 January 1700. [SRO.GD84.Sec.1/22/9B]

KINNAIRD, ELIZABETH, buried in St John's parish, Barbados, 16 April 1679. [H2/74]

KINNAIRD, Mr ROBERT, with 2 slaves and 10 acres in St John's parish, Barbados, 1679. [H2/70]

KINNAIRD, Ensign WILLIAM, son of the laird of Culbin, died at Darien 1700. [DD#325]

KINNEIR, ALEXANDER, from Edinburgh, a sailor on the *Caledonia* from Leith to Darien 14 July 1698, cnf Edinburgh 1707. [SRO.CC8.8.83]

KINNELL, WILLIAM, a tailor in Grangepans, West Lothian, from Leith to Darien on the *St Andrew* 14 July 1698, cnf Edinburgh 7 October 1707. [SRO.CC8.8.83]

KIRK, JAMES, a Covenanter in Largo, Fife, captured after the Battle of Bothwell Bridge 22 June 1679, imprisoned in Edinburgh, banished to the Plantations, transported from Leith on the *Crown of London*, master Thomas Teddico, 27 November 1679, shipwrecked and drowned off Orkney 10 December 1679. [RBM]

KIRK, JOHN, a Covenanter from Ceres, Fife, a prisoner in Edinburgh Tolbooth, transported from Leith to Barbados on the *Crown of London*, master Thomas Teddico 27 November 1679, shipwrecked and drowned off Orkney 10 December 1679. [ETR#162] [RBM]

KIRK, ROBERT, a Covenanter from Orwell, Kinross, captured after the Battle of Bothwell Bridge 22 June 1679, imprisoned in Edinburgh Tolbooth, transported from Leith to the West Indies on the *Crown of London*, master Thomas Teddico, 27 November 1679, shipwrecked off Muil Head of Deerness, Orkney, 10 December 1679, later transported to Jamaica. [CEC#212/5][ETR#162][RBM]

KIRKPATRICK, HUGH, born in Irvine, Ayrshire, 23 October 1671, emigrated to Jamaica 1693, married Ann Goodin, settled in Westmoreland parish, Jamaica, father of Hugh, James, James, Edward and Mary, died 8 December 1746. [Llandilo g/s, Westmoreland parish, Jamaica]

KIRKPATRICK, JOHN, formerly a Lieutenant of the Earl of Argyll's Regiment, to Darien 1699, cnf Edinburgh 22 September 1707. [SRO.CC8.8.83]

KIRKWALL, ELIZABETH, transported from Leith to Jamaica 7 August 1685. [PC.11.329]

KNOLLS, GEORGE, from Bo'ness, West Lothian, from Leith to Darien on the *Caledonia* 14 July 1698, cnf Edinburgh 22 October 1707. [SRO.CC8.8.83]

KRETTS, HENRICK, a trumpeter, from Leith to Darien on the *St Andrew* 14 July 1698, cnf Edinburgh 1707. [SRO.CC8.8.83]

KRETTS, PAUL, a trumpeter, from Leith to Darien on the *St Andrew* 14 July 1698, cnf Edinburgh 1707. [SRO.CC8.8.83]

KYLER, JAMES, master of the *William and James of Saltcoats*, from Port Glasgow to the West Indies with thread, shoes, linen-cloth, plaiding and buttons, November 1681. [SRO.E72.19.6]

LAING, JAMES, a wright, transported from Leith to Barbados on the *St John of Leith* 1 May 1674, died in Barbados 1676. [PC.4.608, 675]

LAING, WILLIAM, a Covenanter and a farmer in Cavers, Roxburghshire, transported from Leith to the West Indies on the *St Michael of Scarborough*, master Edward Johnston, 12 December 1678. [PC.6.76]

LAMB, ALEXANDER, a Covenanter in Straiton, Ayrshire, captured after the Battle of Bothwell Bridge 22 June 1679, imprisoned in Edinburgh, banished to the Plantations, transported from Leith on the *Crown of London*, master Thomas Teddico, 27 November 1679, shipwrecked and drowned off Orkney 10 December 1679. [RBM]

LAMOND, ARCHIBALD, a Covenanter in Kilbride, Argyll, transported from Leith to Jamaica August 1685. [PC.11.307][LC#289]

LAMOND, JOHN, from Kincardine on Forth, Clackmannanshire, a sailor on the *Endeavour* from Leith to Darien 14 July 1698, cnf Edinburgh 1707. [SRO.GD406, bundle 161, 25/6][SRO.CC8.8.83]

LAMOND, SORLEY, a Covenanter in Drum, transported from Leith to Jamaica August 1685. [PC.11.136][LC#289]

LAMONT, ANGUS, from Cowal, Argyll, pro.5 April 1652 Barbados. [RB.6.11.498]

LAMONT, WALTER, husband of Elizabeth Hamilton in Evanachan, Strathlachlan, Argyll, son of John Og Lamont, a soldier who died at Darien 1700. [LC#263]

LAMONT, WILLIAM, Secretary of Curacao 1699. [SPAWI.1699/890.xvi]

LAUGHTON, PATRICK, from Kirkwall, Orkney, a gunner's mate on the *St Andrew* from Leith to Darien 14 July 1698, cnf Edinburgh 27.October 1707. [SRO.GD406, bundle 159, p4/1][SRO.CC8.8.83]

LAUSON, WILLIAM, from Edinburgh, an Ensign who died at Darien 1699, cnf Edinburgh 14 October 1707. [SRO.CC8.8.83]

LAW, JAMES, a Covenanter in Kirkliston, West Lothian, transported from Leith to the West Indies on the *St Michael of Scarborough*, master Edward Johnston, 12 December 1678. [PC.6.76]

LAW, WILLIAM, from Kirkcaldy, Fife, a foremastman on the *Caledonia* from Leith to Darien 14 July 1698, cnf Edinburgh 1707. [SRO.CC8.8.83]

LAWDOR, JOHN, from "Yatem" {Yetholm?}, Scotland, to Barbados 1679. [PRO.C66/3214/7]

LAWSON, MARION, a Covenanter, transported from Leith to Jamaica August 1685. [PC.11.329]

LAWSON, WILLIAM, prisoner in Edinburgh Tolbooth, transported from Leith to Barbados on the *John and Nicholas*, master Edward Barnes, December 1685. [ETR#390]

LEARMONTH, CHARLES, son of Robert Learmonth, a merchant in Edinburgh, a Lieutenant, from the Clyde to Darien on the *Rising Sun* 18 August 1699, died 1699, cnf Edinburgh 7 September 1744. [SRO.CC8.8.109]

LEARMONTH, WILLIAM, soldier of Captain Alleyne's Company of Militia in Barbados 1679. [H2/163]

LEARMONTH, WILLIAM, soldier of Captain Merrell's company of Militia in Barbados 1679. [H2/152]

LECKIE, CATHERINE, guilty of infanticide, transported from Leith to Jamaica August 1685. [PC.11.136]

LECKIE, WILLIAM, a Covenanter and a merchant in Glasgow, husband of Marie Duncan, transported to the West Indies June 1678. [PC.11.136]

LERMONT, PETER, a Covenanter in Shotts, Lanarkshire, captured after the Battle of Bothwell Bridge 22 June 1679, imprisoned in Edinburgh, banished to the Plantations, transported from Leith on the *Crown of London*, master Thomas Teddico, 27 November 1679, shipwrecked and drowned off Orkney 10 December 1679. [RBM]

LESLIE, ANDREW, Lieutenant of Captain Cleaver's company of Militia in Barbados 6 March 1680. [H2/126]

LESLIE, Mrs ANN, with 12 slaves in St John's parish, Barbados, 1679. [H2/70]

LESLIE, Captain JOHN, with 4 servants, 55 slaves and 60 acres in St John's parish, Barbados, 1679, [H2/70]; churchwarden of St John's parish, Barbados, 1679, [H2/72]; Assemblyman for St John's, Barbados, 1684, [SPAWI.1684/1881]; in Barbados 1680. [SPAWI.1680/1336]; soldier of Colonel Colleton's company of Militia in Barbados 9 March 1680,(?) [H2/119]; Captain of a troop of Militia in Barbados 5 January 1679. [H2/208]

LESLIE, Colonel JOHN, Assemblyman in Barbados 24 January 1699. [SPAWI.1699/53]

LESLIE, WALTER, soldier of Captain Morris's company of Militia in Barbados 6 January 1679; sergeant of Captain Thornhill's company of Militia in Barbados 6 January 1680. [H2/179]

LEYDON, JAMES, a Covenanter from Cavers, Roxburghshire, imprisoned in Edinburgh, transported from Leith to the West Indies on the *Crown of London*, master Thomas Teddico, 27 November 1679, shipwrecked off Orkney 10 December 1679, later transported to Jamaica. [CEC#212/5][RBM]

LICKPRIVICK, JAMES, a Covenanter in Cathcart, Glasgow, transported from Leith to the West Indies on the *St Michael of Scarborough*, master Edward Johnston, 12 December 1678. [PC.6.76]

LIDDELL, GEORGE, in Montserrat, pro.1696 PCC [120, Bond]

LIDDELL, JOHN, a clerk on the *Olive Branch* from the Clyde to Darien 18 August 1699, cnf Edinburgh 1708. [SRO.CC8.8.83] ; witness to the testaments of James Troup, George Barclay, and of Patrick Young, 5 May 1699.; "remained at Darien after the colony was abandoned" [APS.14, app114]

LIGHTON, PATRICK, son of Robert Lighton and Christian Hay in Burntisland, Fife, a seaman on the *Rising Sun* from the Clyde to Darien 18 August 1699, cnf Edinburgh 1707. [SRO.CC8.8.83]

LILBOURNE, JAMES, a Covenanter in Shotts, Lanarkshire, captured after the Battle of Bothwell Bridge 22 June 1679, imprisoned in Edinburgh Tolbooth, banished to the Plantations, transported from Leith on the *Crown of London*, master Thomas Teddico, 27 November 1679, shipwrecked and drowned off Orkney 10 December 1679. [RBM][ETR#162]

LINDSAY, ALEXANDER, in Barbados 1649, [SRO.GD39.948]; executor of William Powrie's will, pro.4 April 1649 Barbados

LINDSAY, DANIEL, soldier of Captain Lillington's company of Militia in Barbados 6 January 1679. [H2/154]

LINDSAY, ELIZABETH, in St Philips parish, Barbados, with 4 acres, 1680. [H2/11]

LINDSAY, Captain GEORGE, pro.10 November 1663 Barbados. [RB. 6.15.543]

LINDSAY, GRIZZEL, buried in St Peter's parish, Barbados, 1679. [H2/ 89]

LINDSAY, Major JOHN, instructed to sail from Greenock to Caledonia, Darien, 20 September 1699, killed at Darien 30 March 1700. [SRO.GD406.1][DD#317]

LINKLETTER, WILLIAM, servant to Judge Reid, buried 16 October 1678 in St James, Barbados. [H#498]

LITSTER, HUGH, born 1678, son of Reverend Thomas Litster and Margaret Lindsay in Aberdour, Fife, a sailor on the *Rising Sun* from the Clyde to Darien 18 August 1699, died in Charleston, South Carolina, 3 September 1700, [F.5.3]; cnf Edinburgh 1708. [SRO.CC8.8.84]

LIVINGSTONE, ANDREW, a surgeon in Edinburgh, to Darien on the *Dolphin*, subscribed to a deed of factory at Plaistow, Cornwall, 1 February 1707, imprisoned in Carthagena and in Spain. [SRO.GD406, bundle 163, c24/1][APS.14, app.114]

LOCKHART, GEORGE, a merchant trading from Port Glasgow to the West Indies on the *Walter of Glasgow* February 1683. [SRO.E72. 19.8]

LOCKHART, JOHN, father of John in Prestonpans, East Lothian, a sailor on the *Unicorn* from Leith to Darien 14 July 1698, died at Darien 1699, cnf Edinburgh 1707. [SRO.CC8.8.83]

LOGAN, ANDREW, a sergeant at Darien 1699. [DD#262]

LOGAN, Lieutenant ..., from New York to Darien 1699. [DD#264]

LORNE, PETER, husband of Margaret Robertson in Zealand, the Netherlands, a cooper emigrated from Leith to Darien on the *Unicorn* 14 July 1698, cnf Edinburgh 11 October 1707. [SRO.CC8.8.83]

LOTHIAN, ABRAHAM, a soldier from Renfrew, emigrated to Darien 1699, died there 1699, cnf Edinburgh 1707. [SRO.CC8.8.83]

LOTHIAN, JOHN, Captain's servant on the *St Andrew* to Darien from Leith 1698. [SRO.GD406, bundle 159, p4/15]; admitted to the Scots Charitable Society of Boston, Massachusetts, 1699. [SCS]

LOUGHLAN, DENIS, defaulter from Captain Woodward's company of Militia in Barbados 6 January 1679. [H2/156]

LOUGHLAN, EDWARD, soldier of Lieutenant Colonel Affleck's company of Militia in Barbados 6 January 1680. [H2/148]

LOVE, CHRISTOPHER, a cooper in Ayr, emigrated to Darien on the *Hope* 1698; cnf Edinburgh 1708. [SRO.GD406, bundle 162, p30/28][SRO.CC8.8.84]

LOVET, Captain THOMAS, commander of the Darien Company's hired ship the *Susanna of Bristol* instructed to sail to Glasgow, then to Belfast for provisions, then to Caledonia, Darien, 30 October 1699. [SRO.GD406.1]

LOW, WILLIAM, from Kirkcaldy, Fife, a foremastman on the *Caledonia* from Leith to Darien 14 July 1698, cnf Edinburgh 23 October 1707. [SRO.CC8.8.83]

LOWRIE, ARCHIBALD, in Barbados 1649. [SRO.GD49.948]

LUCKISON, JOHN, a volunteer who died on the voyage to Darien 31 October 1698. [WP#88]

LUKE, WILLIAM, a merchant trading from Port Glasgow to the West Indies in the *Jean of Largs* April 1684. [SRO.E72.19.9]

LUTTONS, HERMAN, a foremastman on the *Caledonia* from Leith to Darien 14 July 1698, cnf Edinburgh 11 October 1707. [SRO.CC8.8.83]

LYELL, JAMES, a sailor on the *St Andrew* 1698. [SRO.GD406, bundle 159, p2/13]

LYON, GEORGE, master of the *Walter of Glasgow*, from Port Glasgow to the West Indies February 1683 with cloth, linen, woollen, hornspoons, thread, buttons, hats, shoes, gloves, tobacco pipes, caps, slippers and candles. [SRO.E72.19.8]

LYON, HENRY, from Edinburgh, a sailor on the *Rising Sun* from the Clye to Darien 18 August 1699, cnf Edinburgh 1707. [SRO.CC8.8.83]

LYON, JAMES, a wright in Barbados, dead by March 1676. [PC#4.674]

LYON, WALTER, a prisoner in Edinburgh Tolbooth, who had returned from Barbados to where he had been exiled, petitioned the Privy Council for his release 16 September 1662; similar 23 September 1662. [PC.1.266][ETR]

MCADAM, QUENTIN, a Covenanter from Dalmellington, Ayrshire, captured after the Battle of Bothwell Bridge 22 June 1679, transported from Leith to the West Indies on the *Crown of London*, master Thomas Teddico, 27 November 1679, shipwrecked off Muil Head of Deerness, Orkney, 10 December 1679, later shipped to Jamaica. [SW#199][RBM]

MCALLESTER, DANIEL, with 5 acres in St Lucy's parish, Barbados, 1678. [H2/42]

MCALLISTER, THOMAS, from Castle Kilcohee, Inverness, with 8 acres in St Lucy's parish, Barbados, 1678, pro.24 March 1684 Barbados. [RB.6.10.337]; soldier of Captain Walley's company of Militia in Barbados 6 January 1680. [H2/137]

MCARTHUR, GILBERT, a Covenanter and a drover in Islay, Argyll, transported from Leith to Jamaica August 1685. [PC.11.329]

MACARTHUR, Major JOHN, born 1648, settled at Figtree, St Thomas, Middle Island, St Kitts, Deputy Governor of St Kitts, father of Gillies, died 4 April 1704 buried in St Thomas, [DP#310] [MWI#182]; in St Kitts, 1699. [SPAWI/1699/282,658]; in St Kitts 22 August 1699. [ActsPCCol]

MACARTNEY, JOHN, a Covenanter from Kirkcudbright, captured after the Battle of Bothwell Bridge 22 June 1679, transported from leith to the West Indies on the *Crown of London*, master Thomas Teddico, 27 November 1679, shipwrecked off Muil Head of Deerness, Orkney, 10 December 1679, later shipped to Jamaica. [SW#202]

MACARTY, ELIZABETH, buried in St Michael's, Barbados, 29 December 1678. [H#431]

MCASKELL, ALLAN, with 20 acres, a soldier in Captain Davies' company of Militia in Barbados 1679, [H2/166]; settled in Barbados before 1702. [SRO.S/H]

MCASKILL, DANIEL, in St Joseph's parish, Barbados, wife Mary, son Daniel, pro.15 March 1710 Barbados. [RB6.5.450]

MCAULAY, ROBERT, servant to ... Riddell, son of Duncan and Agnes McAulay in Glasgow, from Greenock to Darien on the *Rising Sun* 18 August 1699, cnf Edinburgh 21 October 1707. [SRO. CC8.8.83]

MCBRATNEY, JOHN, a Covenanter in Galloway, transported from Leith to the West Indies on the *Crown of London*, master Thomas Teddico, 27 November 1679, shipwrecked off Orkney 10 December 1679, later transported to Jamaica. [CEC#212/5][RBM]

MCCALL, DANIEL, soldier of Colonel Lynne's company of Militia in Barbados 6 January 1679. [H2/109]

MCCALL, WILLIAM, soldier of Captain Allemby's company of Militia in Barbados 6 January 1679. [H2/155]

MCCALLEY, DOUGALL, wounded at Darien 6 February 1699. [DP#86]

MCCALLUM, ARCHIBALD, a Covenanter in Argyll, transported from Leith to Jamaica August 1685. [PC.11.136]

MCCALLUM, NEIL, a Covenanter in Argyll, transported from Leith to Jamaica August 1685, [PC.11.330]

MCCENREE, JOHN, a time-expired indentured servant, emigrated from Barbados to Virginia on the pink *Rebecca*, master Thomas Williams, 7 July 1679. [H#390]

MCCHARLATIE, JOHN, a Covenanter in Argyll, transported from Leith to Jamaica August 1685. [PC.11.136]

MACCLAIRE, JOHN, with 6 acres land and 6 slaves, in St Michael's, Barbados, 1679. [H#456]

MCCLANCE, ARCHIBALD, witness to John Innes's will, pro.14 April 1716 Barbados. [RB6.35.551]

MACCLEIKERAYE, JOHN, a prisoner in Edinburgh Tolbooth, transported from Leith 27 November 1679. [ETR#162]

MCCOLIN, ALEXANDER, sergeant of Colonel Colleton's company of Militia in Barbados 9 March 1680. [H2/119]

MCCOLME, JOHN, merchant on the *James of Ayr*, master James Chalmers, arrived in Ayr 19 September 1673 from Montserrat and the West Indies. [SRO.E72.3.4]

MACCOMBUS, ALEXANDER, soldier of Captain Jack's company of Militia in Barbados 9 March 1680. [H2/123]

MCCONNEL, JAMES, a Covenanter in Kirkmichael, Ayrshire, captured after the Battle of Bothwell Bridge 22 June 1679, imprisoned in Edinburgh Tolbooth, banished to the Plantations, transported from Leith on the *Crown of London*, master Thomas Teddico, 27 November 1679, shipwrecked and drowned off Orkney 10 December 1679. [RBM][ETR#162]

MCCONOCHIE, JOHN, transported from Leith to Jamaica, August 1685. [PC.11.136]

MCCONOCHIE, NEIL, a Covenanter in Argyll, transported from Leith to Jamaica, August 1685. [PC.11.136]

MCCORKADALE, ARCHIBALD, a Covenanter in Argyll, transported from Leith to Jamaica, August 1685. [PC.11.136]

MCCORNOCK, JOHN, a Covenanter in Colmonell, Ayrshire, captured after the Battle of Bothwell Bridge 22 June 1679, imprisoned in Edinburgh, banished to the Plantations, transported from Leith on the *Crown of London*, master Thomas Teddico, 27 November 1679, shipwrecked and drowned off Orkney 10 December 1679. [RBM]

MACCROUGH, JOHN, soldier of Major Williams' company of Militia in Barbados 6 January 1679. [H2/103]

MCCUBBIN, DAVID, a Covenanter in Dalry, Ayrshire, captured after the Battle of Bothwell Bridge 22 June 1679, imprisoned in Edinburgh, banished to the Plantations, transported from Leith on the *Crown of London*, master Thomas Teddico, 27 November 1679, shipwrecked and drowned off Orkney 10 December 1679. [RBM]

MCCULLOCH, JOHN, husband of Sarah McLauchlan in Lochgair, Argyllshire, a sailor on the *Caledonia* from Leith to Darien 14 July 1698, cnf Edinburgh 21.6.1709. [SRO.CC8.8.84]

MCCULLOCH, WILLIAM, a Covenanter in Dalry, Ayrshire, captured after the Battle of Bothwell Bridge 22 June 1679, imprisoned in Edinburgh, banished to the Plantations, transported from Leith on the *Crown of London*, master Thomas Teddico, 27 November 1679, shipwrecked and drowned off Orkney 10 December 1679. [RBM]

MCCUREITH, ARCHIBALD, transported from Leith to Jamaica, August 1685. [PC.11.330]

MCCURRIE, DONALD, transported from Leith to Jamaica, August 1685. [PC.11.330]

MACDANIEL, ALEXANDER, with 13 acres and 1 slave in Christchurch, Barbados, 10 December 1679. [H#481]; referred to in John Innes's will pro.14 April 1716 Barbados. [RB6.35.551]

MCDICHMAYE, WALTER, a prisoner in Edinburgh Tolbooth, transported from Leith 27 November 1679. [ETR#162]

MCDONALD, DAVID, from Lochbank, son of David McDonald of Shangzie, emigrated to Darien 1699, "remained at Darien after the colony was abandoned" [APS.14.app.114], cnf Edinburgh 1709. [SRO.CC8.8.84]

MCDONALD, DONALD, from Buchlyvie, Stirlingshire, transported from Leith to the West Indies on the *St Michael of Scarborough*, master Edward Johnston, 12 December 1678. [PC.6.76]

MCDOUGALL, DUNCAN, a Covenanter in Argyll, transported from Leith to Jamaica, August 1685. [PC.11.136]

MCDOUNIE, JOHN, a Covenanter, transported from Leith to Jamaica, August 1685. [PC.11.136]

MCDOWELL, JOHN, clerk of Captain Woodward's company of Militia in Barbados 6 January 1679. [H2/156]

MCDOWALL, Captain PATRICK, appointed as supercargo on the *Margaret of Dundee* bound to Darien 1700. [SRO.GD406][Erskine's Journal, pp245/246]

MCEWAN, ARCHIBALD, a Covenanter in Argyll, transported from Leith to Jamaica, August 1685. [PC.11.136]

MCEWEN, ARCHIBALD, son of Gilbert McEwen and Katherine Dewar, a foremastman on the *Caledonia* cnf Edinburgh 16 October 1707. [SRO.CC8.8.83]

MCEWAN, DONALD, a prisoner in Edinburgh Tollbooth, transported from Leith to Jamaica, August 1685. [PC.11.136][ETR#373]

MCFARLAND, ISABEL, buried in St Peter's parish, Barbados, 1679. [H2/87]

MCFARLANE, JOHN, soldier of Colonel Baylie's company of Militia in Barbados 1679. [H2/131]

MCFARLANE, JOHN, son of John McFarlane at the Water of Leven, Lennox, Scotland, husband of Alice ..., pro.16 January 1690 Jamaica

MCFARLANE, WALTER, from Tulliallan, Clackmannanshire, a sailor on the *St Andrew* from Leith to Darien 14 July 1698, cnf Edinburgh 21 October 1707. [SRO.CC8.8.83][SRO.GD406, bundle 160, 2/29]

MCFERRAN, PETER, at Darien 18 December 1699. [DD#262]

MCFIE, JOHN, husband of Janet McPherson in Rothesay, Bute, a piper and musician, from the Clyde to Darien on the *Rising Sun* 18 August 1699, cnf Edinburgh 20 January 1710. [SRO.CC8.8.84]

MCGARRON, ROBERT, a Covenanter in Maybole, Ayrshire, captured after the Battle of Bothwell Bridge 22 June 1679, imprisoned in Edinburgh, banished to the Plantations, transported from Leith on the *Crown of London*, master Thomas Teddico, 27 November 1679, shipwrecked and drowned off Orkney 10 December 1679. [RBM]

MCGARRY, WILLIAM, in Jamaica 1694. [SPAWI/1699/443]

MCGEE, JOHN, a Covenanter from Kirkcudbright, captured after the Battle of Bothwell Bridge 22 June 1679, transported from Leith to the West Indies on the *Crown of London*, master Thomas Teddico, 27 November 1679, shipwrecked off Muil Head of

Deerness, Orkney, 10 December 1679, later transported to Jamaica. [CEC#212/5][SW#202][RBM]

MCGERRY, WILLIAM, poor, with 1 acre in St James, Barbados, 20.10 December 1679. [H#504]

MACGHIE, Lieutenant ALEXANDER, sent from Darien as an emissary to the Spanish in Carthagena 11 March 1699. [DD#195]

MCGIBBON, ARCHIBALD, a Covenanter transported from Leith to Jamaica, August 1685. [PC.11.329]

MCGIBBON, HECTOR, a Covenanter transported from Leith to Jamaica, August 1685. [PC.11.329]

MCGIBBON, JOHN, a Covenanter in Glenowkeill, Argyll, transported from Leith to Jamaica, August 1685. [PC.11.329]

MCGILL, ROBERT, a Covenanter from Galashiels, Selkirkshire, captured after the Battle of Bothwell Bridge 22 June 1679, a prisoner in Edinburgh Tolbooth, transported from Leith to the West Indies on the *Crown of London*, master Thomas Teddico, 27 November 1679, shipwrecked off Muil Head of Deerness, Orkney, 10 December 1679, later transported to Jamaica. [CEC#212/5][ETR #162][SW#20][RBM]

MCGILLICH, JOHN, a Covenanter in Argyll, transported from Leith to Jamaica, August 1685. [PC.11.329]

MCGOWAN, JOHN, a Covenanter in Argyll, transported from Leith to Jamaica, August 1685. [PC.11.136]

MCGREGOR, CALLUM, a thief imprisoned in Edinburgh Tolbooth, transported from Leith to Barbados on the *Blossom* 2 August 1680. [ETR#170]

MCGREGOR, DANIEL, from Calton, a sailor on the *Rising Sun* from the Clyde to Darien 18 August 1699, cnf Edinburgh 17 October 1707. [SRO.CC8.8.83]

MCGREGOR, JOHN, soldier of Captain Bowcher's company of Militia in Barbados 6 January 1679. [H2/112]

MCHARIE, JOHN, a Covenanter in Maybole, Ayrshire, captured after the Battle of Bothwell Bridge 22 June 1679, imprisoned in Edinburgh, banished to the Plantations, transported from Leith on the *Crown of London*, master Thomas Teddico, 27 November 1679, shipwrecked and drowned off Orkney 10 December 1679. [RBM]

MCICHAN, JOHN, a Covenanter in Baranazare, Lorne, Argyll, transported from Leith to Jamaica, August 1685. [PC.11.329]

MCILBRYDE, DUNCAN, a Covenanter in Argyll, transported from Leith to Jamaica, August 1685. [PC.11.136]

MCILMOON, DONALD, a Covenanter in Argyll, transported from Leith to Jamaica, August 1685. [PC.11.329]

MCILROY, GILBERT, a Covenanter imprisoned in Edinburgh Tolbooth, transported from Leith to Jamaica, August 1685. [ETR #369]

MCILROY, WILLIAM, transported from Leith to Jamaica, July 1685. [PC.11.329]

MCILSHALLUM, JOHN, transported from Leith to Jamaica, August 1685. [PC.11.330]

MCILVAIN, ARCHIBALD, a Covenanter in Glendaruel, Argyll, transported from Leith to Jamaica, August 1685. [PC.11.329]

MCILVERRAN, DONALD, a Covenanter in Argyll, transported from Leith to Jamaica, August 1685. [PC.11.136]

MCILVORY, DUNCAN, a Covenanter in Argyll, transported from Leith to Jamaica, August 1685. [PC.11.136]

MCILVORY, JOHN, a Covenanter in Cragintyrie, Argyll, transported August 1685. [PC.11.126]

MCINLAY, NEIL, transported from Leith to Jamaica, August 1685. [PC.11.136]

MCINNES, Mr ..., soldier of Captain Allemby's company of Militia in Barbados 6 January 1679. [H2/155]

MCINTOSH, ALESTAIR, buried in St Peter's parish, Barbados, 1679.

MCINTOSH, HENRY, purchased a plantation in Surinam November 1674, petition 8 June 1676, a planter in Surinam, pro.21 January 1679 Barbados [CalSPCol. 1675#683]

MACINTOSH, PETER, a sailor who died on the voyage to Darien 23 October 1698. [WP#88]

MACINTOSH, THOMAS, from Kellochie, Inverness-shire, formerly a Lieutenant of the Earl of Tullibardine's Regiment, died at Darien 1699, cnf Edinburgh 27 April 1709. [SRO.CC8.8.83]

MCINTYRE, ARCHIBALD, a Covenanter in Glendaruel, Argyll, transported from Leith to Jamaica, August 1685. [PC.11.329]

MCIVAR, DONALD, a Covenanter in Argyll, transported from Leith to Jamaica, August 1685. [PC.11.136]

MCIVAR, DUNCAN, a Covenanter in Argyll, transported from Leith to Jamaica, August 1685. [PC.11.136]

MCIVAR, JOHN, a Covenanter in Tulloch, Argyll, transported from Leith to Jamaica, August 1685. [PC.11.136]

MCIVAR, MALCOLM, a Covenanter in Glasary, Argyll, transported from Leith to Jamaica, August 1685. [PC.11.136]

MCKAIRNE, NEIL, a Covenanter in Argyll, transported from Leith to Jamaica, August 1685. [PC.11.136]

MACKAY, DANIEL, appointed as a Member of the Council of Caledonia, Darien, emigrated from Glasgow on the *Speedy Return*, Captain John Baillie, via the Leeward Islands to Caledonia 24 October 1699, [SRO.GD406]; wrote to the Directors of the Darien Company from New Edinburgh, Caledonia, 28 December 1698, [SRO.GD406.1.6489]; wrote to the Earl of Leven from New Edinburgh 28 December 1698, [SRO.GD26.13.101]; admitted to the Scots Charitable Society of Boston, Massachusetts, 1699. [NEHGS]

MACKAY, DONALD, from Aberach, Strathnavaar, died on the voyage to Darien 1699. [BM#174]

MACKAY, DONALD, second son of Murdo Mackay and Jane Mackay in Strathnavaar, emigrated to Darien, later settled in St Kitts 21 January 1700. [BM#249]; Donald Mackay of Anylone subscribed to a document in St Kitts 21 January 1700. [SRO.GD84.sec.1/22/9B]

MACKAY, DONALD, son of Captain William Mackay of Borlay, emigrated from Leith to Darien 17 July 1698, arrived in Darien 28 September 1698, returned to Britain, arrived in London August 1699, in Edinburgh by 28 August 1699, from the Clyde to Darien on the *Rising Sun* 21 September 1699, via Montserrat 9 November 1699, St Kitts, Port Royal, Jamaica, 13 February 1700, drowned in the Caribbean. [BM#174]

MACKAY, Captain HUGH, of Borlay, in St Kitts 21 January 1700. [SRO.GD21.1.1700] [SRO.GD84.Sec.1/22/9B]

MCKAY, MARTIN, transported from Leith to Jamaica, August 1685. [PC.11.136]

MCKEATH, MUNGO, in St Thomas, Jamaica, pro.20 May 1669 Jamaica

MCKECHNIE, WALTER, a Covenanter in Glasgow, captured after the Battle of Bothwell Bridge 22 June 1679, imprisoned in Edinburgh, banished to the Plantations, transported from Leith on the *Crown of London*, master Thomas Teddico, 27 November 1679, shipwrecked and drowned off Orkney 10 December 1679. [RBM]

MCKEICHAN, NEIL, a Covenanter in Baranazare, Lorne, Argyll, transported from Leith to Jamaica, August 1685. [PC.11.136]

MCKELLO, DONALD, a Covenanter in Argyll, transported from Leith to Jamaica, August 1685. [PC.11.136]

MCKELLO, DUGALD, a Covenanter in Argyll, transported from Leith to Jamaica, August 1685. [PC.11.136]

MCKELLO, JOHN, a Covenanter in Argyll, transported from Leith to Jamaica, August 1685. [PC.11.136]

MACKENLOCH, ALESTAR, buried in St Peter's parish, Barbados, 1679. [H2/89]

MCKENNY, ALLISTER, soldier of Captain Woodward's company of Militia in Barbados 6 January 1679. [H2/156]; father of Thomas baptised in St Thomas' parish, Barbados, 13 February 1678. [H2/64]

MACKENNY, DANIEL, with 3 slaves and 3 acres in St Lucy's parish, Barbados, 1678. [H2/43]

MACKENNY, GILBERT, in St Lucy's parish, Barbados, 1678. [H2/43]

MACKENNY, JAMES, a carpenter, husband of Janet Christie in Carsedyke, Renfrewshire, from the Clyde to Darien on the *Speedy Return* 1699, died April 1700, cnf Edinburgh 1707. [SRO.CC8.8.83]

MACKENNY, JOHN, and his wife Susanna, parents of Cornelius, baptised in St Michael's, Barbados, 13 April 1679. [H#424]

MACKENNY, THOMAS, jr., buried in St Joseph's parish, Barbados, 28 January 1678. [H2/31]

MCKENNY, THOMAS, son of Alastair McKenny, baptised in St Thomas's, Barbados, 13 February 1678. [H2/64]

MACKENZIE, ALEXANDER, a soldier, emigrated to Darien 1699, died in the West Indies 1699, cnf Edinburgh 1707. [SRO.CC8.8.83]

MACKENZIE, GEORGE, son of John Mackenzie in Edinburgh, a merchant in Bridgetown, Barbados, before 1698, will subscribed in Barbados 1 December 1710, pro.28 August 1711 Barbados. [RB6/5.546]; [SRO.S/H.25.10.1698]

MACKENZIE, GEORGE, a merchant in Edinburgh, son of George McKenzie and Bethia Law, settled in Barbados before 1704, cnf Edinburgh 1733. [SRO.CC8.8.95][SRO.S/H.20.4.1704]

MACKENZIE, HECTOR, a surgeon on the *Unicorn*, from Leith to Darien 14 July 1698, died at Cape Antonio, America, 12 August 1699, cnf Edinburgh 1707. [SRO.CC8.8.83]

MACKENZIE, JOHN, a gunner on the *Caledonia* from Leith to Darien 14 July 1698, cnf Edinburgh 1707. [SRO.CC8.8.83]

MCKENZIE, THOMAS, a Covenanter from Liberton, Midlothian, captured after the Battle of Bothwell Bridge 22 June 1679, transported from Leith to the West Indies on the *Crown of London*, master Thomas Teddico, 27 November 1679, shipwrecked off Muil Head of Deerness, Orkney, 10 December 1679, later transported to Jamaica. [CEC#212/5][SW#202][RBM]

MACKERNESS, JACOB, with his wife, 2 servants and 4 slaves, in St Michael's, Barbados, 1680, a soldier of Colonel Coddrington's company of Militia in Barbados 6 January 1679. [H#447][H2/174]

MACKERNESS, WILLIAM, with 1 child, 3 servants and 2 slaves, in St Michael's, Barbados, 1680. [H#447]

MACKERVAIL, DAVID, a Covenanter in Glencairn, Dumfries-shire, captured after the Battle of Bothwell Bridge 22 June 1679, imprisoned in Edinburgh, banished to the Plantations, transported from Leith on the *Crown of London*, master Thomas Teddico, 27 November 1679, shipwrecked and drowned off Orkney 10 December 1679. [RBM]

MACKIE, GEORGE, son of James Mackie and Kathrine Lumsden in Fife, a sailor on the *Caledonia* from Leith to Darien 14 July 1698, cnf Edinburgh 1707. [SRO.CC8.8.83]

MCKIE, JAMES, a Covenanter in Denny, Stirlingshire, captured after the Battle of Bothwell Bridge 22 June 1679, imprisoned in Edinburgh, banished to the Plantations, transported from Leith on the *Crown of London*, master Thomas Teddico, 27 November 1679, shipwrecked and drowned off Orkney 10 December 1679. [RBM]

MACKIE, JAMES, a sailor on the *St Andrew* from Leith to Darien 14 July 1698, cnf Edinburgh 10 October 1707. [SRO.CC8.8.83]

MCKILLON, DONALD, a Covenanter in Glendaruel, Argyll, transported from Leith to Jamaica, August 1685. [PC.11.136]

MCKINLAY, NEIL, a Covenanter in Argyll, transported from Leith to Jamaica, August 1685. [PC.11.136]

MCKINNON, ALEXANDER, a pipemaker in Glasgow, guilty of slander, imprisoned in Edinburgh Tolbooth, transported from Leith to Barbados on William Johnston's ship the *Blossom* 10 August 1680. [ETR#171][PC.6.456]

MCKINNON, Dr DANIEL, born 1658, settled in Antigua, married Elizabeth Thomas, father of Samuel, [St John's Town Library MS, Antigua]; admitted as a burgess of Glasgow 1717, [GBR]; died 1720, pro.20 March 1720 Antigua

MCKINNON, JOHN, a Covenanter in Duppen of Kintyre, Argyll, transported from Leith to Jamaica, August 1685. [PC.11.136]

MCKIRRECH, ARCHIBALD, a Covenanter in Argyll, transported from Leith to Jamaica, August 1685. [PC.11.136]

MCLACHLAN, ARCHIBALD, a Covenanter and a farmer in Craigintervie, Argyll, transported August 1685. [PC.11.126]

MCLACHLAN, DONALD, a Covenanter in Argyll, transported from Leith to Jamaica, August 1685. [PC.11.136]

MCLACHLAN, JOHN DOW, a Covenanter in Achahouse, Argyll, transported from Leith to Jamaica, August 1685. [PC.11.329]

MACLAHEN, OWEN, a time-expired indentured servant, emigrated from Barbados to Bristol on the *Society*, master Edmond Ditty, 30 May 1679. [H#390]

MCLANE, Mrs MARY, in Jamaica 1694. [SPAWI/1699/443]

MCLAREN, LAURENCE, a prisoner in Perth Tolbooth, banished to the American Plantations 5 January 1699, bail bond by William Murray of Abercairnie, [SRO.B59.26.11.4]; a prisoner in Stirling awaiting shipment ot America 8 April 1699. [SRO.B66.23.1]

MCLEAN, ANDREW, a Covenanter in Argyll, transported from Leith to Jamaica, August 1685. [PC.11.330]

MCLEAN, ANGUS, a prisoner in Edinburgh Tolbooth, transported by George Hutcheson a merchant in Edinburgh from Leith to Barbados 7 December 1665. [ETR#104]

MCLEAN, DANIEL, from Inverness, a steward's mate on the *Rising Sun*, died in Carolina, cnf Edinburgh 3 October 1707. [SRO.CC8.8.83]

MCLEAN, HUGH, a Covenanter in Argyll, transported from Leith to Jamaica, August 1685. [PC.11.330]

MCLEAN, JOHN, a Covenanter in Portindryan, Argyll, transported from Leith to Jamaica, August 1685. [PC.11.330]

MCLEAN, JOHN, wounded at Darien 6 February 1699. [DP#86]

MCLEAN, LACHLAN, an officer at Darien who sailed from Jamaica to Bristol, in London, January 1700. [DD#297]

MCLEAN, THOMAS, son of Thomas McLean, baptised in St Joseph's parish, Barbados, 9 July 1679. [H2/30]

MCLEAN, ..., Captain, Governor of Crab Island, the Leewards, 4 October 1698. [DSP#78]

MCLELLAN, JOHN, a Covenanter in Colmonell, Ayrshire, captured after the Battle of Bothwell Bridge 22 June 1679, imprisoned in

Edinburgh, banished to the Plantations, transported from Leith on the *Crown of London*, master Thomas Teddico, 27 November 1679, shipwrecked and drowned off Orkney 10 December 1679. [RBM]

MACLELLAN, MATHEW, son of John MacLellan of Orcougule, Galloway, emigrated as a 4 year indentured servant via Bristol to Barbados 13 February 1655. [BRO]

MACLELLAN, WILLIAM, a boy who was drowned at Darien 11 December 1698. [WP#89][NLS.RY2b8/19]

MCLEOD, DANIEL, in St Lucy's parish, Barbados, 1678, soldier of Captain Masson's company of Militia in Barbados 1679. [H2/43/193]

MCLEOD, MALCOLM, pro.4 February 1681 Jamaica

MCLEOD, MATTHEW, buried in St George's, Barbados, 9 February 1679. [H#467]

MCLEOD, WILLIAM, at Darien 18 December 1699. [DD#262]

MCLINE, ALEXANDER, a Covenanter in Argyll, transported from Leith to Jamaica, August 1685. [PC.11.136]

MACLOUGHLIN, EDWARD, buried in St Michael's, Barbados, 11 January 1679. [H#431]

MCLURG, THOMAS, a Covenanter in Colmonell, Ayrshire, captured after the Battle of Bothwell Bridge 22 June 1679, imprisoned in Edinburgh, banished to the Plantations, transported from Leith on the *Crown of London*, master Thomas Teddico, 27 November 1679, shipwrecked and drowned off Orkney 10 December 1679. [RBM]

MCMICHAEL, DUNCAN, a Covenanter in Islay, Argyll, transported from Leith to Jamaica, August 1685. [PC.11.136]

MCMICHAEL, ROGER, a Covenanter in Dalry, Galloway, transported from Leith to Jamaica, August 1685. [PC.11.316]

MCMILLAN, ALEXANDER, a Covenanter in Galloway, imprisoned in Edinburgh Tolbooth, transported from Leith to Barbados December 1685. (probably on the *John and Nicholas*, master Edward Barnes). [ETR#389][PC.11.386]

MCMILLAN, DUNCAN, a Covenanter in Carradale, Kintyre, Argyll, transported from Leith to Jamaica, August 1685. [PC.11.329]

MCMURRIE, JAMES, a Covenanter in Straiton, Ayrshire, captured after the Battle of Bothwell Bridge 22 June 1679, imprisoned in Edinburgh, banished to the Plantations, transported from Leith on the *Crown of London*, master Thomas Teddico, 27 November

1679, shipwrecked and drowned off Orkney 10 December 1679. [RBM]

MCNAB, PATRICK, a thief imprisoned in Crieff and Perth Tolbooths, banished to the American Plantations, transported by William Ritchie, a skipper in Bo'ness, 12 September 1699. [SRO.B59. 26.11.6/8]

MCNAIR, ROBERT, a cooper in Newark of Glasgow, husband of Katherine Purdy, emigrated from Leith to Darien on the *Caledonia* 14 July 1698, cnf Edinburgh 11 October 1707. [SRO.CC8. 8.83]

MCNEIL, ARCHIBALD, a Covenanter in Argyll, transported from Leith to Jamaica, August 1685. [PC.11.136]

MCNEIL, HECTOR, a Covenanter in Argyll, transported from Leith to Jamaica, August 1685. [PC.11.136]

MCNEIL, JOHN, a Covenanter in Argyll, transported from Leith to Jamaica, August 1685. [PC.11.136]

MCNURE, JOHN, a Covenanter in St Ninian's, Stirlingshire, captured after the Battle of Bothwell Bridge 22 June 1679, imprisoned in Edinburgh, banished to the Plantations, transported from Leith on the *Crown of London*, master Thomas Teddico, 27 November 1679, shipwrecked and drowned off Orkney 10 December 1679. [RBM]

MCOLLIN, ALEXANDER, with 2 slaves and 4 acres in St John's parish, Barbados, 1679. [H2/70]

MCOLLIN, DANIEL with 2 slaves and 4 acres in St John's parish, Barbados, 1679. [H2/70]

MCOLLIN, JEAN, buried in St John's parish, Barbados, 9 September 1679. [H2/75]

MCPHERSON ALEXANDER, in St Philips parish, Barbados, with 2 acres, 1680. [H2/12]

MCQUEEN, ANGUS, returned to Scotland from Barbados on the *Love of London* 2 July 1658. [SRO.NRAS.0361/box 24]

MACQUEEN, ARCHIBALD, soldier in Captain Scott's company of Militia in Barbados, 6 January 1679. [H2/191]

MCQUEEN, DUNCAN, a Covenanter in Argyll, transported from Leith to Jamaica, August 1685. [PC.11.136]

MCQUEEN, HUGH, a Covenanter in Argyll, transported from Leith to Jamaica, August 1685. [PC.11.136]

MCQUEEN, JANET, a Covenanter, transported from Leith to Jamaica August, 1685. [PC.11.136]

MACQUHAN, ANDREW, a Covenanter from Kirkcudbright, captured after the Battle of Bothwell Bridge 22 June 1679, transported from Leith to the West Indies on the *Crown of London*, master Thomas Teddico, 27 November 1679, shipwrecked off Muil Head of Deerness, orkney, 10 December 1679, later shipped to Jamaica. [SW#202][RBM]

MCQUHAN, THOMAS, a Covenanter, transported from Leith to the West Indies on the *Crown of London*, master Thomas Teddico, 27 November 1679, shipwrecked off Orkney 10 December 1679, later transported to Jamaica. [CEC#212/5]

MACQUIN, ARCHIBALD, and his wife Frances, parents of Nicholas baptised in St Michael's, Barbados, 20 January 1679. [H#423]

MCREADY, JOHN, a Covenanter in Ratho, Midlothian, transported from Leith to the West Indies, August 1678. [PC.5.488]

MACRERY, ALEXANDER, from Lieutenant Colonel Jelly's, buried in St Michael's, Barbados, 25 September 1679. [H#438]

MCTAGGART, JOHN, a Covenanter in Penninghame, Wigtownshire, captured after the Battle of Bothwell Bridge 22 June 1679, imprisoned in Edinburgh, banished to the Plantations, transported from Leith on the *Crown of London*, master Thomas Teddico, 27 November 1679, shipwrecked and drowned off Orkney 10 December 1679. [RBM]

MACTAILLIOR, DONALD, a Covenanter in Fordie, Perthshire, transported from Leith to Jamaica, August 1685. [PC.11.329]

MCTIRE, JOHN, a Covenanter in Kirkmichael, Ayrshire, captured after the Battle of Bothwell Bridge 22 June 1679, imprisoned in Edinburgh, banished to the Plantations, transported from Leith on the *Crown of London*, master Thomas Teddico, 27 November 1679, shipwrecked and drowned off Orkney 10 December 1679. [RBM]

MCVERRAN, DONALD, transported from Leith to Jamaica, August 1685. [PC.11.136]

MCVIG, DUNCAN, a Covenanter in Argyll, transported from Leith to Jamaica, August 1685. [PC.11.329]

MCWHIDDIE, ALLAN, a Covenanter in Argyll, transported from Leith to Jamaica, August 1685. [PC.11.136]

MCWHIRTIR, JOHN, a Covenanter in Maybole, Ayrshire, captured after the Battle of Bothwell Bridge 22 June 1679, imprisoned in Edinburgh, banished to the Plantations, transported from Leith on the *Crown of London*, master Thomas Teddico, 27 November

1679, shipwrecked and drowned off Orkney 10 December 1679. [RBM]

MCWILLIE, JOHN, a Covenanter imprisoned in Edinburgh Tolbooth, transported from Leith to Jamaica, August 1685. [ETR#369][PC. 11.329]

MACK, JAMES, a Covenanter imprisoned in Edinburgh Tolbooth, transported from Leith to Barbados on the *John and Nicholas*, master Edward Barnes, December 1685. [PC.11.386][ETR#389]

MAIN, ANDREW, and his wife Mary, parents of Mary baptised in St Michael's, Barbados, 2 September 1679. [H#425]

MAIN, JAMES, an interpreter at Darien 1700. [DD#315]

MAITLAND, WILLIAM, son of Patrick Maitland in Linlithgow, West Lothian, a sailor on the *Caledonia* from Leith to Darien 14 July 1698, cnf Edinburgh 1707. [SRO.CC8.8.83]

MAITLAND, WILLIAM, son of John Maitland in Craigmill, Logie, Stirlingshire, a sailor on the *Union* from Leith to Darien 14 July 1698, cnf Edinburgh 1707. [SRO.CC8.8.83]

MALBON, JOHN, a merchant who died on the voyage to Darien 28 October 1698. [WP#88]

MALCOLM, JOHN, a merchant on the *James of Ayr*, master James Chalmers, arrived in Ayr from the West Indies 19 September 1673. [SRO.E72.3.4]

MALCOLM, JOHN, a Covenanter from Dalry, Galloway, captured after the Battle of Bothwell Bridge 22 June 1679, transported from Leith to the West Indies on the *Crown of London*, master Thomas Teddico, 27 November 1679, shipwrecked off Muil Head of Deerness, Orkney,10 December 1679, later transported to Jamaica. [RBM] [CEC#212/5][SW#203]

MALLOCH, JOHN, a skipper from Kirkcaldy, Fife, master of the *Endeavour* from Leith to Darien July 1698; later captain of the *Dolphin*, imprisoned in Carthagena and in Seville accused of piracy, found guilty of piracy and sentenced to death May 1700, released 20 September 1700; subscribed to a deed of factory and testament 1707; later resident in St Botolph without Aldgate, London; cnf. Edinburgh 1709. [SRO.CC8.8.84] [APS.14.app114] [SRO.GD406, bundle 161, 25/1; bundle 163, c23/4/5; 1#4541]

MANSON, ALEXANDER, a prisoner in Edinburgh Tolbooth, transported from Leith to Jamaica, August 1685. [ETR#369][PC. 11.329]

MANUEL, JAMES, a maltman in Glasgow, husband of ... Russell, a Covenanter, transported to the West Indies June 1678. [PC.5.474]

MARJORYBANKS, JOSEPH, a merchant in Edinburgh, son of Joseph Marjorybanks of Lauchrie and Margaret Brown, a sailor on the *St Andrew* from Leith to Darien 14 July 1698, cnf Edinburgh 26 September 1707, witness to the testament of George Calderwood, quartermaster, 16 July 1698. [SRO.CC8.8.83]

MARSHALL, CUTHBERT, with 8 acres in St Phillip's parish, Barbados, 1680; a soldier of Captain Jack's company of Militia in Barbados 6 March 1680. [H2/11, 123]

MARSHALL, JOHN, a Covenanter and a smith in Glasgow, who was banished to the West Indies in June 1678. [PC.5.474]

MARSHALL, Mr JOHN, cavalryman in Captain William Robinson's troop of Militia in Barbados 5 January 1679. [H2/203]

MARSHALL, MARY, daughter of William Marshall, baptised in St Lucy's, Barbados, 6 February 1679. [H2/52]

MARSHALL, Mr ROBERT, with 2 freemen, 11 slaves and 70 acres in St Joseph's parish, Barbados, 1680. [H2/28]

MARSHALL, ROBERT, with 60 acres and 1 servant in Barbados, a soldier of Major Waterman's company of Militia in Barbados 6 January 1679. [H2/160]

MARSHALL, WILLIAM, with 5 acres in St Lucy's parish, Barbados, 30 December 1679; servant of Mr Noake and a soldier of Captain Jack's company in Barbados 1679. [H2/42, 123]

MARSHALL, WILLIAM, a smith from Edinburgh, transported from Leith to Jamaica, August 1685, landed at Port Royal, Jamaica, November 1685. [PC.11.329][LJ#157]

MARTIN, DANIEL, a sailor who died on the voyage to Darien 23 July 1698. [WP#87]

MARTIN, HENRY, master of the *Mayflower of Liverpool*, arrived in Port Glasgow from Barbados with sugar and tobacco October 1683. [SRO.E72.19.8]

MARTIN, JAMES, from Linlithgow, West Lothian, a sailor on the *Hope* from the Clyde to Darien 18 August 1699, cnf Edinburgh 1707. [SRO.CC8.8.83] [SRO.GD406, bundle 162, p39/20]

MARTIN, JOHN, a Covenanter from Borgue, Kirkcudbrightshire, captured after the Battle of Bothwell Bridge 22 June 1679, transported from Leith to the West Indies on the *Crown of London*, master Thomas Teddico, 27 November 1679, shipwrecked off Muil Head of Deerness, Orkney, 10 December 1679, later transported to Jamaica. [CEC#212/5][SW#203][RBM]

MARTIN, JOHN, master of the *Mayflower of Liverpool*, from Port Glasgow to the West Indies with linen, shoes, horseshoes and pipes, January 1682. [SRO.E72.19.6]

MARTIN, JOHN, from Dumfries, emigrated via London to Jamaica March 1684. [CLRO/AIA]

MASON, JOHN, from Burntisland, Fife, a quartier on the *Unicorn* from Leith to Darien 14 July 1698, cnf Edinburgh 17 October 1707. [SRO.CC8.8.83]

MASTERTON, ALEXANDER, son of Alexander Masterton in Linlithgow, West Lothian, bosun on the *Caledonia* from Leith to Darien 14 July 1698, cnf Edinburgh 15 November 1707. [SRO.CC8.8.83]

MASTERTON, WILLIAM, a sailor on the *Hope* to Darien. [SRO. GD406, bundle 162, c39/11]

MATHER, GEORGE, emigrated from Barbados to London on the *Hannah and Elizabeth*, master Richard Pix, 17 May 1679. [H#389]

MATHER, JOHN, a Covenanter in Jedburgh, Roxburghshire, captured after the Battle of Bothwell Bridge 22 June 1679, imprisoned in Edinburgh, banished to the Plantations, transported from Leith on the *Crown of London*, master Thomas Teddico, 27 November 1679, shipwrecked and drowned off Orkney 10 December 1679. [RBM]

MATHIE, THOMAS, a Covenanter in Monklands, Lanarkshire, captured after the Battle of Bothwell Bridge 22 June 1679, imprisoned in Edinburgh, banished to the Plantations, transported from Leith on the *Crown of London*, master Thomas Teddico, 27 November 1679, shipwrecked and drowned off Orkney 10 December 1679. [RBM]

MATHIE, THOMAS, a sailor, from the Clyde to Darien on the *Rising Sun* 18 August 1699, cnf Edinburgh 1707. [SRO.CC8.8.83]

MATHISON, MURDOCH, a thief imprisoned in Crieff and Perth Tolbooths, banished to the American Plantations, transported by William Ritchie, a skipper in Bo'ness, 12 September 1699. [SRO. B59.26.11.6/8]

MAULE, JAMES, a minister, died in Antigua before 1697. [SRO.S/H. 8.5.1697]

MAXWELL, HUMPHREY, soldier of Captain Woodward's company of Militia in Barbados 6 January 1679. [H2/156]

MAXWELL, JAMES, a Covenanter in Cathcart, Glasgow, transported from Leith to the West Indies on the *St Michael of Scarborough*, master Edward Johnston, 12 December 1678. [PC.6.76]

MAXWELL, JAMES, jr., a Covenanter in Cathcart, Glasgow, transported from Leith to the West Indies on the *St Michael of Scarborough* master Edward Johnston, 12 December 1678. [PC.6.76]

MAXWELL, JAMES, sergeant of Captain Burton's company of Militia in Barbados 6 January 1679. [H2/185]

MAXWELL, JOHN, from Glasgow, educated at Edinburgh University 1658, emigrated 1662, a physician and a cleric in Port Royal, husband of Mary ..., father of John, died 1673 Jamaica, pro.17 November 1673 Jamaica (LOS/fo74)[SRA.TPM.113.562]

MAXWELL, JOHN, a merchant on the *James of Ayr*, master James Chalmers, arrived in Ayr 19 September 1673 from Montserrat and the West Indies. [SRO.E72.3.4]

MAXWELL, ROBERT, a Covenanter in Cathcart, Glasgow, transported from Leith to the West Indies on the *St Michael of Scarborough* master Edward Johnston, 12 December 1678. [PC.6.76]

MAXWELL, ROBERT, with 1 servant, 11 slaves and 25 acres in St Peter's parish, Barbados, 1679. [H2/78]

MAXWELL, THOMAS, with 24 acres, 2 servants, and 30 slaves in Christchurch, Barbados, 22 December 1679. [H#481]

MAXWELL, Lieutenant THOMAS, commander of a troop of Horse Militia in Barbados 6 January 1679. [H2/211]

MAXWELL, THOMAS, surgeon of Captain Ely's company of Militia in Barbados 6 January 1679. [H2/178]

MAXWELL, THOMAS, speaker of the Assembly of Barbados, 1 August 1699. [SPAWI.1699.53/691]

MAXWELL, WILLIAM, soldier of Major Lyte's company of Militia in Barbados 6 January 1679. [H2/175]

MAXWELL, WILLIAM, with his wife, 1 child, and 1 slave, in St Michael's, Barbados, 1680. [H#448]

MAXWELL, ..., Lieutenant, in Barbados 1680. [SPAWI.1680/1336]

MEIBLO, JAMES, father of Elspeth in Dysart, Fife, a sailor on the *St Andrew* from Leith to Darien 14 July 1698, cnf Edinburgh 8 October 1707. [SRO.CC8.8.83]

MEIK, WILLIAM, from Bo'ness, West Lothian, a sailor on the *Rising Sun* from the Clyde to Darien 18 August 1699, cnf Edinburgh 3 October 1707. [SRO.CC8.8.83]

MEIKLE, ROBERT, a Covenanter and a minister, transported from Leith to the West Indies on the *St Michael of Scarborough*, master Edward Johnston, 12 December 1678. [PC.6.76]

MEIKLEJOHN, THOMAS, from Queensferry, West Lothian, a cook on the *Duke of Hamilton* from the Clyde to Darien 18 August 1699, died at Darien 1700, cnf Edinburgh 7 May 1712. [SRO.CC8.8.85]

MEIN, PATRICK, appointed as Surveyor General of Barbados 28 May 1692, [ActsPCCol]; appointed a member of the Council of Barbados 15 April 1697, [ActsPCCol]; 17 October 1699. [SPAWI/1699/869, 1012]; a merchant 1699, [SPAWI/1699/559]

MEIN, ..., Miss, in Barbados 1676. [PC#4.674]

MELDRUM, JONATHAN, seaman of the sloop *Friendship*, captured at Crab Island by the Spanish 1699, later escaped. [SPAWI/1699/149]

MELVILLE, JOHN, from Kinghorn, Fife, a sailor on the *Rising Sun* from Greenock to Darien 18 August 1699, cnf Edinburgh 21 October 1707. [SRO.CC8.8.83]

MENZIES, GEORGE, a planter who died on the voyage to Darien 30 August 1698. [WP#87]

MENZIES, JOHN, from Edinburgh, schoolmaster of Colonel Samuel Newton's plantation in Barbados, letter from, dated 20 March 1676. [PC#4.671]

MERCER, ROBERT, born 1656, a baker from Loudoun, Ayrshire, emigrated via London to Jamaica on the *Richard and Sarah* 1683. [CLRO/AIA]

MERCHISTON, ROBERT, from Fife, second mate to a surgeon on the *St Andrew* from Leith to Darien 14 July 1698, cnf Edinburgh 1707. [SRO.CC8.8.83]

MERSTOUN, JOHN, husband of Margaret Colville, formerly in Lord Lindsay's regiment then Lieutenant of the Scots Indian and African Company, wounded at Darien 6 February 1699, cnf Edinburgh 11 September 1707. [SRO.CC8.8.83][DP#86]

MIGGLESTON, THOMAS, husband of Janet Ferguson in Inverkeithing, Fife, a sailor on the *Rising Sun* from the Clyde to Darien 18 August 1699, cnf Edinburgh 1707. [SRO.CC8.8.83]

MILL, JOHN, a surgeon from Aberlady, East Lothian, died at Darien 1699, cnf Edinburgh 1707. [SRO.CC8.8.83]

MILL, WILLIAM, from Haddington, East Lothian, a midshipman on the *Unicorn* from Leith to Darien 14 July 1698, cnf Edinburgh 22 September 1707. [SRO.CC8.8.83]

MILLER, DAVID, a planter who died at Darien 6 December 1698. [WP#89][NLS.RY2b8/19]

MILLER, DAVID, from Kirkcaldy, Fife, a sailor on the *Dolphin* from Leith to Darien 14 July 1698, cnf Edinburgh 1707. [SRO.CC8. 8.83] [SRO.GD406, bundle 163, c23/5/8]

MILLER, JAMES, a Covenanter from Kirkcaldy, transported from Leith to the West Indies on the *St Michael of Scarborough*, master Edward Johnston, 12 December 1678. [PC.6.76]

MILLER, Lieutenant JAMES, master of the *Hope* subscribed to a deed of factory 1699. [SRO.GD406, bundle 162, p39/1]; from Darien via Jamaica bound for Scotland, shipwrecked off Cuba August 1700. [DD#348]

MILLER, JOHN, a Covenanter in Glasford, Lanarkshire, captured after the Battle of Bothwell Bridge 22 June 1679, imprisoned in Edinburgh, banished to the Plantations, transported from Leith on the *Crown of London*, master Thomas Teddico, 27 November 1679, shipwrecked and drowned off Orkney 10 December 1679. [RBM]

MILLER, JOHN, son of John Miller in Auchtertool, Fife, a sailor on the *Dolphin* from Leith to Darien 14 July 1698, cnf Edinburgh 16 October 1707. [SRO.CC8.8.83][SRO.GD406, bundle 163, c23/10]

MILLER, JOHN, son of Isobel Gibson, a sailor on the *Hope*, subscribed to a deed at Greenock 21 August 1699 before sailing to Darien. [SRO.GD406, bundle 162, p39/18]

MILLER, MALCOM, a sailor on the *Caledonia* from Leith to Darien 14 July 1698, subscribed to a testament on the ship *Caledonia* when "sailing for Pennsylvania 28 July 1699", cnf Edinburgh 1 October 1707. [SRO.CC8.8.83]

MILLER, ROBERT, a thief, transported from Ayr to Barbados 1653. [SRO.JC27.10.3]

MILLER, ROBERT, a prisoner in Edinburgh Tolbooth, transported from Leith 27 November 1679. [ETR#162]

MILLER, THOMAS, a soldier of Colonel James Alexander's company of HM Regiment of Guards, guilty of theft and plunder, transported to Barbados 27 February 1668. [PC.2.415]

MILLER, THOMAS, a Covenanter from Ceres, Fife, captured after the Battle of Bothwell Bridge 22 June 1679, imprisoned in Edinburgh Tolbooth, transported from Leith to the West Indies on the *Crown of London*, master Thomas Teddico, 27 November 1679, shipwrecked off Muil Head of Deerness, Orkney, 10 December 1679, later transported to Jamaica. [CEC#212/5][ETR#162][CW#200] [RBM]

MILLER, THOMAS, a Covenanter in Gargunnock, Stirlingshire, captured after the Battle of Bothwell Bridge 22 June 1679, imprisoned in Edinburgh, banished to the Plantations, transported from Leith on the *Crown of London*, master Thomas Teddico, 27 November 1679, shipwrecked and drowned off Orkney 10 December 1679. [RBM]

MILLER, THOMAS, son of baillie Thomas Miller of Stirling, a surgeon's mate on the *Hope* subscribed to a deed of factory in Stirling 15 August 1699 before sailing to Darien. [SRO.GD406, bundle 162, p40/4]

MILLER, WILLIAM, a Covenanter in Glasgow, captured after the Battle of Bothwell Bridge 22 June 1679, imprisoned in Edinburgh, banished to the Plantations, transported from Leith on the *Crown of London*, master Thomas Teddico, 27 November 1679, shipwrecked and drowned off Orkney 10 December 1679. [RBM]

MILLER, WILLIAM, a Covenanter in Monklands, Lanarkshire, captured after the Battle of Bothwell Bridge 22 June 1679, imprisoned in Edinburgh, banished to the Plantations, transported from Leith on the *Crown of London*, master Thomas Teddico, 27 November 1679, shipwrecked and drowned off Orkney 10 December 1679. [RBM]

MILLER, WILLIAM, son of Reverend William Miller {1649–1716} in Kirkliston, a minister in Barbados. [F.1.213]

MILLER, WILLIAM, a volunteer who died on the voyage to Darien 26 October 1698. [WP#88]

MILLIGAN, JOHN, a Covenanter from Glencairn, Nithsdale, captured after the Battle of Bothwell Bridge 22 June 1679, transported from Leith to the West Indies on the *Crown of London*, master Thomas Teddico, 27 November 1679, shipwrecked off Muil Head of Deerness, Orkney, 10 December 1679, later transported to Jamaica. [CEC#212/5][SW#202][RBM]

MILLIGAN, THOMAS, a Covenanter from Glencairn, Nithsdale, captured after the Battle of Bothwell Bridge 22 June 1679, transported from Leith to the West Indies on the *Crown of London*, master Thomas Teddico, 27 November 1679, shipwrecked off Muil Head of Deerness, Orkney, 10 December 1679, later transported to Jamaica. [RBM]

MILLER, WILLIAM, a Covenanter in Glencairn, Dumfriesshire, captured after the Battle of Bothwell Bridge 22 June 1679, imprisoned in Edinburgh, banished to the Plantations, transported from Leith on the *Crown of London*, master Thomas Teddico, 27 November 1679, shipwrecked and drowned off Orkney 10 December 1679. [RBM]

MILLIKEN, JOHN, master of the *Swan of Ayr* arrived in Ayr 27 September 1691 from the Caribee Islands. [SRO.E72.3.23]

MILLIKEN, THOMAS, a merchant trading between Ayr and the Caribee Islands on the *James of Ayr* March 1683. [SRO.E72.3.12]

MILLIKEN, ... Mr, settled on Nevis before 1700. [DP#332]

MILNE, ALEXANDER, a surgeon's assistant on the *Endeavour* bound for Darien. [SRO.GD406, bundle 161, 25/18]

MILNE, GEORGE, first mate of the *Endeavour* bound for Darien. [SRO.GD406, bundle 161, 25/24]

MILNE, WILLIAM, a joiner on the *St Andrew* and later the *Unicorn* assignation by his brother George Milne, mate of the *Royal William* 19 July 1699. [SRO.GD163, bundle 159, p2/12]; died in New York 15 August 1699.

MIRRIE, JAMES, a Covenanter from Cumnock, Ayrshire, captured after the Battle of Bothwell Bridge 22 June 1679, transported from Leith to the West Indies on the *Crown of London*, master Thomas Teddico, 27 November 1679, shipwrecked and drowned off Muil Head of Deerness, Orkney, 10 December 1679. [RBM]

MITCHELL, JAMES, son of John Mitchell in Bo'ness, West Lothian, a mariner from the Clyde to Darien 18 August 1699, cnf Edinburgh 1707. [SRO.CC8.8.83]

MITCHELL, JOHN, a merchant on the *James of Ayr*, master James Chalmers, which arrived in Ayr from the West Indies 19 September 1673. [SRO.E72.3.4]

MITCHELL, JOHN, transported from Leith to Jamaica, August 1685. [PC.11.136]

MITCHELL, WALTER, from Alloway, a sailor on the *Hope* from the Clyde to Darien 18 August 1699, cnf Edinburgh 4 December 1707. [SRO.CC8.8.83][SRO.GD406, bundle 162, c39/21]

MOFFAT, GEORGE, supercargo of the *Caledonia* arrived in New York from Darien, August 1700. [DD#251]

MOFFAT, JAMES, husband of Elizabeth Grozart in Linlithgow, West Lothian, a sailor on the *Rising Sun* from the Clyde to Darien 18 August 1699, cnf Edinburgh 1707. [SRO.CC8.8.83]

MOIR, JOHN, son of Thomas Moir and Christian Ross in Netherpark of Drim, Aberdeenshire, settled in Curacao before 1700. [APB.2.104]

MOIR, MALCOLM, a prisoner in Perth Tolbooth, banished to the American Plantations 9 June 1698, shipped on board the *St Andrew*, master Robert Pennicook. [SRO.B59.26.11.3]

MOIR, WILLIAM, a cooper on the *Dolphin* from Leith to Darien 14 July 1698. [SRO.GD406, bundle 163, c23/5]

MONCRIEFF, DAVID, formerly an Ensign of the Earl of Tullibardine's Regiment, later Deputy Assistant at Darien, to Darien 1699, cnf Edinburgh 24 September 1707. [SRO.CC8.8.83]

MONCRIEFF, GEORGE, a carpenter on the *Rising Sun*, "died abroad", cnf Edinburgh 4 October 1707. [SRO.CC8.8.83]

MONCRIEFF, NATHANIEL, in Christchurch, Barbados, pro.4 August 1687 Barbados. [RB.6.40.461]

MONKE, WILLIAM, a soldier, shipped to Jamaica on the *Grantham* 1659. [SPAWI/1659/126]

MONRO, HUGH, formerly a Lieutenant of Lord Murray's Regiment, emigrated to Darien 1698, an overseer there, cnf Edinburgh 26 September 1707. [SRO.CC8.8.83]

MONTAIN, JOANNES, a sailor on the *Unicorn* from Leith to Darien 14 July 1698, cnf Edinburgh 9 October 1707. [SRO.CC8.8.83]

MONTGOMERY, A., wrote to the Directors of the Darien Company from Caledonia, New Edinburgh, Darien, 28 December 1698. [SRO.GD26.13.119]

MONTGOMERY, HUGH, a Covenanter from Falkirk, Stirlingshire, captured after the Battle of Bothwell Bridge 22 June 1679, transported from Leith to the West Indies on the *Crown of London*, master Thomas Teddico, 27 November 1679, shipwrecked off Muil Head of Deerness, Orkney, 10 December 1679, later transported to Jamaica. [SW#201][CEC#212/5][RBM]

MONTGOMERIE, HUGH, a merchant, died in St Kitts, pro.1700 PCC [11, Noel]

MONTGOMERY, HUGH, of Borland, formerly a Corporal in the Earl of Eglintoun's troop, later a land officer in Captain Andrew Stewart's company in Darien, died there. [APS#14, app.114/127]

MONTGOMERY, JAMES, a merchant, trading from Ayr to the Caribee Islands on the *James of Ayr*, March 1683. [SRO.E72.3.12]

MONTGOMERY, JAMES, died on the voyage to Darien 28 October 1698. [WP#88]

MONTGOMERY, JAMES, a planter who died at Darien 29 November 1698. [WP#89] [NLS.RY2b8/19]

MONTGOMERY, JAMES, a Councillor of Caledonia, Darien, arrived at Gravesend 12 August 1699. [SRO.GD406.1.4427]

MOORE, DONALD, a Covenanter in Argyll, transported from Leith to Jamaica, August 1685. [PC.11.136]

MOOR, HUGH, a passenger on the *James of Ayr*, master James Chalmers, which arrived in Ayr from the West Indies 19 September 1673. [SRO.E72.3.4]

MOORE, ROBERT, from Carluke, Lanarkshire, transported from Leith to Jamaica, August 1685, landed at Port Royal, Jamaica, November 1685. [PC.11.136][LJ#169]

MOORE, SAMUEL, a merchant on the *James of Ayr* from Ayr to the West Indies 20 February 1681. [SRO.E72.3.6]

MOOR, WILLIAM, a merchant on the *James of Ayr*, master James Chalmers, arrived in Ayr from the West Indies 19 September 1673. [SRO.E72.3.4]

MOORE, WILLIAM, a merchant in Barbados, executor of George MacKenzie's will. [see G.Mackenzie's will, 28 August 1711 Barbados]

MORE, ..., a Covenanter from Bothwell, Lanarkshire, captured after the Battle of Bothwell Bridge 22 June 1679, transported from Leith to the West Indies on the *Crown of London*, master Thomas Teddico, 27 November 1679, shipwrecked off Orkney 10 December 1679, later transported to Jamaica. [CEC#212/5][SW#198] [RBM]

MORGAN, JOHN, from Leven, Fife, a sailor on the *St Andrew* from Leith to Darien 14 July 1698, cnf Edinburgh 23 October 1707. [SRO.CC8.8.83] [SRO.GD406, bundle 160, 2/21]

MORISEITE, JOHN, husband of Margaret Gray in Burntisland, Fife, a sailor on the *Unicorn* from Leith to Darien 14 July 1698, cnf Edinburgh 16 October 1707. [SRO.CC8.8.83]

MORRISON, CHRISTOPHER, from Greenock, Renfrewshire, a sailor on the *Dolphin* from Leith to Darien 14 July 1698, cnf Edinburgh 13 October 1707. [SRO.CC8.8.83]

MORRISON, DONALD, a Covenanter in Argyll, transported from Leith to Jamaica, August 1685. [PC.11.136]

MORRISON, JAMES, a prisoner in Barbados 1654, son of Marion Young in Glasgow, petition dated 31 January 1654. [Glasgow Burgh Records]

MORRISON, JOHN, a Covenanter from Airth, Stirlingshire, captured after the Battle of Bothwell Bridge 22 June 1679, transported from Leith to the West Indies on the *Crown of London*, master Thomas Teddico, 27 November 1679, shipwrecked and drowned off Muil Head of Deerness, Orkney, 10 December 1679. [RBM]

MORRISON, Reverend JOHN, emigrated to Nevis 1699, pro 30 September 1704 PCC [EMA#46][DP#335]

MOSSMAN, ARCHIBALD, a volunteer who died at Darien 15 November 1698. [WP#88][NLS.RY2b8/19]

MOSSMAN, JAMES, of Mount, a Covenanter, transported from Leith to the West Indies on the *St Michael of Scarborough*, master Edward Johnston, 12 December 1678. [PC.6.76]

MOUBRAY, THOMAS, a Covenanter in Kirkliston, West Lothian, transported from Leith to the West Indies on the *St Michael of Scarborough*, master Edward Johnston, 12 December 1678. [PC.6.76]

MOULTRIE, WALTER, son of George Moultrie in Markinch, Fife, a sailor on the *Union* from Leith to Darien 14 July 1698, died at Darien, cnf Edinburgh 1707. [SRO.CC8.8.83]

MOWATT, JAMES, soldier of Colonel Lyne's company of Militia in Barbados 6 January 1679. [H2/99]

MOWATT, JOHN, a prisoner in Edinburgh Tolbooth, transported from Leith by Morris Trent a merchant in Leith to Barbados on the *Mary*, master David Couston, 4 May 1663. [EBR#186.13.4]

MOYES, JAMES, a cooper, husband of Janet Spowart in Kinghorn, Fife, a sailor on the *Dolphin* from Leith to Darien 14 July 1698, cnf Edinburgh 1707. [SRO.CC8.8.83] [SRO.GD406, bundle 163, c23/5]

MUDY, PATRICK, soldier of Lieutenant Colonel Lyfe's company of Militia in Barbados 6 January 1679. [H2/173]

MUIR, ALEXANDER, from Auchtermuchty, Fife, a sailor on the *Rising Sun* from Leith to Darien 18 August 1699, cnf Edinburgh 1707. [SRO.CC8.8.83]

MUIR, HUGH, a merchant trading from Ayr to the Caribee Islands on the *James of Ayr* March 1683. [SRO.E72.3.12]

MUIR, WILLIAM, from Portsburgh, Edinburgh, a sailor on the *St Andrew* from Leith to Darien 14 July 1698, cnf Edinburgh 1707. [SRO.CC8.8.83]

MUIRHEAD, JOHN, witnessed James Black's deed when bound for Darien 16 July 1698. [SRO.GD406, bundle 163, c23/11]

MUNCKLAND, ROGER, a volunteer who died at Darien 22 November 1698. [WP#89]

MUNRO, ALEXANDER, with 13 acres in Christchurch, Barbados, 22 December 1679. [H#482]

MUNRO, ALLEN, soldier of Captain Sampson's company of Militia in Barbados 6 January 1680. [H2/150]

MUNRO, ANDREW, with 5 acres and 3 slaves in Christchurch, Barbados, 22 December 1679. [H#481]; soldier of Captain Rawlin's company of Militia in Barbados 6 January 1679. [H2/117]

MUNRO, DANIEL, a soldier of Captain Liston's company of Militia in Barbados 6 January 1679. [H2/143]

MUNRO, DAVID, who left Darien on the *Caledonia* bound for New York August 1699. [SPC.1699.478]; arrived at Sandy Hook on the *Unicorn* August 1699. [PRO.CO5.1043, 2]

MUNRO, DENNIS, with 2 acres in St Lucy's parish, Barbados, 1678; soldier of Captain Walley's company of Militia in Barbados 8 January 1680. [H2/42,137]

MUNRO, DONALD, a prisoner-of-war, son of Robert Munro and Christian Brown, transported to Barbados 1651. [MT#16]

MUNRO, HECTOR, with 4 slaves and 20 acres in St Peter's parish, Barbados, 1679; trooper of Major Stewart's troop of Horse Militia in Barbados 6 January 1679.[H2/79, 209]

MUNRO, HUGH, a prisoner in Edinburgh Tolbooth, transported from Leith to Barbados on the *John and Nicholas*, master Edward Barnes, December 1685. [ETR#390]

MUNRO, JAMES, with 6 acres in St Philip's parish, Barbados, 1680. [H2/11]

MUNRO, JOHN, soldier of Captain Helms' company of Militia in Barbados 6 January 1679. [H2/153]

MUNRO, JOHN, with his wife and 1 slave, in St Michael's, Barbados, 1680. [H#448]; soldier of Major Waterman's company of Militia in Barbados 6 January 1679. [H2/160]

MUNRO, JOHN, soldier of Captain Lyte's company of Militia in Barbados, 6 January 1679. [H2/175]

MUNRO, JOHN, with 2 acres of land in St Lucy's parish, Barbados, 30 December 1679. [H2/43]

MUNRO, THOMAS, soldier of Captain Burton's company of Militia in Barbados 6 January 1679. [H2/183]

MUNROE, WILLIAM, a cordiner in Port Royal, Jamaica, pro.1 December 1697 Jamaica

MURDOCH, ANDREW, a Covenanter from Kinneil, Bo'ness, West Lothian, captured after the Battle of Bothwell Bridge 22 June

1679, transported from Leith to the West Indies on the *Crown of London*, master Thomas Teddico, 27 November 1679, shipwrecked and drowned off Muil Head of Deerness, Orkney, 10 December 1679. [RBM]

MURDOCH, JOHN, a Covenanter from Glencairn, Dumfriesshire, captured after the Battle of Bothwell Bridge 22 June 1679, transported from Leith to the West Indies on the *Crown of London*, master Thomas Teddico, 27 November 1679, shipwrecked off Muil Head of Deerness, Orkney, 10 December 1679, later transported to Jamaica. [CEC#212/5][SW#202][RBM]

MURDOCH, JOHN, a merchant trading from Ayr to the Caribee Islands on the *James of Ayr* March 1683. [SRO.E72.3.12]

MURDOCH, WILLIAM, at Darien 19 October 1699. [SRO.GD45.1. 159]; returned to Scotland on the *Maidstone* 21 April 1699. [DD#352]

MURIE, ANDREW, a Covenanter from Glendevon, Perthshire, captured after the Battle of Bothwell Bridge 22 June 1679, transported from Leith to the West Indies on the *Crown of London*, master Thomas Teddico, 27 November 1679, shipwrecked and drowned off Muil Head of Deerness, Orkney, 10 December 1679. [RBM]

MURIE, JOHN, a Covenanter from Glendevon, Perthshire, captured after the Battle of Bothwell Bridge 22 June 1679, transported from Leith to the West Indies on the *Crown of London*, master Thomas Teddico, 27 November 1679, shipwrecked and drowned off Muil Head of Deerness, Orkney, 10 December 1679. [RBM]

MURRAY, ALEXANDER, a Covenanter from Penningham, Wigtownshire, captured after the Battle of Bothwell bridge 22 June 1679, transported from Leith to the West Indies on the *Crown of London*, master Thomas Teddico, 27 November 1679, shipwrecked off Muil Head of Deerness, Orkney, 10 December 1679, later transported to Jamaica. [CEC#212/5][SW#202][RBM]

MURRAY, ALEXANDER, householder and soldier of Colonel Stanfast's company of Militia in Barbados 6 January 1679. [H2/ 158]

MURRAY, ANNA, imprisoned in Edinburgh Tolbooth on a charge of infanticide, transported from Leith to Jamaica, August 1685. [PC.11.330][ETR#369]

MURRAY, DANIEL, soldier of Captain Dent's company of Militia in Barbados 6 January 1679. [H2/104]

MURRAY, HUTHEN (?), freeman and soldier of Captain Burton's company of Militia in Barbados 6 January 1679, [H2/183]

MURRAY, Mrs ISABEL, resident of Port Royal, Jamaica, 1700. [DD#324]

MURRAY, JAMES, householder and soldier of Captain Johnstone's company of Militia in Barbados 6 January 1679. [H2/165]

MURRAY, JOHN, with 3 acres of land in St Joseph's parish, Barbados, 1680; soldier of Major Foster's company of Militia in Barbados 6 January 1680. [H2/28, 134]

MURRAY, JOHN, soldier of Colonel Lyne's company of Militia in Barbados 6 January 1679. [H2/100]

MURRAY, LEWIS, a planter in St Thomas, Jamaica, pro. 9 October 1692 Jamaica

MURRAY, WILLIAM, mariner on the *Josiah*, pro. 24 October 1693 Jamaica

MURRAY, Captain WILLIAM, sailed from Darien on the *Unicorn* bound for New York August 1699. [SPC.1699.478]; from Sandy Hook to Scotland 12 October 1699 on the *Caledonia*, arrived at Islay, Argyll, 20 November 1699, from there to Edinburgh with news of Darien. [DSP#108][PRO.CO5.1043, 2]

MURROE, JOHN, with 3 acres in St Joseph's parish, Barbados, 1680. [H2/28]

MUTRAY, ALEXANDER, a Covenanter from Midcalder, Midlothian, captured after the Battle of Bothwell Bridge 22 June 1679, transported from Leith to the West Indies on the *Crown of London*, master Thomas Teddico, 27 November 1679, shipwrecked and drowned off Muil Head of Deerness, Orkney, 10 December 1679. [RBM]

NAISMITH, WILLIAM, father of Agnes in Bo'ness, West Lothian, a sailor on the *Caledonia* sailed from Leith to Darien 14 July 1698, cnf Edinburgh 7 October 1707. [SRO.CC8.8.83]

NEILSON, JOHN, a Covenanter from St Ninian's, Stirlingshire, captured after the Battle of Bothwell Bridge 22 June 1679, transported from Leith to the West Indies on the *Crown of London*, master Thomas Teddico, 27 November 1679, shipwrecked and drowned off Muil Head of Deerness, Orkney, 10 December 1679. [RBM]

NEILSON, THOMAS, clerk to the Captain of the *Unicorn* from Leith to Darien 14 July 1698, cnf Edinburgh 1707. [SRO.CC8.8.83]

NESMITH, Captain ROBERT, an Assemblyman in St Kitts 10 September 1677. [SPAWI.1678/741]

NEWBIGGING, ANDREW, a Covenanter from Bowden, Roxburgh-shire, captured after the Battle of Bothwell Bridge 22 June 1679, imprisoned in Edinburgh Tolbooth, transported from Leith to the West Indies on the *Crown of London*, master Thomas Teddico, 27 November 1679, shipwrecked and drowned off Muil Head of Deerness, Orkney, 10 December 1679. [RBM] [ETR#162]

NEWLANDS, DAVID, a Captain of the Scots Colony in America 1701, [SRO.RD3.98.1131]

NICHOLSON, ALEXANDER, with 4 slaves and 7 acres in St Thomas's parish, Barbados, 1679. [H2/61]

NICOLL, JOHN, transported from Leith to Jamaica, August 1685. [PC.11.136]

NISBET, SAMUEL, a Covenanter from Nenthorn, Berwickshire, cap-tured after the Battle of Bothwell Bridge 22 June 1679, impris-oned in Edinburgh, transported from Leith to the West Indies on the *Crown of London*, master Thomas Teddico, 27 November 1679, shipwrecked and drowned off Muil Head of Deerness, Orkney, 10 December 1679. [RBM]

NIMMO, ANDREW, son of James Nimmo in Airth, Stirlingshire, a foremastman on the *Caledonia* from Leith to Darien 14 July 1698, cnf Edinburgh 1707. [SRO.CC8.8.83]

NIVEN, WILLIAM, from Cathcart, Glasgow, transported from Leith to the West Indies on the *St Michael of Scarborough*, master Edward Johnston, 12 December 1678. [PC.6.76]

NOBLE, WALTER, master of the *Mayflower of Glasgow*, from Port Glasgow to the Caribee Islands with linen, shoes, cloth, coal, gloves, butter, and thread, March 1685. [SRO.E72.19.9]

NORRIE, ROBERT, from Dalkeith, Midlothian, a sailor on the *Unicorn* from Leith to Darien 14 July 1698, cnf Edinburgh 14 October 1707. [SRO.CC8.8.83]

OCHILTREE, DAVID, a Covenanter, transported from Leith to Jamaica August 1685. [PC.11.329]

OCKFORD, JANET, a prisoner in Edinburgh Tolbooth, transported by George Hutcheson a merchant in Edinburgh from Leith to Barba-dos 7 December 1665. [ETR#104]

OGILBY, Mr JOHN, and his wife Elizabeth, parents of Frances baptised in St Michael's, Barbados, 22 March 1678, buried 12 July 1678; with 4 servants and 6 slaves 1680. [H#424/427/440]

OGILVY, JOHN, an overseer who died at Darien 1699, cnf Edinburgh 1707. [SRO.CC8.8.83]

OLIPHANT, JOHN, son of James Oliphant and Isobel Wyse in Kirkcaldy, Fife, a foremastman on the *Caledonia* from Leith to Darien 14 July 1698, cnf Edinburgh 23 October 1707. [SRO.CC8. 8.83]

OLIPHANT, LAURENCE, from Williamstown, a sailor on the *Caledonia* from Leith to Darien 14 July 1698, cnf Edinburgh 1707. [SRO.CC8.8.83]

OLIPHANT, THOMAS, son of Patrick Oliphant in the Shetland Islands, a sailor on the *Unicorn* from Leith to Darien 14 July 1698, cnf Edinburgh 1708. [SRO.CC8.8.84]

OLIVER, JAMES, a Covenanter in Jedburgh Forest, Roxburghshire, transported from Leith to Jamaica August 1685, landed at Port Royal, Jamaica, November 1685. [PC.11.329][LJ#175]

OLIVER, JOHN, a Covenanter from Hobkirk, Roxburghshire, captured after the Battle of Bothwell Bridge 22 June 1679, imprisoned in Edinburgh, transported from Leith to the West Indies on the *Crown of London*, master Thomas Teddico, 27 November 1679, shipwrecked and drowned off Muil Head of Deerness, Orkney, 10 December 1679. [RBM]

ORROCK, ALEXANDER, husband of Rachel Simpson in Fife, a sailor on the *St Andrew* from Leith to Darien 14 July 1698, cnf Edinburgh 1707. [SRO.CC8.8.83]

ORROCK, JOHN, son of Isabel Steedman or Orrock in Kinghorn, Fife, a sailor on the *St Andrew* from Leith to Darien 14 July 1698, cnf Edinburgh 1707. [SRO.CC8.8.83][SRO.GD406, bundle 159, p4/12]

OSBURNE, ADAM, merchant on the *James of Ayr*, master James Chalmers, arrived in Ayr 19 September 1681 from the West Indies. [SRO.E72.3.7]

OSWALD, ROGER, son of George Oswald of Prestoun, who wrote from New Edinburgh, Darien Colony, to Thomas Aikman 17 February 1699. [SRO.NRAS#0174]

PANTON, ROBERT, from Dalmeny, West Lothian, transported from Leith to the West Indies on the *St Michael of Scarborough*, master Edward Johnstone, 12 December 1678. [PC.6.76]

PARGILLIS, WILLIAM, husband of Agnes Brown, a sailor on the *Hope* subscribed to a deed at Greenock when bound for Darien 18 August 1699. [SRO.GD406, bundle 162, c39/10]

PARK, ISABEL, a prisoner in Edinburgh Correction House, transported from Leith by Morris Trent a merchant in Leith to Barbados on the *Mary*, master David Couston, 4 May 1663. [EBR#186.13.4]

PARK, JOHN, a Covenanter and a weaver in Lanark, a prisoner in Edinburgh Tolbooth, transported from Leith to Barbados on the *John and Nicholas*, master Edward Barnes, December 1685. [PC.11.254][ETR#389]

PARK, PATRICK, a merchant from Glasgow who emigrated from Leith to Darien on the *Caledonia* 14 July 1698, and died at Darien, cnf Edinburgh 1707. [SRO.CC8.8.83]

PARRIS, ..., Mr, a merchant in London, authorised to transport 500 Scots prisoners to Barbados 20 May 1654. [Rawl.MS.A.328,p.46]

PATRICK, JAMES, a Covenanter in Kilmarnock, imprisoned in Edinburgh Tolbooth, transported from Leith to Barbados on the *John and Nicholas*, master Edward Barnes, December 1685. [PC.11. 386][[ETR#389]

PATERSON, ALEXANDER, a Covenanter from Muirkirk, Ayrshire, captured after the Battle of Bothwell Bridge 22 June 1679, imprisoned in Edinburgh, transported from Leith to the West Indies on the *Crown of London*, master Thomas Teddico, 27 November 1679, shipwrecked and drowned off Muil Head of Deerness, Orkney, 10 December 1679. [RBM]

PATTERSON, DAVID, a Covenanter in Eaglesham, Renfrewshire, imprisoned in Edinburgh Tolbooth, transported from Leith to Barbados on the *John and Nicholas*, master Edward Barnes, January 1685. [PC.11.254][ETR#389]

PATERSON, Mrs ELIZABETH TURNER or, died at Darien 14 November 1698. [WP#88]

PATTERSON, JAMES, a volunteer who died on the voyage to Darien 7 October 1698. [WP#87]

PATTERSON, JOHN, in St Andrew's parish, Jamaica, pro.3 October 1692 Jamaica

PATERSON, JONAS, chief carpenter of the *Hope* from Greenock to Darien 18 August 1699, cnf Edinburgh 17 October 1707. [SRO. CC8.8.83][SRO.GD406, bundle 406, c39/5]

PATERSON, PETER, a sailor who died on the voyage to Darien 28 October 1699. [WP#88]

PATTERSON, WILLIAM, a merchant in Edinburgh, petitioned the Privy Council for the loss of his ship the *Crown of London*, master Thomas Teddico, which sailed from Leith for the West Indies on 24 October 1679 with 258 Covenanter prisoners but was wrecked off Deer Sound, Orkney, with loss of the ship and all but 30 of the prisoners. Petition dated 6 March 1680. [PC#6.331/415]

PATTERSON, WILLIAM, wrote to the Directors of the Darien Company from Caledonia, New Edinburgh, Darien, 28 December 1698; wrote from Fort St Andrew, Caledonia, Darien, to Sir Patrick Scott of Ancrum 20 February 1699. [SRO.NRAS#0479/3; GD406.1.6489] ; arrived in New York from Darien on the *Unicorn* 23 August 1699. [PRO.CO5.1043, 2] [DSP#119]

PATTON, ANDREW, in St Andrews, Jamaica, pro.28 April 1685 Jamaica

PATTON, HENRY, from Bo'ness, West Lothian, a mate, from Leith to Darien 14 July 1698, cnf Edinburgh 1707. [SRO.CC8.8.83]

PATTON, WILLIAM, a gentleman in Barbados, pro.27 May 1671 Barbados. [RB.6.8.238]

PEARSON, MICHAEL, emigrated from Leith to Darien 14 July 1698, settled on Crab Island in the West Indies 7 October 1698. [DSP#80]

PEARSON, ROBERT, died in Kingston, Jamaica, 1 July 1700. [DP#352]

PEARSON, WILLIAM, seaman on the *Margaret of Dundee* at Darien 1700. [DD#328]

PEDDIN, ALEXANDER, transported from Leith to the West Indies on the *St Michael of Scarborough*, master Edward Johnstone, 12 December 1678. [PC.6.76]

PEDDEN, JAMES, from Prestonpans, East Lothian, a sailor on the *Rising Sun* from the Clyde to Darien 18 August 1699, cnf Edinburgh 22 October 1707. [SRO.CC8.8.83]

PEEBLES, ALEXANDER, a passenger on the *James of Ayr* from Ayr to the West Indies February 1681. [SRO.E72.3.6]

PENDAR, JOHN, a Covenanter from Torpichen, West Lothian, captured after the Battle of Bothwell Bridge 22 June 1679, transported from Leith to the West Indies on the *Crown of London*, master Thomas Teddico, 27 November 1679, shipwrecked off Muil Head of Deerness, Orkney, 10 December 1679, later transported to Jamaica. [CEC#212/5][SW#201][RBM]

PENDREICK, ROBERT, from Leith to Darien 14 July 1698, drowned at Darien 11 December 1698. [WP#89][NLS.RY2b8/19]

PENICUIK, JAMES, captain's servant on the *St Andrew* bound for Darien. [SRO.GD406, bundle 159, p4.14]

PENICUIK, ROBERT, Captain of the *St Andrew* wrote from Caledonia, New Edinburgh, Darien, to the Directors of the Darien Company 28 December 1698; witness to the testament of George Calderwood, quartermaster of *St Andrew*, 16 July 1698. [SRO.GD406. 1.6489]

PENMAN, JAMES, a Covenanter from Quathquan, Lanarkshire, captured after the Battle of Bothwell Bride 22 June 1679, transported from Leith to the West Indies on the *Crown of London*, master Thomas Teddico, 27 November 1679, shipwrecked off Orkney 10 January 1679, later transported to Jamaica. [CEC#212/5][SW #199][RBM]

PHILLIPS, ROBERT, from Leven, Fife, a sailor on the *Rising Sun* from the Clyde to Darien 18 August 1699, cnf Edinburgh 1707. [SRO. CC8.8.83]

PHILP, THOMAS, a Covenanter from Muiravonside, Stirlingshire, captured after the Battle of Bothwell Bridge 22 June 1679, transported from Leith to the West Indies on the *Crown of London*, master Thomas Teddico, 27 November 1679, shipwrecked off Muil Head of Deerness, Orkney, 10 December 1679. [RBM]

PINKERTON, ROBERT, from Liberton, Edinburgh, master of the pink *Endeavour* from Leith to Darien 14 July 1698; wrote to the Directors of the Darien Company from Caledonia, New Edinburgh, Darien, 28 December 1698; settled at Darien, later imprisoned at Carthgena and in Seville on a charge of piracy May 1700, released September 1700; cnf Edinburgh 1707. [APS.14, app114] [SRO. GD406.1.4541/6489][SRO.CC8.8.83][DSP#69/332][DD#332]

PIRIE, ALEXANDER, a Covenanter from Glasgow, captured after the Battle of Bothwell Bridge 22 June 1679, imprisoned in Edinburgh, transported from Leith to the West Indies on the *Crown of London*, master Thomas Teddico, 27 November 1679, shipwrecked off Muil Head of Deerness, Orkney, 10 December 1679. [RBM]

PIRIE, ANDREW, a Covenanter from Fife, captured after the Battle of Bothwell Bridge 22 June 1679, imprisoned in Edinburgh, transported from Leith to the West Indies on the *Crown of London*, master Thomas Teddico, 27 November 1679, shipwrecked off Muil Head of Deerness, Orkney, 10 December 1679. [RBM]

PIERY, ALEXANDER, a planter who died on the voyage to Darien 23 July 1698. [WP#87]

PITSCOTTIE, COLIN, son of John Pitscottie of Craigduchie, a sailor on the *Rising Sun* from the Clyde to Darien 18 August 1699, cnf Edinburgh 14 October 1707. [SRO.CC8.8.83]

POTT, ANTHONY, of Headshope, a thief imprisoned in Jedburgh Tolbooth, Roxburghshire, 7 January 1666, and later 17 April 1666 in Edinburgh Tolbooth, banished to Barbados to be sold as a slave, 1666. [ETR#10]

POWER, EDWARD, a seaman on the *St Andrew* from Leith to Darien 14 July 1698, cnf Edinburgh 23 September 1707. [SRO.CC8. 8.83]

POWRIE, ALEXANDER, son of Andrew Powrie in Edinburgh, husband of Elizabeth Smith, a druggist burgess of Edinburgh and a sailor on the *St Andrew*, from Leith to Darien 14 July 1698, cnf Edinburgh 22 November 1707. [SRO.CC8.8.83]

POWRIE, ANDREW, a sailor on the *St Andrew* bound for Darien 1698. [SRO.GD406, bundle 160, 2/20]

POWRIE, WILLIAM, planter in Barbados, 5 October 1640. [SRO. GD34.932]; will subscribed 17 August 1647, references to his father Richard Powrie, Gilbert Powrie, John Powrie, Richard Powrie, Elizabeth Powrie and Jean Powrie, uncle Archibald Hay, pro.4 April 1649 Barbados. [RB3.3.532]; pro.1651 PCC [95, Grey]; testimonial re Richard Powrie of Dawick, Peebles-shire, father of William Powrie late of Barbados, gentleman, deceased, Elizabeth and Jane Powrie sisters and heirs of the said William and of Archibald Hay Esq, deceased, having sold Spring Plantation, Barbados, and all other plantations in Barbados and the Caribee Islands to Sir James Halket and John, natural son of the said William Powrie., 1663, [Edinburgh Burgh Records, 30 October 1644; 25 March 1663]

PRATT, THOMAS, son of Alexander Pratt in Bo'ness, West Lothian, a sailor on the *Dolphin* from Leith to Darien 14 July 1698, cnf Edinburgh 1708. [SRO.CC8.8.83]

PRINGLE, JOHN, a Covenanter from Castletoun, Roxburghshire, captured after the Battle of Bothwell Bridge 22 June 1679, imprisoned in Edinburgh, transported from Leith to the West Indies on the *Crown of London*, master Thomas Teddico, 27 November 1679, shipwrecked off Muil Head of Deerness, Orkney, 10 December 1679. [RBM]

PRINGLE, THOMAS, a Covenanter from Stow, Midlothian, captured after the Battle of Bothwell Bridge 22 June 1679, imprisoned in Edinburgh Tolbooth, transported from Leith to the West Indies on the *Crown of London*, master Thomas Teddico, 27 November 1679, shipwrecked off Muil Head of Deerness, Orkney, 10 December 1679. [RBM] [ETR#162]

PRINGLE, WILLIAM, purchased a plantation in Surinam November 1674, petition 8 June 1676. [Cal.SPCol.1675#683, 1676#943]

PRYDE, JAMES, a Covenanter and a weaver in Strathmiglo, Fife, transported from Leith to the West Indies on the *St Michael of Scarborough*, master Edward Johnstone, 12 December 1678. [PC.6.76]

PURDY, RICHARD, deceased, husband of Agnes Napier in Edinburgh, late in service of the West India Company of Flanders, 1640. [EBR#239]

PYOTT, ALEXANDER, pro 14 January 1651 PCC.

RAE, ADAM, a merchant burgess of Edinburgh, trading from Leith to the West Indies 1611. [SRO.E71.29.6]

RAE, JAMES, a Covenanter in Uddingston, Lanarkshire, imprisoned in Edinburgh Tolbooth, transported from Leith to Barbados on the *John and Nicholas*, master Edward Barnes, 12 December 1685. [PC.11.254][ETR#389]

RAE, JOHN, a tailor in Falkirk, transported from Leith to the West Indies on the *St Michael of Scarborough*, master Edward Johnstone, 12 December 1678. [PC.6.76]

RAE, WILLIAM, a weaver in Glasgow, transported from Leith to the West Indies on the *St Michael of Scarborough*, master Edward Johnstone, 12 December 1678. [PC.6.76]

RAIT, JAMES, born 1653, son of Reverend John Rait and Elizabeth Beattie {died 1 December 1661} in Inverkeilor, Angus, died in Nevis 1675. [Inverkeilor g/s][F.3.439]

RALTOUN, DAVID, a Covenanter from Bathgate, West Lothian, captured after the Battle of Bothwell Bridge 22 June 1679, imprisoned in Edinburgh, transported from Leith to the West Indies on the *Crown of London*, master Thomas Teddico, 27 November 1679, shipwrecked off Muil Head of Deerness, Orkney, 10 December 1679. [RBM]

RAMSAY, CICELLA, a prisoner in Edinburgh Correction House, transported from Leith by Morris Trent a merchant in Leith to Barbados on the *Mary*, master David Couston, 4 May 1663. [EBR#186. 13.4]

RAMSAY, DAVID, jr., Ensign of Colonel Thornhill's company of Militia in Barbados 6 January 1679. [H2/146]

RAMSAY, DAVID, appointed a Councillor of Barbados 15 April 1697. [ActsPCCol]; petition 1704. [Rawl.MS.A.271 pp1-6]

RAMSAY, GEORGE, soldier of Captain Hackett's company of Militia in Barbados 1680. [H2/128]

RAMSAY, GILBERT, born 1650s, educated at King's College, Aberdeen, 1673, ordained by the Bishop of Galloway 1686, emigrated to Antigua 1688, minister of St Paul's, Antigua, 1688–1692, minister of Christchurch parish, Barbados, 1692–1724+, died in Bath, England, 5 May 1728. pro.1720 PCC [122, Brook], [Bath Abbey g/s] [SRO.RD3.142.274; RD3.143.507] [Car.3.268][KCA.2.243]

RAMSAY, JAMES, wounded at Darien 6 February 1699. [DP#86]

RAMSAY, JAMES, a volunteer at Darien, wrote William Milne's disposition possibly in New York 9 July 1699. [SRO.GD406, bundle 159, p2/12]

RAMSAY, JOHN, in St Philips parish, Barbados, with 4 acres, 1680; soldier of Captain Rawling's company of Militia in Barbados 6 January 1679. [H2/14, 118]

RAMSAY, MARGARET, a prisoner in Edinburgh Correction House, transported from Leith by Morris Trent a merchant in Leith to Barbados on the *Mary*, master David Couston, 4 May 1663. [EBR#186.13.4]

RAMSAY, ROBERT, in Barbados 19 October 1670. [SPAWI/1670/910]; buried in St Michael's, Barbados, 8 April 1678. [H#425]

RAMSAY, ROBERT, a Covenanter from Kirkmichael, Ayrshire, captured after the Battle of Bothwell Bridge 22 June 1679, imprisoned in Edinburgh, transported from Leith to the West Indies on the *Crown of London*, master Thomas Teddico, 27 November 1679, shipwrecked off Muil Head of Deerness, Orkney, 10 December 1679. [RBM]

RAMSAY, ROSE, with 20 acres, 1 servant and 29 slaves in St James, Barbados, 20 December 1679. [H#505][H2/148]

RAMSAY, WILLIAM, a soldier of Captain Hackett's company of Militia in Barbados 1680. [H2/128]

RANKEILLER, THOMAS, son of James Rankeiller in Wemyss, Fife, a sailor, from the Clyde to Darien 18 August 1699, cnf Edinburgh 1708. [SRO.CC8.8.84]

RANKIN, JOHN, a Covenanter from Biggar, Lanarkshire, captured after the Battle of Bothwell Bridge 22 June 1679, imprisoned in Edinburgh, transported from Leith to the West Indies on the *Crown of London*, master Thomas Teddico, 27 November 1679, shipwrecked off Muil Head of Deerness, Orkney, 10 December 1679. [RBM]

RANKEN, JOHN, from Ayr, a sailor on the *Rising Sun* from the Clyde to Darien 18 August 1699, cnf Edinburgh 1708. [SRO.CC8.8.84]

READY, JOHN, a sailor on the *St Andrew* 1698 bound for Darien. [SRO.GD406, bundle 160, 2/2]

REID, ADAM, poor, with 6 acres in St James, Barbados, 20 December 1679. [H#505]

REID, ANDREW, a Covenanter in Argyll, imprisoned in Edinburgh Tolbooth, transported from Leith to Jamaica August 1685. [PC.11. 328][ETR#369]

REID, GEORGE, a planter in Jamaica, formerly factor of the Royal African Company in Barbados, 1684. [SPAWI.1684/2030]

REID, GEORGE, a petitioner in Jamaica, 19 November 1691. [ActsPCCol]

REID, HUGH, arrived in Ayr from Montserrat on the *Unity of Ayr*, master John Hodgson, 2 September 1673. [SRO.E72.3.3]

REID, JOHN, trooper of Colonel Lambert's Leeward Island Regiment of Militia 5 January 1679, [H2/199]; with 198 acres, 2 servants and 85 slaves in St James, Barbados, 20 December 1679, [H#505]; Judge of Spight's Court of Common Pleas in Barbados, 1680. [H2/93]; Judge of the Five Precincts of Barbados 22 March 1681, [SPAWI.1681/53]; Assemblyman for St James', Barbados, 1684. [SPAWI.1684/1881]; a gentleman in Barbados reference to in Richard Trant's will pro.18 May 1705 Barbados. [RB6.16.250]

REID, JOHN, born 1663, a groom, emigrated via London to Jamaica March 1684. [CLRO/AIA]

REID, MALCOLM, imprisoned in Perth Tolbooth, banished to the American Plantations 9 June 1698, shipped on board the *St Andrew*, master Robert Pennicuik. [SRO.B59.26.11.3]

REID, ROBERT, a weaver in Langside, Glasgow, transported from Leith to the West Indies on the *St Michael of Scarborough*, master Edward Barnes, 12 December 1678. [PC.6.76]

REID, ROBERT, a weaver in Cathcart, Glasgow, transported from Leith to the West Indies on the *St Michael of Scarborough*, master Edward Johnstone, 12 December 1678. [PC.6.76]

REID, THOMAS, from Edinburgh, a gunner on the *Unicorn* from Leith to Darien 14 July 1698, cnf Edinburgh 1708. [SRO.CC8.8.84]

REID, WILLIAM, pro.26 May 1675 Jamaica

REID, WILLIAM, a Covenanter from Mauchline, Ayrshire, captured after the Battle of Bothwell Bridge 22 June 1679, imprisoned in Edinburgh, transported from Leith to the West Indies on the *Crown of London*, master Thomas Teddico, 27 November 1679, shipwrecked off Muil Head of Deerness, Orkney, 10 December 1679. [RBM]

REID, WILLIAM, a Covenanter from Musselburgh, Midlothian, captured after the Battle of Bothwell Bridge 22 June 1679, imprisoned in Edinburgh, transported from Leith to the West Indies on the *Crown of London*, master Thomas Teddico, 27 November 1679, shipwrecked off Muil Head of Deerness, Orkney, 10 December 1679. [RBM]

REID, WILLIAM, a prisoner in Edinburgh Tolbooth, transported from Leith to Barbados on the *John and Nicholas*, master Edward Barnes, 12 December 1685. [ETR#390]

RICHARD, THOMAS, a Covenanter in Greenock Mains, Muirkirk, Ayrshire, imprisoned in Edinburgh Tolbooth, transported from Leith to Jamaica August 1685. [ETR#369][PC.11.329]

RICHARDSON, JOHN, a Covenanter from Borgue, Kirkcudbrightshire, captured after the battle of Bothwell Bridge 22 June 1679, transported from Leith to the West Indies on the *Crown of London*, master Thomas Teddico, 27 November 1679, shipwrecked off Muil Head of Deerness, Orkney, 10 December 1679, later transported to Jamaica. [CEC#212/5][SW#203][RBM]

RICHARDSON, WALTER, husband of Elizabeth Orrock in Kirkcaldy, Fife, a sailor on the *Endeavour* bound for Darien. [SRO.GD406, bundle 161, 26/16]

RICHARDSON, WILLIAM, transported from Leith 17 November 1679. [PC.6.343]

RICHMOND, ANDREW, a Covenanter from Auchenleck, Ayrshire, captured after the Battle of Bothwell Bridge 22 June 1679, imprisoned in Edinburgh, transported from Leith to the West Indies on the *Crown of London*, master Thomas Teddico, 27 November 1679, shipwrecked off Muil Head of Deerness, Orkney, 10 December 1679. [RBM]

RIDDELL, JAMES, wounded at Darien 6 February 1699. [DP#86]

RIDDELL, JAMES, son of John Riddell in Sauchieglass, St Ninian's, Stirlingshire, a sailor on the *Unicorn* from Leith to Darien 14 July 1698, cnf Edinburgh 1707. [SRO.CC8.8.83]

RIDDELL, THOMAS, from Leith, mate on the *Rising Sun* from the Clyde to Darien 18 August 1699, cnf Edinburgh 1707. [SRO.CC8. 8.83]

RIDDOCH, ALEXANDER, son of David Riddoch of Aberlechoch, captured and imprisoned by the Turks when on a trading voyage to the West Indies, before 1645. [APS.VI(1)457]

RIDDOCH, ALEXANDER, Colonel in Barbados with 200 acres of land in 1673, [H2/216]; with 8 servants, 70 slaves and 188 acres in St Peter's parish, Barbados, 1679; Lieutenant Colonel of Militia in Barbados 1679. [H2/159]; appointed as Judge of Common Pleas in Scotland, Barbados, 11 March 1680, [ActsPCCol.][H2/93]; Judge of the Five Precincts of Barbados 22 March 1681. [SPAWI.1681/53]

RIDDOCH, CATHERINE, buried in St Peter's parish, Barbados, 1678. [H2/87]

RIDDOCH, JAMES, son of David Riddoch of Aberlechoch, captured and imprisoned by the Turks when on a trading voyage to the West Indies, before 1645. [APS.VI(1)457]

RIDPATH, JOHN, a tinker, guilty of adultery and imprisoned in Edinburgh Tolbooth, transported December 1662. [ETR#80]

RITCHIE, Dr ..., in Montserrat and St Kitts ca1642. [SRO.GD34.932]

ROBERTSON, CHARLES, from Aberdeen, pro.26 October 1697 Barbados. [RB6.1.22]

ROBERTSON, JOHN, from Burntisland, Fife, a sailor on the *St Andrew* from Leith to Darien 14 July 1698, cnf Edinburgh 1707. [SRO.CC8.8.83][SRO.GD406, bundle 160, 2/25]

ROBERTSON, LEONARD, Captain of the *Margaret of Dundee* which sailed from Dundee to New Edinburgh, Darien, with supplies March 1700. [SRO.GD406]

ROBERTSON, ROBERT, surgeon of the *Lyon*, pro.24 May 1692 Jamaica

ROBERTSON, Reverend ROBERT, born 18 March 1681, from Edinburgh, emigrated 1706, settled in St Paul's, Charlestown, Nevis, married Mary Podgson, father of Mary and Elizabeth, buried in St Paul's, Nevis. [EMA#52][CAR.1.9]

ROBERTSON, THOMAS, a sailor on the *Caledonia* from Leith to Darien 14 July 1698, cnf Edinburgh 25 November 1707. [SRO.CC8.8.83]

ROBERTSON, WILLIAM, a sergeant at Darien 18 December 1699. [DD#262]

ROBERTSON, ..., Captain, a planter in Northside, Jamaica, before 1700. [DP#305, 313]

RODGER, WILLIAM, a Covenanter from Maybole, Ayrshire, captured after the Battle of Bothwell Bridge 22 June 1679, imprisoned in Edinburgh, transported from Leith to the West Indies on the *Crown of London*, master Thomas Teddico, 27 November 1679, shipwrecked off Muil Head of Deerness, Orkney, 10 December 1679. [RBM]

RODGER, WILLIAM, a Covenanter from Kilbride, Lanarkshire, captured after the Battle of Bothwell Bridge 22 June 1679, imprisoned in Edinburgh, transported from Leith to the West Indies on the *Crown of London*, master Thomas Teddico, 27 November 1679, shipwrecked off Muil Head of Deerness, Orkney, 10 December 1679. [RBM]

RODRIE, THOMAS, husband of Janet Beattie, a gunner on the *Unicorn* from Leith to Darien 14 July 1698, cnf Edinburgh 6 January 1707. [SRO.CC8.8.83]

ROLLOCK, ANDREW, with 18 slaves and 44 acres in Barbados 30 December 1679; a trooper of Colonel Lambart's troop of Militia in Barbados 6 January 1679. [H2/44, 197]

RONALD, WILLIAM, father of William and Elizabeth in Grangepans, West Lothian, a mariner on the *Dolphin* from Leith to Darien 14 July 1698, cnf Edinburgh 6 October 1707. [SRO.CC8.8.83]

RONALD, WILLIAM, jr., son of William Ronald in Grangepans, West Lothian, a mariner on the *Dolphin* from Leith to Darien 14 July 1698, died 1699, cnf Edinburgh 6 October 1707. [SRO.CC8.8.83]

ROSEWELL, ANTHONY, a merchant in Leith and in Barbados, 1666. [SRO.RD2.16.323; RD4.16.874]

ROSPER, THOMAS, a Covenanter from Glencairn, Dumfriesshire, captured after the Battle of Bothwell Bridge 22 June 1679, imprisoned in Edinburgh, transported from Leith to the West Indies on the *Crown of London*, master Thomas Teddico, 27 November 1679, shipwrecked off Muil Head of Deerness, Orkney, 10 December 1679. [RBM]

ROSS, ALEXANDER, son of Agnes Ross in Junesner{?}, Scotland, pro.4 July 1688 Barbados. [RB.6.41.8]

ROSS, DANIEL, (1), with 5 acres in St Thomas's parish, Barbados, 1679. [H2/62]

ROSS, DANIEL (2), with 1 acre at the Spring, St Thomas's parish, Barbados, 1679. [H2/62]

ROSS, DANIEL, soldier of Captain Merrell's company of Militia in Barbados 6 January 1680. [H2/152]

ROSS, GEORGE, soldier of Captain Bowcher's company of Militia in Barbados 6 January 1679. [H2/112]

ROSS, HUGH, writer and secretary of the Darien Company, died in New England, cnf Edinburgh 1708. [SRO.CC8.8.84]

ROSS, JOHN, from Ellon, Aberdeenshire, emigrated to Barbados February 1670. [EPR#130]

ROSS, JOHN, soldier of Captain Woodward's company of Militia in Barbados 6 January 1679. [H2/156]

ROSS, JOHN, soldier of Captain Thornhill's company of Militia in Barbados 6 January 1679. [H2/151]

ROSS, JOHN, soldier of Captain Bowcher's company of Militia in Barbados 6 January 1679. [H2/112]

ROSS, JOHN, soldier of Major Williams' company of Militia in Barbados 6 January 1679. [H2/103]

ROSS, JOHN, with 1 acre in Christchurch, Barbados, 22 December 1679. [H#484]

ROSS, JOHN, with 1 slave and 3 acres in St Thomas's parish, Barbados, 1679. [H2/62]

ROSS, MARGARET, daughter of George Ross, buried in St Philips parish, Barbados, 23 February 1678. [H2/23]

ROSS, PHILIP, with 4 acres in St Thomas's parish, Barbados, 1679. [H2/62]

ROSS, Mr PHILIP, with 12 acres and 4 slaves in St Andrew's, Barbados, 1680. [H#471]

ROSS, ROBERT, buried in St Lucy's parish, Barbados, 6 October 1678. [H2/55]

ROSS, THOMAS, son of David Ross, baptised in St Thomas's, Barbados, 28 April 1678. [H2/64]

ROSS, Dr THOMAS, with 20 acres and 9 slaves in St James, Barbados, 20 December 1679. [H#505]

ROSS, WILLIAM, a time-expired indentured servant, emigrated from Barbados to New England on the ketch *William and Susan*, master Ralph Parker, 21 March 1678. [H#399]

ROSS, WILLIAM, a soldier of Captain Merrell's company of Militia in Barbados 6 January 1679. [H2/152]

ROSS, WILLIAM, from Kirkwall, Orkney Islands, settled in New Scotland, Barbados, dead by 1683, father of Alexander. [SRO.S/H]

ROSS, WILLIAM, a cooper in Port Royal, Jamaica, pro.7 January 1694 Jamaica

ROSS, WILLIAM, from Linktown of Abbotshall, Kirkcaldy, Fife, a sailor on the *Endeavour* bound for Darien. [SRO.GD406, bundle 161, 25/15]

ROY, JOHN, with 2 acres in St Philip's parish, Barbados, 1680. [H2/14]

RUGBIE, JOHN, a merchant in Barbados, 1666. [SRO.RD2.16.323]

RULE, ELIZABETH, buried in St Michael's, Barbados, 25 September 1679. [H#438]

RUSSELL, GEORGE, a Covenanter and a cordwainer in Glasgow, son of George Russell, transported to the West Indies June 1678. [PC.5.474]

RUSSELL, GEORGE, a sailor on the *Unicorn* from Leith to Darien 14 July 1698, cnf Edinburgh 1707. [SRO.CC8.8.83]

RUSSELL, JAMES, a prisoner in Edinburgh Tolbooth, transported from Leith by Morris Trent a merchant in Leith to Barbados on the *Mary*, master David Couston, 4 May 1663. [EBR#186.13.4]

RUSSELL, JAMES, a soldier of Major Lyte's company of Militia in Barbados 1679. [H2/175]

RUSSELL, JAMES, soldier of Captain Burrow's company of Militia in Barbados 1679. [H2/181]

RUSSELL, JAMES, from Edinburgh, a sailor on the *Caledonia* from Leith to Darien 14 July 1698, died at Darien 1699, cnf Edinburgh 1707. [SRO.CC8.8.83]

RUSSELL, JOHN, a Covenanter from Calder, Midlothian, captured after the Battle of Bothwell Bridge 22 June 1679, imprisoned in Edinburgh, transported from Leith to the West Indies on the *Crown of London*, master Thomas Teddico, 27 November 1679, shipwrecked off Muil Head of Deerness, Orkney, 10 December 1679. [RBM]

RUSSELL, JOHN, a Covenanter from Calder, Midlothian, captured after the Battle of Bothwell Bridge 22 June 1679, imprisoned in Edinburgh Tolbooth, transported from Leith to the West Indies on the *Crown of London*, master Thomas Teddico, November 1679, shipwrecked off Muil Head of Deerness, Orkney, 10 December 1679. [RBM][ETR#162]

RUSSELL, ROBERT, from Stirling, was issued with a birthbrief by Stirling Town Council prior to emigrating to Darien 18 June 1698. [RBS, MS]

RUTHERFORD, GEORGE, a Covenanter from Ancrum, Roxburghshire, captured after the Battle of Bothwell Bridge 22 June 1679, imprisoned in Edinburgh, transported from Leith to the West Indies on the *Crown of London*, master Thomas Teddico, 27 November 1679, shipwrecked off Muil Head of Deerness, Orkney, 10 December 1679. [RBM]

RUTHERFORD, GEORGE, from Jedburgh, Roxburghshire, a surgeon's assistant on the *St Andrew*, from Leith to Darien 14 July

1698, cnf Edinburgh 23 March 1709. [SRO.CC8.8.84][SRO. GD406, bundle 159, p4/5]

RUTHERFORD, JOHN, a gentleman in Port Royal, Jamaica, pro.18 October 1692 Jamaica

RUTHVEN, JAMES, Captain of Colonel Francis Collingwood's Regiment of Foot, died in Nevis, pro.1699 PCC.

SAMPLE, WILLIAM, a surgeon and a planter in St Kitts, son of Agnes Sample in Edinburgh, settled in Nevis before 1709, died 1712, father of John, pro. 1713 St Kitts. [PRO.CO243.4.f49]

SAMUEL, DAVID, a Covenanter from East Calder, Midlothian, captured after the Battle of Bothwell Bridge 22 June 1679, transported from Leith to the West Indies on the *Crown of London*, master Thomas Teddico, 27 November 1679, shipwrecked off Muil Head of Deerness, Orkney, 10 December 1679, later transported to Jamaica. [CEC#212/5][SW#202][RBM]

SANDERSON, WILLIAM, from Kinghorn, Fife, an Ensign who died at Darien 1699, cnf Edinburgh 1707. [SRO.CC8.8.83]

SANDS, JAMES, a Covenanter from Gargannock, Stirlingshire, captured after the Battle of Bothwell Bridge 22 June 1679, transported from Leith to the West Indies on the *Crown of London*, master Thomas Teddico, 27 November 1679, shipwrecked off Muil Head of Deerness, Orkney, 10 December 1679, later transported to Jamaica. [CEC#212/5][SW#201][RBM]

SANDS, ROBERT, a Covenanter from Orwell, Kinross, captured after the Battle of Bothwell Bridge 22 June 1679, transported from Leith to the West Indies on the *Crown of London*, master Thomas Teddico, 27 November 1679, shipwrecked off Muil Head of Deerness, Orkney, 10 December 1679, later transported to Jamaica. [RBM][CEC#212/5][SW#200]

SANDS, WILLIAM, from Culross, Fife, a sailor on the *Hope* bound for Darien. [SRO.GD406, bundle 162, c39/11]

SANDS, WILLIAM, from Dunfermline, Fife, a sailor on the *Rising Sun* from the Clyde to Darien 18 August 1699, cnf Edinburgh 1707. [SRO.CC8.8.83]

SCHOALLA, ROBERT, a joiner, son of James Schoalla in Papa, Orkney Islands, from Leith to Darien on the *Unicorn* 14 July 1698, cnf Edinburgh 1707. [SRO.CC8.8.83]

SCHOWRMAN, JASPER, arrived in New York from Darien on board the *Caledonia* 8.1699. [DSP#1118][PRO.CO5.1043,2]

SCOTT, ADAM, born in Roxburghshire, educated at the University of Edinburgh 1691, licenced by the Presbytery of Jedburgh 14 August 1695, chaplain to the 1st Expedition to Darien 6 July 1698, died at sea 20 November 1698. [F.7.665][WP#88][NLS.RY2b8/19]

SCOTT, ANDREW, a merchant trading from Ayr to the Caribee Islands on the *James of Ayr,* March 1683. [SRO.E72.3.12]

SCOTT, ANDREW, a Covenanter in Teviotdale, Roxburghshire, transported from Leith to Jamaica July 1685, landed in Port Royal, Jamaica, November 1685. [PC.11.329][LJ#195]

SCOTT, BENJAMIN, a time-expired indentured servant, emigrated from Barbados to London on the *Expedition*, master John Harding, 31 March 1679. [H#404]

SCOTT, BENJAMIN, gentleman of Lieutenant Maxwell's troop of Militia in Barbados 6 January 1679, [H2/211]; with 10 acres in St Michael's, Barbados, 1679, and 108 acres, 2 servants and 41 slaves in Christchurch, Barbados, 10 December 1679. [H#458/485]

SCOTT, EDWARD, soldier of Captain Ely's company of Militia in Barbados 1679. [H2/177]

SCOTT, GEORGE, soldier of Colonel Baylie's company of Militia in Barbados 1679. [H2/131]

SCOTT, HUGH, brother to ... Scott of Galashiels, "remained at Darien after the colony was abandoned", (1700). [APS.14, app114]; son of Hugh Scott of Gala, Selkirkshire, an Ensign who died at Darien, cnf Edinburgh 1708. [SRO.CC8.8.84]

SCOTT, JAMES, soldier of Captain Woodward's company of Militia in Barbados 6 January 1679; with 6 slaves and 5 acres in Barbados 18 October 1679. [H2/156, 72]

SCOTT, JAMES, from Falkirk, Stirlingshire, a foremastman on the *Caledonia* from Leith to Darien 14 July 1698, cnf Edinburgh 6 October 1707. [SRO.CC8.8.83]

SCOTT, JOHN, a gentleman in Nevis, bound for Barbados on the *Golden Lion of London*, pro.1654 PCC.

SCOTT, JOHN, master of the *Good Intent* petitioned the Privy Council for felons from Edinburgh, Leith and Canongate Tolbooths for shipment to Virginia or Barbados November 1667. [PC.2.358]

SCOTT, JOHN, a Covenanter from Ancrum, Roxburghshire, captured after the Battle of Bothwell Bridge 22 June 1679, imprisoned in Edinburgh Tolbooth, transported from Leith to the West Indies on the *Crown of London*, master Thomas Teddico, 27 November 1679, shipwrecked off Muil Head of Deerness, Orkney, 10 December 1679. [RBM][ETR#162]

SCOTT, JOHN, a soldier of Captain Hall's company of Militia in Barbados 10 December 1679. [H2/136]

SCOTT, JOHN, with 10 acres and 1 slave in St James, Barbados, 20.10 December 1679. [H#505]

SCOTT, JOHN, passenger on the *James of Ayr*, master James Chalmers, arrived in Ayr from the West Indies 19 September 1681. [SRO. E72.3.7]

SCOTT, JOHN, in Montserrat, 1699. [SPAWI/1699/658]; appointed a Councillor of Montserrat 22 August 1699. [ActsPCCol]

SCOTT, JOHN, son of John Scott of Thirleston, Berwickshire, died at Darien, cnf Edinburgh 1707. [SRO.CC8.8.83]

SCOTT, MARGARET, daughter of James Scott, baptised in St Thomas's, Barbados, 10 May 1679. [H2/65]

SCOTT, MATTHEW, soldier of Lieutenant Colonel Affleck's company of Militia in Barbados 1679. [F2/148]

SCOTT, MATTHEW, born 1660, emigrated via London to Barbados on the *Barbados Merchant* February 1683. [CLRO/AIA]

SCOTT, Mr PHILLIP, trooper of Colonel Lambard's Leeward Island Militia in Barbados 5 January 1679. [H2/199]

SCOTT, RICHARD, Captain of Militia in Barbados 6 January 1679. [H2/170]

SCOTT, ROBERT, pro.25 January 1685 Jamaica

SCOTT, ROBERT, appointed a Councillor of Barbados 8 October 1695. [ActsPCCol]

SCOTT, ROBERT, son of John Scott in Linlithgow, West Lothian, a mariner on the *Rising Sun* from the Clyde to Darien 18 August 1699, cnf Edinburgh 1707. [SRO.CC8.8.83]

SCOTT, THOMAS, with 10 slaves in St Lucy's parish, Barbados, 1678. [H2/46]

SCOTT, THOMAS, soldier of Captain Harrison's company of Militia in Barbados 1679. [H2/141]

SCOTT, THOMAS, a time-expired indentured servant, emigrated from Barbados to Virginia on the pink *Rebecca*, master Thomas Williams, 15 July 1679. [H#407]

SCOTT, THOMASIN, buried in St Philips parish, Barbados, 21 September 1679. [H2/25]

SCOTT, THOMAS, in St Elizabeth's, Jamaica, pro.12 August 1684 Jamaica

SCOTT, THOMAS, a surgeon in Port Royal, Jamaica, pro.25 April 1695 Jamaica

SCOTT, Captain WALTER, with 107 acres, 2 servants and 52 slaves in St James, Barbados, 10 December 1679. [H#505]; of Major Farmer's troop of Horse Militia in Barbados 5 January 1679. [H2/199]

SCOTT, WILLIAM, a prisoner in Edinburgh Tolbooth, transported from Leith or Buckhaven to Barbados 22 December 1665 on Edward Burd's ship the *Margaret of Leith*{?}. [ETR#104]

SCOTT, WILLIAM, a Covenanter from Castletoun, Roxburghshire, captured after the Battle of Bothwell Bridge 22 June 1679, imprisoned in Edinburgh, transported from Leith to the West Indies on the *Crown of London*, master Thomas Teddico, 27 November 1679, shipwrecked off Muil Head of Deerness, Orkney, 10 December 1679. [RBM]

SCOULLER, WILLIAM, a Covenanter from Cambusnethan, Lanarkshire, captured after the Battle of Bothwell Bridge 22 June 1679, transported from Leith to the West Indies on the *Crown of London*, master Thomas Teddico, 27 November 1679, shipwrecked off Orkney 10 December 1679, later transported to Jamaica. [RBM] [CEC#212/5][SW#198]

SCROGGIE, ALEXANDER, a sailor on the *Rising Sun* from the Clyde to Darien 18 August 1699, cnf Edinburgh 1707. [SRO.CC8.8.83]

SCROGGIE, ROBERT, husband of Helen Ferrier, a sailor on the *St Andrew* from Leith to Darien 14 July 1698, cnf Edinburgh 1707. [SRO.CC8.8.83]

SEATON, JOHN, buried in St James, Barbados, 22 December 1678. [H#498]

SEATON, JOHN, son of James Hutton or Seaton in Chapel Lauder, Berwickshire, a minister who emigrated from Leith to Darien on the *Caledonia* 14 July 1698, cnf Edinburgh 25 September 1707. [SRO.CC8.8.83]

SERANDA, JOANNES, a sailor on the *Unicorn* from Leith to Darien 14 July 1698, cnf Edinburgh 1707. [SRO.CC8.8.83]

SETON, ALEXANDER, captain's clerk on the *St Andrew* from Leith to Darien 14 July 1698, cnf Edinburgh 1707; witness to the testament of William Muir, a sailor, 11 July 1698. [SRO.CC8.8.83]

SETON, GEORGE, son of John Seton a shipmaster in Burntisland, Fife, a sailor on the *St Andrew*, cnf Edinburgh 11 October 1707. [SRO.CC8.8.83]

SHAIRP, ROBERT, son of Thomas Shairp of Houston, an Ensign who died at Darien 1699, cnf Edinburgh 1707. [SRO.CC8.8.83]

SHARP, ROBERT, a Covenanter, transported from Leith to Jamaica August 1685. [PC.11.329]

SHAW, ANGUS, soldier of Captain Bounes' company of Militia in Barbados 1679. [H2/130]

SHAW, DANIEL, poor, with 6 acres in St James, Barbados, 20 December 1679. [H#506]

SHIELDS, ALEXANDER, born 1661 son of James Shields, a miller, and Helen Brown in Heughhead, Earlston, Berwickshire, educated at Edinburgh University 1675 and at Utrecht University, ordained a Puritan minister in London 1685, imprisoned in Newgate prison, London, Edinburgh Tolbooth and on the Bass Rock, chaplain to the Cameronian Regiment in the Netherlands, a minister in St Andrews 1697, appointed chaplain to the Second Expedition to Darien 1699, emigrated from Greenock to Darien on the *Rising Sun* 21.7.1699, wrote from on board the *Rising Sun* in Caledonia Bay, Darien, 2 February 1700; died in the house of Isobel Murray, Port Royal, Jamaica, 14 June 1700. [F.7.655] [F.5.239][Erskine's Journal #240/244]

SHIELD, GEORGE, a prisoner in Edinburgh Tolbooth, transported from Leith or Buckhaven to Barbados 22 December 1665, on Edward Burd's ship the *Margaret of Leith*{?}. [ETR#104]

SHIELDS, MICHAEL, son of James Shields, a miller, and Helen Brown in Heughhead, Earlston, Berwickshire, emigrated to Darien 1699, later settled in Jamaica. [F#5.239]

SHIRREFF, GILBERT, from Prestonpans, East Lothian, a seaman aboard the *Royal William* discharged 12 November 1696 to join the Darien Company. [OSN#226]

SIM, JOHN, a sailor who died at Darien 16 November 1698. [WP#88] [NLS.RY2b8/19]

SIME, ARCHIBALD, from Bo'ness, West Lothian, a sailor on the *Rising Sun* from the Clyde to Darien 18 August 1699, cnf Edinburgh 7 October 1707. [SRO.CC8.8.83]

SIMPSON, ALEXANDER, father of Elizabeth in Dysart, Fife, a mariner on the *St Andrew* from Leith to Darien 14 July 1698, cnf Edinburgh 1707. [SRO.CC8.8.83]

SIMPSON, GEORGE, in St Andrew's, Jamaica, pro.13 September 1693 Jamaica

SIMPSON, HUGH, a Covenanter from Dalmellington, Ayrshire, captured after the Battle of Bothwell Bridge 22 June 1679, imprisoned in Edinburgh, transported from Leith to the West Indies on the *Crown of London*, master Thomas Teddico, 27 November

1679, shipwrecked off Muil Head of Deerness, Orkney, 10 December 1679. [RBM]

SIMPSON, JOHN, a Covenanter from Garieside, Roxburghshire, imprisoned in Edinburgh Tolbooth, transported from Leith to Jamaica August 1685, landed at Port Royal, Jamaica, November 1685. [PC.11.330][ETR#369][LJ#15]

SIMSON, THOMAS, son of John Simson of Balchrystie, died at Darien 1699, cnf Edinburgh 1708. [SRO.CC8.8.84]

SIMPSON, THOMAS, "remained at Darien after the colony was abandoned", (1700). [APS.14.app.114]

SIMPSON, WILLIAM, from Leith, a seaman on the *Royal William* discharged to join the Darien Company 12 November 1696; a sailor on the *Rising Sun* from the Clyde to Darien 18 August 1699, cnf Edinburgh 1707. [SRO.CC8.8.83][OSN#226]

SINCLAIR, ADAM, with 10 slaves and 10 acres in St Lucy's parish, Barbados, 1678. [H2/45]

SINCLAIR, ALEXANDER, with 10 acres, 1 servant and 7 slaves, in St Michael's, Barbados, 1679. [H#458]

SINCLAIR, DUNCAN, a Covenanter, transported from Leith to Jamaica August 1685. [PC.11.136]

SINCLAIR, EDWARD, in St Michael's, Barbados, March 1681. [SPAWI.1681/58]; in Barbados, pro.25 November 1682 Jamaica

SINCLAIR, JOHN, from Inverkip, Renfrewshire, coxswain on the *Rising Sun* from the Clyde to Darien 18 August 1699, cnf Edinburgh 1707. [SRO.CC8.8.83]

SINCLAIR, PATRICK, pro.12 December 1674 Barbados [RB.6.4.209]

SINCLAIR, RICHARD, sergeant of Captain Scott's company of Militia in Barbados 1679. [H2/190]

SKEEN, ANDREW, in Clarendon, Jamaica, pro.15 November 1692 Jamaica

SKENE, A., a secretary, emigrated to Barbados before 1705. [SPAWI. 1705.409]

SLEIMAN, GABRIEL, from Paisley, Renfrewshire, a sailor on the *Rising Sun* from the Clyde to Darien 18 August 1699, cnf Edinburgh 1707. [SRO.CC8.8.83]

SMART, ROBERT, in Vere, Jamaica, pro.17 September 1694 Jamaica

SMEWREY, CORNELIUS, a weaver from Berwick, emigrated via London to Barbados 15 May 1686. [CLRO/AIA]

SMITH, DAVID, a merchant on the *James of Ayr* arrived in Ayr from Montserrat 23 September 1678. [SRO.E72.3.4]

SMITH, JAMES, son of James Smith a servant of the Earl of Haddington, a sailor on the *St Andrew* from Leith to Darien 14 July 1698, cnf Edinburgh 20 November 1707. [SRO.GD406, bundle 406, 4/21][SRO.CC8.8.83]

SMITH, JOHN, a Covenanter from Glencairn, Nithsdale, captured after the Battle of Bothwell Bridge 22 June 1679, transported from Leith to the West Indies on the *Crown of London*, master Thomas Teddico, 27 November 1679, shipwrecked off Muil Head of Deerness, Orkney, 10 December 1679, later transported to Jamaica. [CEC#212/5][SW#202]

SMITH, JOHN, a Covenanter from Dalry, Galloway, captured after the Battle of Bothwell Bridge 22 June 1679, transported from Leith to the West Indies on the *Crown of London*, master Thomas Teddico, 27 November 1679, shipwrecked off Muil Head of Deerness, Orkney, 10 December 1679, later transported to Jamaica. [RBM] [CEC#212/5][SW#203]

SMITH, JOHN, a Covenanter from Glencairn, Dumfriesshire, captured after the Battle of Bothwell Bridge 22 June 1679, imprisoned in Edinburgh, transported from Leith to the West Indies on the *Crown of London*, master Thomas Teddico, 27 November 1679, shipwrecked off Muil Head of Deerness, Orkney, 10 December 1679, later transported to Jamaica. [RBM]

SMITH, JOHN, a passenger, from Ayr to the West Indies on the *James of Ayr* February 1681; returned to Ayr 19 September 1681 on the *James of Ayr*, master James Chalmers. [SRO.E72.3.6/7]

SMITH, JOHN, a sailor who died on the voyage to Darien 23 September 1698. [WP#87]

SMITH, JOHN, who was wounded at Darien 6 February 1698. [DP#86]

SMYTH, ROBERT, a minister educated in Aberdeen, a preacher in Ireland, later in the Caribbean Islands in Bermuda 1646 on way to visit his wife in Middleburg, Zealand. [MCA.1.177]

SMITH, THOMAS, a prisoner in Edinburgh Tolbooth, who had returned from Barbados, to where he had been exiled, petitioned the Privy Council for his release 16 September 1662; also 23 September 1662. [PC.1.266][ETR]

SMITH, WILLIAM, a Covenanter, son of John Smith in Kimgatyhill, Cambusnethan, Lanarkshire, transported from Leith to Jamaica August 1685, died at sea. [PC.11.329][LJ#203]

SNODGRASS, ANDREW, a Covenanter from Govan, Lanarkshire, captured after the Battle of Bothwell Bridge 22 June 1679, imprisoned in Edinburgh, transported from Leith to the West Indies on the *Crown of London*, master Thomas Teddico, 27 November 1679, shipwrecked off Muil Head of Deerness, Orkney, 10 December 1679. [RBM]

SOMERVILLE, JAMES, a Covenanter and a fermorer in Cambusnethan, Lanarkshire, imprisoned in Edinburgh Tolbooth, transported from Leith to Barbados on the *John and Nicholas*, master Edward Barnes, December 1685. [PC.11.254][ETR#389]

SOMERVILLE, JAMES, son of George Somerville and Agnes Scoon in Dalkeith, Midlothian, an assistant armorer on the *Unicorn* from Leith to Darien 14 July 1698, cnf Edinburgh 20 October 1707. [SRO.CC8.8.83]

SOMERVILLE, PATRICK, a Covenanter and a tailor in the Canongate, Edinburgh, transported from Leith to the West Indies on the *St Michael of Scarborough*, master Edward Johnston, 12 December 1678. [PC.6.76]

SOMERVILLE, WILLIAM, a Covenanter from Cambusnethan, Lanarkshire, imprisoned in Edinburgh Tolbooth, transported from Leith to Barbados on the *John and Nicholas*, master Edward Barnes, December 1685. [PC.11.254][ETR#389]

SOMERVILLE, WILLIAM, husband of Isobel Dalgleish in Culross, Fife, a sailor on the *St Andrew* from Leith to Darien 14 July 1698, cnf Edinburgh 1707. [SRO.CC8.8.83][SRO.GD406, bundle 159, p2/11]

SPALSIE, JOHN, a surgeon from Kirkcudbright, father of Margaret, died in Darien, cnf Edinburgh 1708. [SRO.CC8.8.84]

SPANKIE, Captain ANDREW, master of the *Elizabeth of Leith* petitioned the Privy Council for felons for shipment to Virginia or Barbados 7 November 1667. [PC.2.446]

SPENSE, BENJAMIN, a translator in service of the Darien Company, captured by the Spanish in Cuba, imprisoned in Seville, found guilty of piracy and sentenced to death May 1700, released 20 September 1700. [DD#346]

SPENCE, JAMES, a bosun at Darien 2.1700. [DD#283]

SPENCE, JAMES, a schoolmaster and minister, son of George Spence and Christian Thorn in Inch, Aberdeenshire, emigrated 1698, settled in St Mary's, Jamaica, died 1737. [APB.3.57][EBR.162/6294]

SPENCE, JEREMY, a sailor who died on the voyage to Darien 27 September 1698. [WP#87]

SPENCE, JOHN, son of John Spence in Leith, a boatman on the *Rising Sun* from the Clyde to Darien 18 August 1699, died on the

Darien Expedition, cnf Edinburgh 7 October 1707. [SRO.CC8. 8.83]

SPENCE, JOHN, a sailor from Leith, from the Clyde to Darien on the *Rising Sun* 18 August 1699, cnf Edinburgh 1707. [SRO.CC8.8.83]

SPENCER, BENJAMIN, to Darien, from Darien 1699, landed at Matanzas, Cuba, subscribed to a deposition 25 September 1699, [Audienca de Panama, General Archives of the Indies, Seville, #160/1, 2540, 69-6-6]; imprisoned in Seville, Spain, accused of piracy. [SRO.GD406.1.4541]

SPIERS, JOSEPH, a tailor's servant in Barbados 1676. [PC#4.674]

SPROT, ANDREW, a Covenanter from Borgue, Kirkcudbrightshire, captured after the Battle of Bothwell Bridge 22 June 1679, imprisoned in Edinburgh, transported from Leith to the West Indies on the *Crown of London*, master Thomas Teddico, 27 November 1679, shipwrecked off Muil Head of Deerness, Orkney, 10 December 1679. [RBM]

STANDBURGH, RECOMPENCE, mate on the *St Andrew*, witness to the testament of quartermaster George Calderwood 16 July 1698; died at Darien 10 December 1698. [WP#89]

STARK, ALEXANDER, Captain of the *Hopeful Binning of Bo'ness* to Darien 12 May 1699, arrived there August 1699, took settlers from Darien to Jamaica. [OSN#202]DD#255]

STEEL, JAMES, a Covenanter from Calder, Midlothian, captured after the Battle of Bothwell Bridge 22 June 1679, imprisoned in Edinburgh, transported from Leith to the West Indies on the *Crown of London*, master Thomas Teddico, 27 November 1679, shipwrecked off Muil Head of Deerness, Orkney, 10 December 1679. [RBM]

STEEL, JOHN, a sailor on the *Rising Sun* from the Clyde to Darien 18 August 1699, cnf Edinburgh 1708. [SRO.CC8.8.84]

STEEL, WILLIAM, servant of Alexander Dunlop of Dunlop, from Ayrshire to Antigua on the *Richard and John of London* 4 March 1686, sent to South Carolina with goods from Antigua, [WLClements Library, Misc. Bound Collections, University of Michigan]

STENHOUSE, GEORGE, from Burntisland, Fife, a sailor on the *Caledonia* from Leith to Darien 14 July 1698, cnf Edinburgh 3 October 1707. [SRO.CC8.8.83]

STEVEN, JOHN, a Covenanter from Livingston, West Lothian, captured after the Battle of Bothwell Bridge 22 June 1679, imprisoned in Edinburgh, transported from Leith to the West Indies on the *Crown of London*, master Thomas Teddico, 27 November 1679, shipwrecked off Muil Head of Deerness, Orkney, 10 December 1679. [RBM]

STEVEN, WILLIAM, a Covenanter from Glasgow, transported from Leith to the West Indies on the *St Michael of Scarborough*, master Edward Johnston, 12 December 1678. [PC.6.76]

STEVENSON, JAMES, a sailor on the *St Andrew* from Leith to Darien 14 July 1698, cnf Edinburgh 1707. [SRO.CC8.8.83]

STEVENSON, JAMES, from Culross, Fife, quartermaster of the *Rising Sun* from the Clyde to Darien 18 August 1698, cnf Edinburgh 1708. [SRO.CC8.8.84]

STEVENSON, JOHN, master of the *James of Wairwater*, from Port Glasgow to the Caribees 15 February 1682. [SRO.E72.19.6]

STEWART, ABRAHAM, soldier of Captain Brown's company of Militia in Barbados 6 January 1679. [H2/106]

STEWART, ADAM, a planter in St David's, Jamaica, pro.11 November 1696 Jamaica

STEWART, AGNES, a prisoner in Edinburgh Correction House, transported from Leith by Morris Trent a merchant in Leith to Barbados on the *Mary*, master David Couston, 4 May 1663. [EBR#186.13.4]

STEWART, ALEXANDER, a Covenanter in Kirkliston, transported from Leith to the West Indies on the *St Michael of Scarborough*, master Edward Johnston, 12 December 1678. [PC.6.76]

STEWART, ALEXANDER, subscribed to an agreement, on St Thomas 27 October 1699. [SPAWI.1699/902]

STEWART, ALEXANDER, from Kincarrochie, gun-room tailor on the *St Andrew* from Leith to Darien 14 July 1698, cnf Edinburgh 15 October 1707. [SRO.CC8.8.83]

STEWART, Captain ANDREW, brother of the Earl of Galloway, at Darien. [DD#246]

STEWART, ARCHIBALD, a surgeon who was instructed to go to New York on William Kincaid's galley to check on the men who had arrived there from Caledonia, Darien, 10 October 1699. [SRO.GD406][DP#175]

STEWART, ARCHIBALD, HM Hospital in Jamaica, 1704. [NLS.Melville.MS5163.f13]

STEWART, CHARLES, a Captain of the Darien Company, from the Clyde to Darien 1699, from Darien bound for Scotland on the *Little Hope*, shipwrecked off Cuba, captured by the Spanish and imprisoned in Havanna and in Cadiz, petitioned Parliament in Edinburgh 10 March 1707. [APS.XI.441, app.113]

STEWART, DANIEL, buried in St Philips parish, Barbados, 18 September 1678. [H2/23]

STEWART, DANIEL, from West Lothian, a sailor on the *Unicorn* from Leith to Darien 14 July 1698, cnf Edinburgh 3 October 1707. [SRO.CC8.8.83]

STEWART, DAVID, from Inverkeilor, Angus, died in Barbados before 1698. [SRO.PC2.27.109]

STEWART, Captain GABRIEL, of Captain Lewgar's company of Militia in Barbados 6 January 1679; with 4 servants, 37 slaves and 97 acres in St Peter's parish, Barbados, 1679. [H2/77, 138, 209]

STEWART, JAMES, sergeant of Captain Scott's company of Militia in Barbados 1679. [H2/191]

STEWART, JAMES, in Jamaica 1694. [SPAWI/1699/443]

STEWART, Mr JOHN, and his wife Margaret, parents of John baptised in St Michael's, Barbados, 3 June 1679; with 8 slaves 1680. [H#424/441]

STEWART, Major JOHN, with 55 slaves and 147 acres in Barbados 10 December 1679; buried in St Peter's parish, Barbados, 1679. [H2/78,89]

STEWART, JOHN, a volunteer who died on the voyage to Darien 21 September 1698. [WP#87]

STEWART, JOHN, of Kingarrochie, a soldier who died at Darien 1699, cnf Edinburgh 1707. [SRO.CC8.8.83]

STEWART, ROBERT, a clerk, settled in Barbados before 1705. [SPAWI.1705.409]

STEWART, Colonel ROBERT, in Barbados, admitted as a burgess of Glasgow 1706. [GBR]

STEWART, ROBERT, born in Bute, died June 1714, pro.1 November 1714 Barbados.

STEWART, THOMAS, born in Galloway 1666, a merchant in Bridgetown, Barbados, died in Chelsea, England, 12 November 1722, pro.23 February 1723 Barbados. [Chelsea g/s] Executor of George Mackenzie 1710. [see G.Mackenzie's will 28 August 1711 Barbados]

STEWART, ..., Major, in Barbados 1680. [SPAWI.1680.1336]

STEWART, Dr ..., settled in Port Morant, Jamaica, before 1700. [DP#305]

STIRKE, GEORGE, a minister, emigrated 1623, settled in Bermuda, died there 1637. [ACL#1.342][AP#90]

STIRLING, ALEXANDER, of Achyle, formerly a Lieutenant in the Earl of Tullibardine's Regiment, father of John in the Port of Menteith, Perthshire, a soldier who died at Darien 1699, cnf Edinburgh 23 August 1710. [SRO.CC8.8.84]

STIRLING, ROBERT, a merchant from Glasgow who died "abroad" {Darien?}, cnf Edinburgh 22 August 1707. [SRO.CC8.8.83]

STIRLING, WILLIAM, a sailor on the *Caledonia*, witnessed the testament of Malcolm Miller when "sailing to Pennsylvania" 28 July 1699.

STITT, EDWARD, a Covenanter from Durisdeer, Dumfries-shire, imprisoned in Edinburgh Tolbooth, transported from Leith to Jamaica, August 1685. [PC.11.145][ETR#372]

STOBIE, ADAM. a Covenanter in Lascar, Stirlingshire, transported from Leith to the West Indies on the *St Michael of Scarborough*, master Edward Johnston, 12 December 1678. [PC.6.76]

STOBO, ARCHIBALD, born 1674, educated at Edinburgh University, graduated MA 1697, married Elizabeth Jean Park, father of Jean and Richard, appointed chaplain to the Second Expedition to Darien 1699, from the Clyde to Darien on the *Rising Sun* 18 August 1699, from Darien on the *Rising Sun* bound for Scotland but shipwrecked at Charleston, South Carolina, settled there as a Puritan minister, later in Willtown, Carleton County, SC, died there 1741. [F.7.665][SHR#1.416][SRO.RD4.99.47]

STORIE, FRANCIS, from Linlithgow, West Lothian, a sailor on the *St Andrew* from Leith to Darien 14 July 1698, died in the West Indies 1699, cnf Edinburgh 1707. [SRO.CC8.8.83]

STRACHAN, ADAM, a schoolmaster, emigrated to the Leeward Islands 1700. [EMA#57]

STRAWNE, HENRY, with 5 acres and 2 slaves in Christchurch, Barbados, 22 December 1679. [H#485]

STRACHAN, WILLIAM, born 1666 in "Fitsit"(!), a tailor, emigrated to Darien on the *Caledonia*, deserted but captured by the Spanish and signed a deposition in Panama 15 January 1700. [Audienca de Panama, Archives of the Indies, L#164, Seville][DD#274]

STRENNOH, ALEXANDER, a surgeon in Nevis, pro.1700 PCC.

STRETTON, Captain ..., returned from Darien via Jamaica, in London 1700. [DD#297]

STRUTHERS, JOHN, a Covenanter from Kilbride, Lanarkshire, captured after the Battle of Bothwell Bridge 22 June 1679, impris-

oned in Edinburgh, transported from Leith to the West Indies on the *Crown of London*, master Thomas Teddico, 27 November 1679, shipwrecked off Muil Head of Deerness, Orkney, 10 December 1679. [RBM]

STUART, ARTHUR, died in Jamaica, pro.1658 PCC.

STUART, DAVID, in Barbados, 1696, pro. 5/5813 PCC.

STUART, Major JOHN, with 55 slaves and 147 acres in St Peter's parish, Barbados, 1679; buried in St Peter's parish, Barbados, 1679.

STUART, JOHN, in St Philips parish, Barbados, with 4 acres and 2 slaves, 1680. [H2/14]

STUART, ROBERT, a schoolmaster, emigrated to Jamaica 3 January 1689. [Rawl.MS#A306/93]

SUSHAN, WILLIAM, from Edinburgh, a yeoman on the *Caledonia* from Leith to Darien 14 July 1698, cnf Edinburgh 28 November 1707. [SRO.CC8.8.83]

SUTHERLAND, ISAAC, soldier of Lieutenant Colonel Tidcom's company of Militia in Barbados 11 October 1679. [H2/132]

SUTHERLAND, ROGER, soldier of Lieutenant Colonel Lyne's company of Militia in Barbados 6 January 1679. [H2/101]

SUTHERLAND, THOMAS, soldier of Colonel Colleton's company of Militia in Barbados 9 March 1679. [H2/119]

SUTTIE, DAVID, a son of James Suttie and Bessie Law in Kirkcaldy, Fife, a mariner on the *Caledonia* from Leith to Darien 14 July 1698, cnf Edinburgh 21 October 1707. [SRO.CC8.8.83]

SWAN, JOHN, with 12 acres in St Thomas's parish, Barbados, 1679. [H2/62]

SWAN, THOMAS, a Covenanter from Carstairs, Lanarkshire, captured after the Battle of Bothwell Bridge 22 June 1679, transported from Leith to the West Indies on the *Crown of London*, master Thomas Teddico, 27 November 1679, shipwrecked off Muil Head of Deerness, Orkney 10 December 1679, later transported to Jamaica. [RBM] [CEC#212/5][SW#199]

SWANSTON, WILLIAM, a Covenanter from Loudoun, Ayrshire, transported from Leith to the West Indies on the *Crown of London*, master Thomas Teddico, 27 November 1679, shipwrecked off Muil Head of Deerness, Orkney 10 December 1679, later transported to Jamaica. [CEC#212/5] [SRO.JC27.10.3][RBM]

SWINTON, ALEXANDER, son of William Swinton and Jean Wright in Glasgow, an Ensign who was killed at Darien 6 February 1699, cnf Edinburgh 4 October 1707. [SRO.CC8.8.83][DP#86]

SWINTON, JOHN, a joiner in Port Royal, Jamaica, pro.26 February 1678 Jamaica

SWINTON, WILLIAM, a merchant from Stirling, who with his wife and children emigrated from the Clyde to Darien on the *Risng Sun* 18 August 1699. [RSB#91]

SYME, JOHN, husband of Katherine Downie in Earlsferry, Fife, a cook on the *Rising Sun* from the Clyde to Darien 18 August 1699, cnf Edinburgh 1707. [SRO.CC8.8.83]

SYME, PATRICK, a prisoner in Edinburgh Tolbooth, transported by George Hutcheson a merchant in Edinburgh from Leith to Barbados 7 December 1665. [ETR#104]

TAGGART, ALEXANDER, with 4 acres and 2 slaves, in St Michael's, Barbados, 1679. [H#458]

TAGGART, ELIZABETH, buried in St Michael's, Barbados, 18 June 1679. [H#434]

TAGGART, JAMES, with his wife and 4 slaves, in St Michael's, Barbados, 1680. [H#445]

TAILFAIR, JOHN, Captain SIAC, witnessed a document in St Kitts 21 January 1700. [SRO.GD84.Sec.1/22/9B]

TAIT, JAMES, son of William Tait and Bethia Hunter in Burntisland, Fife, a sailor on the *Endeavour* from Leith to Darien 14 July 1698, cnf Edinburgh 3 October 1707. [SRO.CC8.8.83] [SRO.GD406, bundle 161, 25/14]

TAYLOR, ALEXANDER, from Burntisland, Fife, witness to the testament of Edward Power 15 July 1698; a sailor on the *St Andrew* died on the voyage to Darien 28 October 1698, cnf Edinburgh 1707. [SRO.CC8.8.83][SRO.GD406, bundle 160, 7/2][WP#88]

TAYLOR, JAMES, from Greenock, Renfrewshire, a sailor on the *Hope* from the Clyde to Darien 18 August 1699, cnf Edinburgh 11 October 1707. [SRO.CC8.8.83]

TAYLOR, JOHN, master of a vessel arrived in Leith with a cargo of sugar from Barbados for Morris Trent a merchant in Leith June 1661, petition 6 February 1662. [PC#1/154]

TAYLOR, JOHN, a sailor on the *St Andrew* bound for Darien 1698. [SRO.GD406, bundle 160, 2/4]

TAYLOR, WILLIAM, husband of Katherine Gray, second mate and gunner of the *Hope* bound for Darien 1699. [SRO.GD406, bundle 406, c39/3]

TATE, ANN, wife of John Tate, buried in St Lucy's parish, Barbados, 4 October 1679. [H2/55]

TELFER, PETER, a planter who died at Darien 24 December 1698. [NLS.RY2b8/19][WP#89]

TEMPLE, WILLIAM, from Linton, Roxburghshire, transported from Leith to the West Indies on the *St Michael of Scarborough*, master Edward Johnston, 12 December 1678. [PC.6.76]

TENTER, WILLIAM, who was drowned at Darien 11 December 1699. [NLS.RY28/19][WP#89]

THARE, ..., a council clerk, settled in Barbados before 1705. [SPAWI. 1705.410]

THOMSON, ANDREW, a Covenanter from Dundonald, Ayrshire, captured after the Battle of Bothwell Bridge 22 June 1679, transported from Leith to the West Indies on the *Crown of London*, master Thomas Teddico, 27 November 1679, shipwrecked off Muil Head of Deerness, Orkney 10 December 1679, later transported to Jamaica. [CEC#212/5][SW#199][RBM]

THOMSON, ANDREW, a Covenanter from St Ninian's, Stirlingshire, captured after the Battle of Bothwell Bridge 22 June 1679, transported from Leith to the West Indies on the *Crown of London*, master Thomas Teddico, 27 November 1679, shipwrecked off Muil Head of Deerness, Orkney 10 December 1679, later transported to Jamaica. [SW#199][RBM]

THOMSON, ANDREW, from Leith, a sailor on the *Dolphin* from Leith to Darien 14 July 1698, cnf Edinburgh 1707. [SRO.CC8.8.83]

THOMSON, ARCHIBALD, a Covenanter, transported from Leith to Jamaica, August 1685. [PC.11.329]

THOMSON, DAVID, baillie of Inverkeithing, Fife, husband of Janet ..., emigrated from Leith to Darien on the *Unicorn* 14 July 1698, cnf Edinburgh 16 October 1707. [SRO.CC8.8.83]

THOMSON, DONALD, a Covenanter in Argyll, transported from Leith to Jamaica, August 1685. [PC.11.329]

THOMSON, DUNCAN, a Covenanter in Argyll, transported from Leith to Jamaica, August 1685. [PC.11.130]

THOMSON, GABRIEL, a Covenanter and a merchant in Glasgow, transported from Leith to the West Indies on the *St Michael of Scarborough*, master Edward Johnston, 12 December 1678. [PC.6.76]

THOMSON, HENRY, a sailor on the *Unicorn* from Leith to Darien 14 July 1698, cnf Edinburgh 1707. [SRO.CC8.8.83]

THOMSON, JAMES, a Covenanter from Quathquan, Lanarkshire, captured after the Battle of Bothwell Bridge 22 June 1679, impris-

oned in Edinburgh, transported from Leith to the West Indies on the *Crown of London*, master Thomas Teddico, 27 November 1679, shipwrecked off Muil Head of Deerness, Orkney, 10 December 1679. [RBM]

THOMSON, JAMES, from Aberdour, Fife, a sailor on the *Rising Sun* from the Clyde to Darien 18 August 1699, cnf Edinburgh 7 October 1707. [SRO.CC8.8.83]

THOMSON, JAMES, from Edinburgh, a sailor on the *St Andrew* from Leith to Darien 14 July 1698, cnf Edinburgh 1707. [SRO.CC8. 8.83]

THOMSON, JOHN, a Covenanter from Shotts, Lanarkshire, imprisoned in Edinbugh, transported from Leith to the West Indies on the *Crown of London*, master Thomas Teddico, 27 November 1679, shipwrecked off Orkney 10 December 1679, later transported to Jamaica. [RBM][CEC#212/5]

THOMSON, JOHN, a Covenanter from Dalmeny, West Lothian, captured after the Battle of Bothwell Bridge 22 June 1679, imprisoned in Edinburgh, transported from Leith to the West Indies on the *Crown of London*, master Thomas Teddico, 27 November 1679, shipwrecked off Muil Head of Deerness, Orkney, 10 December 1679. [RBM]

THOMSON, JOHN, a Covenanter from Torpichen, West Lothian, captured after the Battle of Bothwell Bridge 22 June 1679, imprisoned in Edinburgh, transported from Leith to the West Indies on the *Crown of London*, master Thomas Teddico, 27 November 1679, shipwrecked off Muil Head of Deerness, Orkney, 10 December 1679. [RBM]

THOMSON, NEIL, a Covenanter in Argyll, transported from Leith to Jamaica, August 1685. [PC.11.136]

THOMSON, THOMAS, a Covenanter from St Ninian's, Stirlingshire, captured after the Battle of Bothwell Bridge 22 June 1679, transported from Leith to the West Indies on the *Crown of London*, master Thomas Teddico, 27 November 1679, shipwrecked off Muil Head of Deerness, Orkney, 10 December 1679, later transported to Jamaica. [SW#201][RBM]

THOMSON, WALTER, brother of David Thomson in Bo'ness, West Lothian, a sailor on the *Duke of Hamilton*, from the Clyde to Darien 18 August 1699, cnf Edinburgh 22 June 1709. [SRO.CC8. 8.84]

THOMSON, WILLIAM, a Covenanter from Borgue, Kirkcudbrightshire, captured after the Battle of Bothwell Bridge 22 June 1679, imprisoned in Edinburgh, transported from Leith to the West Indies on the *Crown of London*, master Thomas Teddico, 27 November 1679, shipwrecked off Muil Head of Deerness, Orkney, 10 December 1679. [RBM]

THOMSON, WILLIAM, son of John Thomson in Irvine, Ayrshire, a sailor on the *Rising Sun* from the Clyde to Darien 18 August 1699, cnf Edinburgh 17 February 1710. [SRO.CC8.8.84]

THOMSON, WILLIAM, from Hopetoun, West Lothian, a sailor on the *Rising Sun* from the Clyde to Darien 18 August 1699, cnf Edinburgh 16.October 1707. [SRO.CC8.8.83]

THOMSON, WILLIAM, from Edinburgh, a sailor on the *Caledonia* from Leith to Darien 14 July 1698, cnf Edinburgh 10 October 1707. [SRO.CC8.8.83]

TIBERNING, (?), JOHN, a merchant in Barbados, dead by 1710, sisters Mary and Margaret in Scotland. [see G.Mackenzie's will, pro.28 August 1711 Barbados]

TINTO, JAMES, a Covenanter from Temple, Midlothian, captured after the Battle of Bothwell Bridge 22 June 1679, imprisoned in Edinburgh, transported from Leith to the West Indies on the *Crown of London*, master Thomas Teddico, 27 November 1679, shipwrecked off Muil Head of Deerness, Orkney, 10 December 1679. [RBM]

TOD, JAMES, a Covenanter from Dunbar, East Lothian, captured after the Battle of Bothwell Bridge 22 June 1679, imprisoned in Edinburgh, transported from Leith to the West Indies on the *Crown of London*, master Thomas Teddico, 27 November 1679, shipwrecked off Muil Head of Deerness, Orkney, 10 December 1679. [RBM]

TOD, QUENTIN, a goat-thief in Kirkcudbright, ordered to be scourged and transported to Barbados January 1666. [PC.2.134]

TOD, ROBERT, a Covenanter from Fenwick, Ayrshire, captured after the Battle of Bothwell Bridge 22 June 1679, imprisoned in Edinburgh, transported from Leith to the West Indies on the *Crown of London*, master Thomas Teddico, 27 November 1679, shipwrecked off Muil Head of Deerness, Orkney, 10 December 1679. [RBM]

TODSHALL, JOHN, a prisoner in Edinburgh Tolbooth, transported from Leith or Buckhaven, Fife, to Barbados 22 December 1665, on Edward Burd's ship the *Margaret of Leith*{?}. [ETR#104]

TORRANCE, ANDREW, a Covenanter from Avondale, Lanarkshire, captured after the Battle of Bothwell Bridge 22 June 1679, impris-

oned in Edinburgh, transported from Leith to the West Indies on the *Crown of London*, master Thomas Teddico, 27 November 1679, shipwrecked off Muil Head of Deerness, Orkney, 10 December 1679. [RBM]

TOWARD, HENRY, son of John Toward in Bo'ness, West Lothian, a seaman on the *Unicorn* from Leith to Darien 14 July 1698, cnf Edinburgh 1707. [SRO.CC8.8.83]

TRAQUAIR, JAMES, from Torpichen, West Lothian, a sailor on the *Caledonia* from Leith to Darien 14 July 1698, cnf Edinburgh 20 October 1707. [SRO.CC8.8.83]

TRENT, LAWRENCE, a merchant from Newbattle, Midlothian, settled in Barbados before 1689. [SRO.SH.1703]; will subscribed to in St Peter's parish, Barbados, 11 July 1692, reference to his sons John, William, Andrew, Lawrence, daughters Elizabeth and Agnes, goddaughter Sarah, daughter of Colonel William Forster, and to William Cleland, pro.23 March 1693 Barbados. [RB6.2.60]

TRENT, LAWRENCE, son of Lawrence Trent, referred to as an overseer in Richard Trent's will, pro.18 May 1705 Barbados. [RB6.16.250]

TRENT, MORRIS, a merchant in Leith, transported 17 felons from Edinburgh via Leith to Barbados on the *Mary*, master David Couston, 4 May 1663. [EBR#186.13.4]

TRENT, MORRIS, militiaman in Barbados 1679. [H2/171]

TRENT, RICHARD, (?), with 1 servant and 4 slaves in St Michael's, Barbados, 1680. [H#441]; father of John Trent, executor Patrick Trent in London, reference to Lawrence Trent and Thomas Trent in Barbados, pro.18 May 1705 Barbados. [RB6.16.250]

TRENT, THOMAS, in Barbados, 1684, reference to in Richard Trent's will, pro.18 May 1705 Barbados. [RB6.16.250]

TROUP, JAMES, from Edinburgh, a sailor on the *Olive Branch* from the Clyde to Darien May 1699, cnf Edinburgh 4 October 1707. [SRO.CC8.8.83]

TURNBULL, ROBERT, a Lieutenant of the Darien Company, from the Clyde to Darien 1698, arrived November 1698, wrote from Fort St Andrew, Darien, to Colonel John Erskine, Governor of Stirling Castle 11 April 1699, sailed to New York 20 June 1699 but returned to Darien November 1699, left Darien bound for Scotland on the *Little Hope* but shipwrecked on Cuba, subsequently imprisoned in Havanna and in Cadiz, returned to Scotland July 1701, petitioned Parliament in Edinburgh 10 March 1707. [APS#XI, 441a, app.113][SHR#XI.404]

TURNBULL, THOMAS, a Covenanter in Argyll, imprisoned in Edinburgh Tolbooth, transported from Leith to Jamaica, August 1685. [PC.11.330][ETR#369]

TURNBULL, WILLIAM, transported from Leith or Newhaven to the West Indies on the *St Michael of Scarborough*, master Edward Johnston, 12 December 1678. [PC.6.76]

TURNBULL, WILLIAM, husband of Bessie Dempster, bosun's mate on the *St Andrew* from Leith to Darien 14 July 1698, cnf Edinburgh 1707. [SRO.CC8.8.83]

TURNER, JAMES, from Alloway, a sailor on the *Rising Sun* from the Clyde to Darien 18 August 1699, cnf Edinburgh 5 December 1707. [SRO.CC8.8.83]

UNNES, JOHN, a Covenanter from Castletoun, Roxburghshire, captured after the Battle of Bothwell Bridge 22 June 1679, imprisoned in Edinburgh, transported from Leith to the West Indies on the *Crown of London*, master Thomas Teddico, 27 November 1679, shipwrecked off Muil Head of Deerness, Orkney, 10 December 1679. [RBM]

URIE, JOHN, a Covenanter in Blairgorts, transported from Leith to the West Indies on the *St Michael of Scarborough*, master Edward Johnston, 12 December 1678. [PC.6.76]

URIE, WILLIAM, a Covenanter in Cathcart, Glasgow, transported from Leith to the West Indies on the *St Michael of Scarborough*, master Edward Johnston, 12 December 1678. [PC.6.76]

URQUHART, ALEXANDER, a time-expired indentured servant, emigrated from Barbados to Antigua on the sloop *Hopewell*, master William Murphy, 8 November 1679. [H#413]

URQUHART, THOMAS, with 4 slaves and 10 acres in St Lucy's parish, Barbados, 1678; buried in St Lucy's parish, Barbados, 25 June 1679. [H2/47, 56]

URQUHART, ..., late of Captain in the Darien Company's Service, 1707. [APS.14, app.114]

VASS, CHARLES, son of Patrick Vass and Margaret Hamilton in Edinburgh, a sailor on the *Caledonia* {600 tons, 50 guns}, from Leith to Darien 14 July 1698, cnf Edinburgh 13 October 1707. [SRO.CC8.8.83]

VASS, WILLIAM, with 1 slave in St Thomas's parish, Barbados, 1679.

VEIZY, RICHARD, arrived in New York from Darien on board the *Caledonia* August 1699. [DSP#118][PRO.CO5.1043, 2]

VERNER, JOHN, passenger on the *James of Ayr*, master James Chalmers, arrived in Ayr 19 September 1681 from the West Indies. [SRO.E72.3.7]

VETCH, Captain SAMUEL, arrived at New York from Darien August 1699. [DSP#122].

VETCH, Captain WILLIAM, son of Reverend William Vetch in Dumfries, formerly a Lieutenant of the Earl of Angus's Regiment, appointed as a Member of the Council of Caldeonia, Darien, 20 October 1699, died on the *Hope* 1699, cnf Edinburgh 22 July 1709. [SRO.CC8.8.84] [SRO.GD406]

WADDELL, ALEXANDER, a Covenanter from Castletoun, Roxburghshire, captured after the Battle of Bothwell Bridge 22 June 1679, imprisoned in Edinburgh, transported from Leith to the West Indies on the *Crown of London*, master Thomas Teddico, 27 November 1679, shipwrecked off Muil Head of Deerness, Orkney, 10 December 1679. [RBM]

WADDELL, JAMES, a Covenanter from Monklands, Lanarkshire, captured after the Battle of Bothwell Bridge 22 June 1679, imprisoned in Edinburgh Tolbooth, banished to the American Plantations, transported from Leith on the *Crown of London*, master Thomas Teddico, bound for Barbados 27 November 1679, shipwrecked and drowned off Muil Head of Deerness, Orkney, 10 December 1679. [RBM] [ETR#162]

WADDELL, THOMAS, son of William Waddell and Margaret Cuby in Prestonpans, East Lothian, a sailor on the *Rising Sun* from the Clyde to Darien 18 August 1699, died at Darien 1699, cnf Edinburgh 1707. [SRO.CC8.8.83]

WADDELL, WALTER, a Covenanter from Sprouston, Roxburghshire, captured after the Battle of Bothwell Bridge 22 June 1679, imprisoned in Edinburgh, banished to the American Plantations, transported from Leith on the *Crown of London*, master Thomas Teddico, bound for Barbados 27 November 1679, shipwrecked and drowned off Muil Head of Deerness, Orkney, 10 December 1679. [RBM]

WADDELL. WILLIAM, a Covenanter from Monklands, Lanarkshire, captured after the Battle of Bothwell Bridge 22 June 1679, transported from Leith to the West Indies on the *Crown of London*, master Thomas Teddico, 27 November 1679, shipwrecked off Orkney 10 December 1679, later transported to Jamaica. [RBM] [CEC#212/5][SW#198]

WALDROP, WILLIAM, in St Thomas, Barbados, pro.17 July 1702 Barbados. [RB.6.37.508]

WALKER, ADAM, son of ... Walker and Janet Handiesyde in Edinburgh, a tailor on the *St Andrew* from Leith to Darien 14 July 1698, cnf Edinburgh 1707. [SRO.CC8.8.83]

WALKER, ALEXANDER, a Covenanter from Shotts, Lanarkshire, captured after the Battle of Bothwell Bridge 22 June 1679, imprisoned in Edinburgh, banished to the American Plantations, transported from Leith on the *Crown of London*, master Thomas Teddico, bound for Barbados 27 November 1679, shipwrecked and drowned off Muil Head of Deerness, Orkney, 10 December 1679. [RBM]

WALKER, DONALD, a Covenanter and a farmer in Otter, Argyll, a prisoner in Edinburgh Tolbooth, transported from Leith to Jamaica August 1685. [ETR#373]

WALKER, DUNCAN, a Covenanter in Argyll, transported from Leith to Jamaica, August 1685. [PC.11.136]

WALKER, GEORGE, a butcher in Edinburgh, emigrated from Leith to Darien on the *Caledonia* 14 July 1698, cnf Edinburgh 1707. [SRO.CC8.8.83]

WALKER, ROBERT, purser on the *Caledonia*, witnessed Malcolm Miller's testament while "sailing to Pennsylvania" 28 July 1699.

WALKER, SIMEON, husband of Janet Scott in Burntisland, Fife, cook's mate on the *Caledonia* from Leith to Darien 14 July 1698, cnf Edinburgh 8 October 1707. [SRO.CC8.8.83]

WALKER, WILLIAM, transported from Leith to Jamaica August 1685. [PC.11.136]

WALKER, WILLIAM, son of William Walker in Coaltown of Durie, Fife, a sailor on the *Unicorn* from Leith to Darien 14 July 1698, cnf Edinburgh 23 October 1707. [SRO.CC8.8.83]

WALLACE, ANDREW, a prisoner in Edinburgh Tolbooth, transported from Leith 27 November 1679. [ETR#162]

WALLACE, ANDREW, physician and surgeon in Barbados, executor of George Drummond, 1701. [see G. Drummond's will, pro.23 May 1701 Barbados]. [RB6.43.269]

WALLACE, ELIZABETH, daughter of Archibald Wallace, buried in St Philips parish, Barbados, 30 July 1679. [H2/24]

WALLACE, JAMES, born in Kirkwall, Orkney Islands, 1673, son of Reverend James Wallace and Elizabeth Cuthbert, a physician at Darien and later with the East India Company, died 1724. [DSP #271][F.7.222]

WALLACE, JANET, guilty of infanticide, imprisoned in Edinburgh Tolbooth, transported from Leith to Jamaica, August 1685. [ETR #369][PC.11.330]

WALLACE, JOHN, husband of Katherine Carmichael in Musselburgh, Midlothian, (executor to James Gordon), quartermaster of the *Unicorn* from Leith to Darien 14 July 1698, cnf Edinburgh 11 November 1707. [SRO.CC8.8.83]

WALLACE, ROBERT, a Covenanter from Fenwick, Ayrshire, captured after the Battle of Bothwell Bridge 22 June 1679, transported from Leith to the West Indies on the *Crown of London*, master Thomas Teddico, 27 November 1679, shipwrecked off Muil Head of Deerness, Orkney, 10 December 1679, later transported to Jamaica. [CEC#212/5][SW#199][RBM]

WALLACE, ROBERT, master of the *Great Hope of Boston*, arrived in Port Glasgow from Barbados with ginger July 1683. [SRO.E72. 19.8]

WALLET, ANDREW, a Covenanter from Irongray, Dumfriesshire, captured after the Battle of Bothwell Bridge 22 June 1679, imprisoned in Edinburgh, banished to the American Plantations, transported from Leith on the *Crown of London*, master Thomas Teddico, bound for Barbados 27 November 1679, shipwrecked off Muil Head of Deerness, Orkney, 10 December 1679. [RBM]

WARDEN, NINIAN, mate of the *Hope* bound to Darien 1698. [SRO. GD406, bundle 162, c39/2]

WARDEN, WILLIAM, passenger on the *James of Ayr* from Ayr to the West Indies 20 February 1681. [SRO.E72.3.6]

WARDROPE, JAMES, a passenger, from Ayr to the West Indies on the *James of Ayr* 20 February 1681 and on April 1684. [SRO.E72.3.6]

WARDROPE, JAMES, a merchant trading from Port Glasgow to the West Indies on the *Jean of Largs* April 1684. [SRO.E72.19.9]

WARRACK, JAMES, father of Robert Warrack in Canongate, Edinburgh, a sailor on the *Rising Sun* from the Clyde to Darien 18 August 1699, cnf Edinburgh 1707. [SRO.CC8.8.83]

WARRENDER, WILLIAM, from East Wemyss, Fife, a foremastman on the *Caledonia* from Leith to Darien 14 July 1698, cnf Edinburgh 22 October 1707. [SRO.CC8.8.83]

WATSON, JAMES, in Port Royal, Jamaica, pro.25 May 1669 Jamaica

WATSON, JAMES, from Burntisland, Fife, a sailor on the *Caledonia* from Leith to Darien 14 July 1698, cnf Edinburgh 7 October 1707. [SRO.CC8.8.83]

WATSON, JOHN, a Covenanter from Avondale, Lanarkshire, captured after the Battle of Bothwell Bridge 22 June 1679, imprisoned in Edinburgh, banished to the American Plantations, transported from Leith on the *Crown of London*, master Thomas Teddico, bound for Barbados 27 November 1679, shipwrecked off Muil Head of Deerness, Orkney, 10 December 1679. [RBM]

WATSON, JOHN, a merchant trading from Ayr to the Caribee Islands on the *James of Ayr* March 1683. [SRO.E72.3.12]

WATSON, JOHN, from Hamilton, emigrated via Bristol to Barbados on the *Maryland Merchant*, 2 October 1684. [BRO]

WATSON, WILLIAM, a Covenanter from Islay, transported from Leith to Jamaica, August 1685. [PC.11.136]

WATSON, WILLIAM, from Aberdeen, a merchant in Port Royal, Jamaica, 1689, executor to John McFarlane pro.1690 Jamaica

WATT, ALEXANDER, soldier of Captain Bowcher's company of Militia in Barbados 6 January 1679; with 1 slave and 3 acres in St Philip's parish, Barbados, 1680. [H2/16, 112]

WATT, DAVID, soldier of Colonel Lyne's company of Militia in Barbados 6 January 1679; in St Philip's parish, Barbados, with 4 acres, 1680. [H2/17, 101]

WATT, GILBERT, buried in St Peter's parish, Barbados, 1679. [H2/89]

WATT, JOHN, husband of Elizabeth Smith in Newcastle-upon-Tyne, an armorer on the *Caledonia* from Leith to Darien 14 July 1698, cnf Edinburgh 16 October 1707. [SRO.CC8.8.83]

WATT, MARY, baptised in St Peter's parish, Barbados, 1679. [H2/86]

WATT, PATRICK, a Covenanter from Kilmarnock, Ayrshire, captured after the Battle of Bothwell Bridge 22 June 1679, transported from Leith to the West Indies on the *Crown of London*, master Thomas Teddico, 27 November 1679, shipwrecked off Orkney 10 December 1679, later transported to Jamaica. [CEC#212/5][SW #199][RBM]

WATT, THOMAS, from Cairsay Knowe, Auchtervale, Fife, a foremastman on the *Caledonia* from Leith to Darien 14 July 1698, cnf Edinburgh 27 October 1707. [SRO.CC8.8.83]

WEBSTER, BESSIE, a prisoner in Edinburgh Tolbooth, transported by George Hutcheson a merchant in Edinburgh from Leith to Barbados 7 December 1665. [ETR#104]

WEEMS, JAMES, a volunteer who died at Darien 9 November 1698. [WP#88] [NLS.RY2b8/19]

WEIR, GEORGE, a Covenanter from Lesmahagow, Lanarkshire, captured after the Battle of Bothwell Bridge 22 June 1679, imprisoned in Edinburgh, banished to the American Plantations, transported from Leith on the *Crown of London*, master Thomas Teddico, bound for Barbados 27 November 1679, shipwrecked off Muil Head of Deerness, Orkney, 10 December 1679. [RBM]

WEIR, JOHN, a Covenanter, transported from Leith to Jamaica August 1685. [PC.11.130]

WEIR, JOHN, land grant in St John's, Antigua, 3 November 1699. [SPAWI/1699/927]

WEIR, JOHN, husband of Mary Brown in Canongate, Edinburgh, father of Thomas Weir, a gunner on the *Rising Sun* from the Clyde to Darien 18 August 1699, cnf Edinburgh 1707. [SRO.CC8.8.83]

WEIR, ROBERT, a Covenanter from Lesmahagow, Lanarkshire, captured after the Battle of Bothwell Bridge 22 June 1679, imprisoned in Edinburgh, banished to the American Plantations, transported from Leith on the *Crown of London*, master Thomas Teddico, bound for Barbados 27 November 1679, shipwrecked off Muil Head of Deerness, Orkney, 10 December 1679. [RBM]

WEIR, THOMAS, a Covenanter in Lesmahagow, Lanarkshire, transported from Leith to Jamaica August 1685, landed at Port Royal, Jamaica, November 1685. [PC.11.329][LJ#225]

WELSH, ANDREW, a Covenanter from Ochiltree, Ayrshire, captured after the Battle of Bothwell Bridge 22 June 1679, imprisoned in Edinburgh, banished to the American Plantations, transported from Leith on the *Crown of London*, master Thomas Teddico, bound for Barbados 27 November 1679, shipwrecked off Muil Head of Deerness, Orkney, 10 December 1679. [RBM]

WELSH, ANDREW, soldier of Captain Burrow's company of Militia in Barbados 1679. [H2/181]

WELSH, SUSAN, daughter of Walter Welsh, baptised in St Lucy's parish, Barbados, 9 October 1678. [H2/51]

WELSH, WALTER, soldier of Captain Liston's company of Militia in Barbados 1679. [H2/143]

WEMYSS, JAMES, an Ensign, father of Helen Wemyss, died at Darien 1699, cnf Edinburgh 1707. [SRO.CC8.8.83]

WEMYSS, JOHN, son of Alexander Wemyss and Bessie Innes in Canongate, Edinburgh, a sailor on the *Caledonia* from Leith to Darien 14 July 1698, cnf Edinburgh 1707. [SRO.CC8.8.83]

WETHERHEAD, DAVID, in St Philips parish, Barbados, with 10 acres and 7 slaves, 1680. [H2/17]

WHITE, DAVID, a planter who died at Darien 24 December 1698. [WP#89] [NLS.RY2b8/19]

WHITE, JAMES, a minister, son of Reverend George White in Maryculter, Aberdeenshire, emigrated to Kingston, Jamaica, before 1692. [APB.2.188]

WHITE, JOHN, a Covenanter from Kirkoswald, Ayrshire, captured after the Battle of Bothwell Bridge 22 June 1679, imprisoned in Edinburgh, banished to the American Plantations, transported from Leith on the *Crown of London*, master Thomas Teddico, bound for Barbados 27 November 1679, shipwrecked off Muil Head of Deerness, Orkney, 10 December 1679. [RBM]

WHITEHEAD, WILLIAM, captain's servant on the *Hope* to Darien 1698. [SRO.GD406, bundle 162, p39/26]

WHITELAW, ELSPETH, a prisoner in Edinburgh Correction House, transported from Leith by Morris Trent a merchant in Leith to Barbados on the *Mary*, master David Couston, 4 May 1663. [EBR #186.13.4]

WHYTE, ARCHIBALD, from Clackmannan, a sailor on the *Rising Sun* from the Clyde to Darien 18 August 1699, cnf Edinburgh 1708. [SRO.CC8.8.84]

WHYTE, JOHN, a Covenanter from Fenwick, Ayrshire, captured after the Battle of Bothwell Bridge 22 June 1679, imprisoned in Edinburgh, banished to the American Plantations, transported from Leith on the *Crown of London*, master Thomas Teddico, bound for Barbados 27 November 1679, shipwrecked off Muil Head of Deerness, Orkney, 10 December 1679. [RBM]

WHYTE, MALCOLM, a Covenanter in Argyll, transported from Leith to Jamaica, August 1685. [PC.11.126]

WHYTE, WALTER, from Glasgow to Barbados 1675. [GR#195]

WIGHTON, HENRY, son of Henry Wighton and Isobel Ogilvie in Kirkcaldy, Fife, a foremastman on the *Caledonia* from Leith to Darien 14 July 1698, cnf Edinburgh 23 October 1707. [SRO.CC8.8.83]

WILKIE, DAVID, buried in St Philips parish, Barbados, 14 July 1678. [H2/22]

WILLIAMS, ALISTER, soldier of Captain Woodward's company of Militia in Barbados 6 January 1679. [H2/156]

WILLIAMS, ROBERT, master of the *Barbados Merchant*, bound from Barbados to Berwick, arrived in Leith 7 July 1665. [SPAWI/1666/66]

WILLIAMS, THOMAS, husband of Margaret Tod in Leith, bosun of the *Caledonia* from Leith to Darien 14 July 1698, cnf Edinburgh 1707. [SRO.CC8.8.83]

WILLIAMSON, JOHN, son of James Williamson in Cardenden, Fife, a sailor on the *Unicorn* from Leith to Darien 14 July 1698, cnf Edinburgh 9 October 1707. [SRO.CC8.8.83]

WILLIAMSON, THOMAS, a Covenanter from Cranston, Midlothian, captured after the Battle of Bothwell Bridge 22 June 1679, imprisoned in Edinburgh Tolbooth, banished to the American Plantations, transported from Leith on the *Crown of London*, master Thomas Teddico, bound for Barbados 27 November 1679, shipwrecked off Muil Head of Deerness, Orkney, 10 December 1679. [RBM] [ETR#162]

WILLOCK, WILLIAM, in St Philips parish, Barbados, with 10 acres and 7 slaves, 1680. [H2/17]

WILSON, CHARLES, from Coaltown of Balgonie, Fife, second mate on the *Olive Branch* from the Clyde to Darien 1698, cnf Edinburgh 25 November 1707. [SRO.CC8.8.83]

WILSON, DAVID, from Wemyss, Fife, a sailor on the *Caledonia* from Leith to Darien 14 July 1698, cnf Edinburgh 8 October 1707. [SRO.CC8.8.83]

WILSON, DAVID, a boy at Darien, captured by the Spanish and imprisoned in Seville, Spain, on a charge of piracy petitioned the Directors of the Darien Company in Edinburgh 1700. [SRO. GD406.1.4540]

WILSON, GEORGE, son of James Wilson and Margaret McEwan in Dysart, Fife, a sailor on the *Rising Sun* from the Clyde to Darien 18 August 1699, died at Darien, cnf Edinburgh 1707. [SRO.CC8. 8.83]

WILSON, JOHN, a sailor on the *Dolphin*, testament dative 1707. [SRO. GD406, bundle 163, c23/5]

WILSON, JOHN, from Coaltown of Balgonie, Fife, bosun on the *Dolphin* from the Clyde to Darien 1698, cnf Edinburgh 1708. [SRO.CC8.8.84][SRO.GD406, bundle 163, c23/4]

WILSON, PATRICK, a Covenanter from Livingston, West Lothian, captured after the Battle of Bothwell Bridge 22 June 1679, imprisoned in Edinburgh, banished to the American Plantations, transported from Leith on the *Crown of London*, master Thomas Teddico, bound for Barbados 27 November 1679, shipwrecked off Muil Head of Deerness, Orkney, 10 December 1679. [RBM] [ETR#162]

WILSON, ROBERT, passenger on the *James of Ayr*, master James Chalmers, arrived in Ayr 19 September 1673 from Montserrat and the West Indies. [SRO.E72.3.4]

WILSON, ROBERT, son of James Wilson in Linlithgow, West Lothian, a sailor on the *St Andrew* from Leith to Darien 14 July 1698, cnf Edinburgh 1708. [SRO.CC8.8.84]

WILSON, THOMAS, a Covenanter from Quathquan, Lanarkshire, captured after the Battle of Bothwell Bridge 22 June 1679, imprisoned in Edinburgh, banished to the American Plantations, transported from Leith on the *Crown of London*, master Thomas Teddico, bound for Barbados 27 November 1679, shipwrecked off Muil Head of Deerness, Orkney, 10 December 1679. [RBM] [ETR#162]

WINDRAM, GEORGE, a distiller, died at Darien 1700. [DD#325]

WINDRAM, ROBERT, from Leith, a foremastman on the *Caledonia* from Leith to Darien 14 July 1698, cnf Edinburgh 1707. [SRO. CC8.8.83]

WINTER, EDWARD, husband of Elizabeth McMath in Edinburgh, imprisoned in Edinburgh Tolbooth, transported from Leith to Barbados on the *John and Nicholas*, master Edward Barnes,17 December 1685. [ETR#390]

WINTON, DAVID, from Edinburgh, mate of the *Olive Branch* from the Clyde to Darien May 1699, cnf Edinburgh 1707. [SRO.CC8. 8.83]; witness to the testaments of James Troup and of Patrick Young.

WISHART, ANDREW, with 3 slaves in St Peter's parish, Barbados, 1679; militiaman under Major William Foster January 1680. [H2/82/134]

WISHART, WILLIAM, a sailor on the *Hope* bound for Darien 1698. [SRO.GD406, bundle 159, p40/2]

WITHARDS, MICHAEL, from Edinburgh, a sailor on the *Unicorn* from Leith to Darien 14 July 1698, cnf Edinburgh 9 October 1707. [SRO.CC8.8.83]

WODDROP, WILLIAM, Assemblyman in St Kitts 26 January 1684. [SPAWI.1684/1520]

WODROW, FRANCIS, a Covenanter from Glasgow, Lanarkshire, captured after the Battle of Bothwell Bridge 22 June 1679, imprisoned in Edinburgh, banished to the American Plantations, transported from Leith on the *Crown of London*, master Thomas Teddico, bound for Barbados 27 November 1679, shipwrecked off Muil Head of Deerness, Orkney, 10 December 1679. [RBM]

145

WOOD, ISAAC, court marshal, settled in Barbados before 1705. [SPAWI.1705.410]

WOOD, JANET, a prisoner in Edinburgh Tolbooth, transported by Morris Trent a merchant in Leith from Leith to Barbados on the *Mary*, master David Couston, 4 May 1663. [EBR#186.13.4]

WOOD, JOHN, a prisoner in Edinburgh Tolbooth, transported by George Hutcheson a merchant in Edinburgh from Leith to Barbados 7 December 1665. [ETR#104]

WOOD, WILLIAM, a passenger on the *Unity of Ayr*, master John Hodgson, which arrived in Ayr from Montserrat 2 September 1673. [SRO.E72.3.3]

WOODRUPP, WILLIAM, a merchant in Nevis 1675. ["Isle of Wight County, Virginia, Will and Deed Book" 1/573]

WOODRUP, WILLIAM, a merchant from Glasgow, son of William Woodrup, settled in St Kitts, father of Margaret, Barbara, and William, died 15 May 1687, buried at St Anne's, Sandy Point, St Kitts. [MWI#154]

WRIGHT, ARCHIBALD, a volunteer who died at Darien 6 November 1698. [NLS.RY2b8/19][WP#88]

WRIGHT, JAMES, from Carriden, West Lothian, a sailor on the *St Andrew* from Leith to Darien 14 July 1698, cnf Edinburgh 11 March 1708. [SRO.CC8.8.84]

WRIGHT, JOHN, from Edinburgh, a sailor on the *Olive Branch* from the Clyde to Darien 5.1699, cnf Edinburgh 13 October 1707. [SRO.CC8.8.83]

WRIGHT, JOHN, son of George Wright and Agnes Grant in Keith, Banffshire, a sailor on the *St Andrew* from Leith to Darien 14 July 1698, cnf Edinburgh 3 January 1733. [SRO.CC8.8.95] [SRO. GD406, bundle 160, 2/6]

WYLLIE, ALEXANDER, son of Alexander Wyllie a weaver in Grahamshall, Orkney Islands, a sailor on the *Endeavour* from Leith to Darien 14 July 1698, cnf Edinburgh 23 October 1707. [SRO.CC8.8.83] [SRO.GD406, bundle 161, 25/19]

WYLLIE, ANDREW, a Covenanter from Stewarton, Ayrshire, captured after the Battle of Bothwell Bridge 22 June 1679, imprisoned in Edinburgh, banished to the American Plantations, transported from Leith on the *Crown of London*, master Thomas Teddico, bound for Barbados 27 November 1679, shipwrecked off Muil Head of Deerness, Orkney, 10 December 1679. [RBM]

WYLLIE, JOHN, a Covenanter from Fenwick, Ayrshire, captured after the Battle of Bothwell Bridge 22 June 1679, imprisoned in

Edinburgh, banished to the American Plantations, transported from Leith on the *Crown of London*, master Thomas Teddico, bound for Barbados 27 November 1679, shipwrecked off Muil Head of Deerness, Orkney, 10 December 1679. [RBM]

WYLLIE, ROBERT, a Covenanter from Stewarton, Ayrshire, captured after the Battle of Bothwell Bridge 22 June 1679, imprisoned in Edinburgh, banished to the American Plantations, transported from Leith on the *Crown of London*, master Thomas Teddico, bound for Barbados 27 November 1679, shipwrecked off Muil Head of Deerness, Orkney, 10 December 1679. [RBM]

WYLLIE, THOMAS, a Covenanter from Loudoun, Ayrshire, captured after the Battle of Bothwell Bridge 22 June 1679, imprisoned in Edinburgh Tolbooth, banished to the American Plantations, transported from Leith on the *Crown of London*, master Thomas Teddico, bound for Barbados 27 November 1679, shipwrecked off Muil Head of Deerness, Orkney, 10 December 1679. [RBM]

WYLLIE, THOMAS, a Covenanter from Stewarton, Ayrshire, captured after the Battle of Bothwell Bridge 22 June 1679, imprisoned in Edinburgh, banished to the American Plantations, transported from Leith on the *Crown of London*, master Thomas Teddico, bound for Barbados 27 November 1679, shipwrecked off Muil Head of Deerness, Orkney, 10 December 1679. [RBM]

WYLLIE, THOMAS, a Covenanter, imprisoned in Edinburgh Tolbooth, transported from Leith to Barbados on the *John and Nicholas*, master Edward Barnes, December 1685. [PC.11.254][ETR#389]

WYNET, JOHN, a Covenanter from Monklands, Lanarkshire, captured after the Battle of Bothwell Bridge 22 June 1679, imprisoned in Edinburgh, banished to the American Plantations, transported from Leith on the *Crown of London*, master Thomas Teddico, bound for Barbados 27 November 1679, shipwrecked off Muil Head of Deerness, Orkney, 10 December 1679. [RBM]

YEAMAN, JOHN, a Covenanter and a farmer in Edington, Berwickshire, transported from Leith to the West Indies on the *St Michael of Scarborough*, master Edward Johnston, 12 December 1678. [PC.6.76]

YORKLAND, JACOB, a volunteer who died on the voyage to Darien 11 October 1698. [WP#87]

YOUNG, ANDREW, a Covenanter from Airth, Stirlingshire, captured after the Battle of Bothwell Bridge 22 June 1679, imprisoned in Edinburgh, banished to the American Plantations, transported from Leith on the *Crown of London*, master Thomas Teddico, bound for Barbados 27 November 1679, shipwrecked off Muil Head of Deerness, Orkney, 10 December 1679. [RBM]

YOUNG, CHARLES, son of Robert Young and Margaret McFarlane in Kippen, Stirlingshire, surgeon's mate on the *St Andrew* from Leith to Darien 14 July 1698, cnf Edinburgh 1707. [SRO.CC8.8.83]; issued with a birthbrief by Stirling Burgh Council 6 July 1698 before emigrating to Darien. [RBS#343]

YOUNG, GEORGE, a Covenanter in Teviotdale, Roxburghshire, transported from Leith to Jamaica August 1685, landed in Port Royal, Jamaica, November 1685. [PC.11.329][LJ#17]

YOUNG, JAMES, a Covenanter in Irvine, Ayrshire, transported 1679. [Irvine g/s]

YOUNG, JAMES, a Covenanter in Cavers, Roxburghshire, captured after the Battle of Bothwell Bridge 22 June 1679, transported from Leith to the West Indies on the *Crown of London*, master Thomas Teddico, 27 November 1679, shipwrecked off Muil Head of Deerness, Orkney, 10 December 1679, later shipped to Jamaica. [SW#203][RBM]

YOUNG, JAMES, a Covenanter in Netherfield, Avondale, Lanarkshire, imprisoned in Edinburgh Tolbooth, transported from Leith to Jamaica August 1685. [ETR#373][PC.11.129]

YOUNG, JAMES, a sailor who died at Darien 27 November 1698. [WP#89] [NLS.RY2b8/19]

YOUNG, JAMES, from Abbotshall, Fife, a foremastman on the *Caledonia* from Leith to Darien 14 July 1698, cnf Edinburgh 23 October 1707. [SRO.CC8.8.83]

YOUNG, JASON, a Covenanter, transported from Leith to the West Indies on the *Crown of London*, master Thomas Teddico, 27 November 1679, shipwrecked off Orkney 10 December 1679, later transported to Jamaica. [CEC#212/5]

YOUNG, JOHN, a Covenanter from Melrose, Roxburghshire, captured after the Battle of Bothwell Bridge 22 June 1679, imprisoned in Edinburgh, banished to the American Plantations, transported from Leith on the *Crown of London*, master Thomas Teddico, bound for Barbados 27 November 1679, shipwrecked off Muil Head of Deerness, Orkney, 10 December 1679. [RBM]

YOUNG, PATRICK, from Edinburgh, a sailor on the *Olive Branch* from the Clyde to Darien 5 1699, cnf Edinburgh 6 October 1707. [SRO.CC8.8.83]